Professional Ethics in Education Series

Kenneth A. Strike, Editor

The Ethics of School Administration
Kenneth A. Strike, Emil J. Haller, and Jonas F. Soltis

Classroom Life as Civic Education: Individual Achievement and Student Cooperation in Schools
David C. Bricker

The Ethics of Special Education
Kenneth R. Howe and Ofelia B. Miramontes

The Ethics of Multicultural and Bilingual Education
Barry L. Bull, Royal T. Freuhling, and Virgie Chattergy

Ethics for Professionals in Education: Perspectives for Preparation and Practice
Kenneth A. Strike and P. Lance Ternasky, Editors

Ethics for Professionals in Education

Perspectives for Preparation and Practice

Edited by
Kenneth A. Strike
and
P. Lance Ternasky

Teachers College, Columbia University
New York and London

Published by Teachers College Press, 1234 Amsterdam Avenue
New York, New York

Library of Congress Cataloging-in-Publication Data

Ethics for professionals in education : perspectives for preparation
and practice / edited by Kenneth A. Strike and P. Lance Ternasky.
p. cm. — (Professional ethics in education series)
Includes bibliographical references and index.
ISBN 0-8077-3216-8 (alk. paper). — ISBN 0-8077-3215-X (pbk. : alk. paper)
1. Teachers—Professional ethics—United States. 2. School administration—Professional ethics—United States. 3. Moral education—United States. I. Strike, Kenneth A. II. Ternasky, P. Lance. III. Series.
LB1779.E74 1993
174.'93711—dc20 92-28997

ISBN 0-8077-3216-8
ISBN 0-8077-3215-X (pbk)

Printed on acid-free paper

Manufactured in the United States of America

99 98 97 96 95 94 93 7 6 5 4 3 2 1

Contents

Ethics for Professionals in Education

Perspectives for Preparation and Practice

INTRODUCTION: Ethics in Educational Settings

KENNETH A. STRIKE AND P. LANCE TERNASKY
Cornell University

Ethics might be applied to education in three broad ways. First, ethical deliberation should be part of the process of reflection on educational policy. When we consider matters of educational policy, we need to ask such questions as whether the policy is just and whether it serves worthy goals. Various political-educational theories—liberalism, Marxism, feminism, and postmodernism, for example—have a strong normative core and provide various ways to appraise the merits and judge the significance of educational policy. There are a variety of "hot topics" that seem largely ethical: What is the role of religion in the schools? Can or should we teach creationism? What kinds of things are suitable or unsuitable for children to read? What constitutes a multicultural curriculum? What is the role of schooling in preparing children to be citizens in a democratic society? All of these questions seem to raise ethical concerns.

A second domain in which ethics seems vital is moral education. In a society in which such moral influences as family and religion are much weakened and in which children's time is spent mostly in school, it seems inevitable that schools should be expected to engage in some form of moral education. They may be expected to teach respect for law, democratic values and skills, tolerance, and a wide range of other ethical values. The schools may be expected to develop character and to teach responsible attitudes toward sex. All the while, they will also be expected to remain neutral about the controversial issues that divide Americans. Programs that promise to allow schools to engage in moral education while retaining a semblance of neutrality, such as Values Clarification or Kohlberg's Just Schools program, have seemed quite attractive to many educators. While these enterprises are influenced by different psychological theories, they too have a strong normative core and require appraisal from an ethical perspective.

These two kinds of enterprises are well represented in educational scholarship and in the training of educational professionals. Although it is possible for teachers and administrators to go through their training programs without encountering a course in philosophy of education, few teachers or administrators are likely to escape the necessity to reflect on the justice of some social policy or what the school's role in moral education should be.

A third domain, which has been somewhat neglected until recently, is professional ethics. As we understand it, professional ethics concerns those norms, values, and principles that should govern the professional conduct of teachers, administrators, and other educational professionals. Thus understood, professional ethics is distinguishable from both the ethical appraisal of educational policy and from issues of moral education, although it certainly has connections to both domains. Examples of questions of professional ethics are: What constitutes fairness in grading or in evaluation? What counts as an equitable distribution of teacher time between students with different kinds of needs? Is it ever appropriate for teachers to punish a group of children for the misbehavior of one child? What are appropriate standards of due process in discipline? What is the nature of a child's right to privacy? The reader should note that this initial characterization of professional ethics is contested and, we suppose, would be rejected by some of the authors of the chapters in this book. We do not wish this characterization to function as a preemptive strike against the views of our colleagues. Here its merit is that it provides a starting place for discussion and reflection.

We do not, of course, wish to claim that these three domains are sharply distinct. Obviously, reflection on the ethical aspects of policy or of moral education will produce judgments that bear on the professional responsibilities of educators. Our purpose is rather to note that the kinds of questions we have asked above seem distinguishable from broad matters both of policy and of moral education and that they, unlike these other areas of ethical reflection, seem neglected. What seems noteworthy to us is that until recently professional ethics has not been a matter of significant emphasis either in educational literature or in instruction in training programs for educational professionals. Of course this judgment would be difficult to demonstrate. It may be that discussion of such matters is common but is woven into other topics and other areas of the curriculum in ways that make it hard to identify. Nevertheless, despite more than half a decade of interest in professional ethics, we have found only a few articles, and even fewer books and courses, that seem analogous to the kinds of enterprises in teaching ethics to practitioners that have sprung up in medical schools, law schools, and business schools.

It is true that the National Education Association (NEA) has a code of ethics for teachers. There are also codes of ethics for administrators. However, the NEA code is platitudinous and perfunctory. Moreover, there is little evidence that it is taught or that most teachers are aware of its existence. It is even more doubtful that it has a role in any real deliberations about the professional conduct of teachers in schools. Codes of ethics do not currently seem to play a significant role in training educators or in their professional lives.

Perhaps this is changing. The existence of the series of books by Teachers College Press on professional ethics in education, in which this volume appears, is one indication of the growing interest in this topic. This series emerged, in part, from the success of *The Ethics of Teaching* (Strike & Soltis, 1985). Also, the American Educational Research Association (AERA) has sponsored several quite successful sessions dealing with professional ethics. Equally noteworthy is that AERA has recently established, under the capable leadership of Nel Noddings, a committee to consider a code of ethics for educational research. Finally, a smattering of articles have begun to appear on the topic. Thus there is reason to suppose that there is a good deal of latent interest in professional ethics, and that this latent interest is starting to produce a literature and has the potential to become a factor in professional training programs.

What is the source of this interest? Three possibilities occur. First, notable cases of public misconduct frequently generate demands for instruction in ethics. Insider trading scandals have led to the proliferation of ethics courses in business schools. Educators too have had their share of such visible scandals. There have been reports claiming that educators are quite capable of such nefariousness as fraud, theft, drug pushing, and child abuse.

A second source of interest may be the push to conceptualize education as a profession. One of the reforms of the 1980s has been the view that teaching will be more effective if teachers are treated as professionals. One characteristic of a profession is that its members are self-governing. Often, part of the idea of being self-governing is that the members of a profession police their own ethics. Generally professionals are supposed to have internalized a client-centered ethic by virtue of their training. Many professions also have detailed and enforceable codes of ethics. Education, it seems, has neither deliberate and systematic instruction in ethics nor an enforceable code of ethics. It may be that more attention to instruction in professional ethics and to the development of codes of ethics would help advance the status of teaching as a profession.

A third factor may be a growing rejection of a vision of teaching as a largely technical endeavor in favor of a vision of teaching as a moral pursuit linked to the ethical structure of schools. We have had several decades of research on better techniques for teaching. This research has consumed thousands of hours and millions of dollars. It is unclear that the quality of schooling has been much improved thereby. Perhaps this has increased the willingness to see teaching as a "moral craft." Furthermore, some recent research has emphasized the extent to which the effectiveness of schooling depends on the organizational characteristics of schools and on the characteristics of school communities. Communities are, first and foremost, human associations organized around shared values, and the organizational characteristics of schools are generated in part by assumptions about the nature of legitimate authority in organizations. One may suppose that issues of professional ethics would be found to be entangled with concern for the organizational characteristics of schools or for the quality of community to be found in schools. Nothing erodes community more quickly than a pervasive feeling that an organization is routinely unfair. One of the central concerns about organizational characteristics of schools is the authority relationships between elected officials, administrators, and teachers. A concern for professional ethics, it seems, must be part of these concerns for the quality of organizational life.

Whereas there may be a variety of reasons for being interested in professional ethics in education, it is not at all clear that these reasons point to a coherent agenda or that there is much clarity concerning what professional ethics should be about. Indeed, some intractable dilemmas may well be involved in squaring what can reasonably be done in teaching professional ethics with what might be expected of the enterprise.

We suppose that what the general public wants from ethics courses taught in professional schools is that those to whom they are taught would behave better as a consequence. It is not at all clear, however, that we know how to improve behavior by classroom instruction. Indeed, among philosophers, the connection between reflection or cognition and moral behavior has historically been a matter of considerable controversy. Consider that it is very likely that business people who engage in insider trading, administrators who steal from their school districts, and teachers who engage in child abuse already know that these activities are wrong. A course that spends a few weeks asserting that they are wrong is not clearly relevant to the prevention of such abuses. Nor is it evident that people who engage in patently immoral activity are often dissuaded from doing so by the power of good arguments. If what the public wants are courses that make people better, they are quite likely to be disappointed by courses in professional ethics.

The public is likely to be even more disappointed in such courses if they are essentially philosophy courses. Academic philosophy has been dominated recently by questions that are more about ethics than they are ethical. Philosophers are more likely to worry about the structure of ethical argumentation or the meaning of ethical terms than about what is right and what is wrong. These are not independent concerns. Nevertheless the connection between the interests of philosophers and the ethical behavior of educational professionals is sufficiently remote that it strains credulity to believe that people will behave better as a result of studying the products of academic philosophy about ethics. It is an unusual person who will be motivated by the study of Kant's arguments for the categorical imperative to practice it more faithfully.

Perhaps the principal reason why courses that tell people what they already know about morality or that seek to argue people into good behavior are likely to be inefficacious is that good behavior is as much a matter of character as of belief. Character is usually formed slowly over many years and is at least as much a matter of habituation and training as it is of cognition and reflection. This is the kind of story that Aristotle might have told, and it is one worth serious consideration.

That ethical conduct depends on character as well as cognition suggests that there are dangers involved in teaching professional ethics. Instruction in ethics to those of nefarious disposition may actually enhance their capacity for rationalization, obfuscation, and self-justification. A program of instruction that makes people more sophisticated about ethics but does not make them better people is not self-evidently a good thing. Also, instruction in professional ethics can serve hidden agendas and inhibit needed reform. Consider that professional training programs may often form character or reinforce predilections in those enrolled in them. And they may do so quite inadvertently because of the prevailing ethos of the profession or various structural factors in the lives of professionals. It may be, then, that the implicit role for professional ethics is to contain the kinds of values or character traits that are formed or reinforced elsewhere in the professional program. One supposes, for example, that those who are trained in business administration learn in the process to have a healthy regard for the importance of the bottom line. Perhaps one purpose of professional ethics in business is to convey what count as acceptable and unacceptable ways of the pursuit of profit. Thus far there is no difficulty. The aspirations of any enterprise can become vices when carried to excess. Thus it is morally appropriate for business people to pursue profit and commendable that they should be taught the difference between just and unjust ways of doing so.

But what if the moral environment of some business schools encourages the pursuit of profit by any means, and students come to feel that the real morality of the business world is the so-called eleventh commandment, "Thou shalt not get caught." If so, instruction in professional ethics may partake of several vices. First, it may simply serve to notify students concerning what will be found unacceptable, but do so in a way that divorces the study of ethics from any concern for doing the right thing. We believe that no program of professional ethics is adequate that functions merely as a notice board about unacceptable conduct, but fails to encourage genuine commitment to reasonable moral standards. Second, courses in professional ethics may function as a mere ruse, placed before the public to persuade them that attention is being paid to the moral failings of members of the profession. At the same time, the institutionalization of such courses may inhibit a more searching analysis of the kinds of socialization provided young professionals. Some professions, perhaps including education, may require scrutiny of their structure, their prevailing ethos, and the pursuant socialization that initiation into the profession provides. We are not optimistic about the potential of instruction in professional ethics to counter a morally unhealthy ethos. And we are concerned that its availability can serve as a substitute for more intensive soul searching and reform.

Despite these caveats it doesn't follow that teaching about professional ethics has no point. One might argue that, given a presumption that those who are undergoing instruction are persons of goodwill or of good character (a presumption that we feel is reasonable in education), instruction in professional ethics can help them to a clearer understanding of what counts as proper conduct. In many ethics courses in professional schools, the concern seems more for hard cases than for the affirmation of generally accepted standards. Perhaps this is sensible. It seems more plausible to believe that classroom instruction can help people think through ethical dilemmas than to believe that it can make them better persons. We should recognize, however, that if we act on such assumptions we are unlikely to do what the public wants. There is little to be taught in university classrooms that is likely to diminish the incidence of theft and child abuse.

We do not, however, think that this settles the issue of what our aspirations for professional ethics should be. Some will see the comments in the previous paragraph as presupposing a certain view of what ethics is about. Some feminist scholars, for example, have recently focused on the contrast between an ethic of principle and an ethic of relationships and caring. And they have held that an ethic of caring should supplement or supplant an ethic of principle. Our preceding comments might be taken (correctly) to indicate that we see ethics as having to do more with the application of principles, largely principles of justice, to cases. That is not, however, to say that we are against caring, or that we do not think it a good thing for teachers to be caring people. The justice/caring dichotomy is one of the things that need to be discussed in order to develop a coherent set of aspirations for professional ethics.

Moreover, although we have thus far talked a lot about *professional* ethics and have suggested that the desire to professionalize teaching is one motive for an interest in ethics, we do not take it for granted that teaching or administration should be fully professionalized. It may be argued that the professionalization of teachers tends to be inconsistent with the development of schools as genuinely democratic communities, and that the development and elaboration of codes of ethics is part of a process that removes reflection on education from parents and students. Or it may be that the elaboration of codes of ethics is likely to make teaching more rule-bound and less caring. Anyone who has had the experience of being terrorized by the medical profession's legally inspired concern for informed consent should be impressed with the difference between following the rules and treating people humanely. It is far from certain that teaching is or should be a profession in the same sense as are law and medicine, and that attempting to make teaching a profession modeled after law or medicine will have an altogether benign effect.

We should also note that some of the incentives that have generated an interest in ethics in other professions do not seem to apply to education. In medicine, for example, among the factors that may have generated an increased interest in ethics are new medical technologies, a growing resistance to medical paternalism, and a legal context that requires clear ethical standards. None of these factors, except perhaps the concern for paternalism, seems to have an analogue in education. Educators have not suddenly developed new techniques of instruction whose dramatic effectiveness raises profound questions with respect to what counts as an ethical use of these technologies. Nor have educators been successfully sued for malpractice.

The need for thinking about professional ethics in education is more commonplace. Here, as in most other areas of human conduct, we stand in need of wisdom about how we should treat one another and about how we may become the kinds of persons we want to be. Insofar as we have failed to achieve a consensus about such matters, we have a need to learn and to teach about how to think responsibly about them. Insofar as we have achieved some wisdom on these matters, we need to know how this wisdom is to be imparted to aspirant educational practitioners.

We hope that these comments will have served to suggest two thoughts. The first is that there are some reasons for hoping that instruction in ethics will come to occupy a more prominent place in the preparation of teachers and administrators. After all, teachers and administrators have considerable power over our children. Children, being more vulnerable and powerless than most other human beings, are easily mistreated. Although instruction in ethics may not have the capacity to rectify every evil, we should not assume that it is an unimportant part of the preparation of teachers and administrators. Second, it is not evident that we have identified a coherent and achievable set of aspirations for teaching ethics. Achieving a coherent set of aspirations will take some study.

These two thoughts are the principal motives for this book and for the way we have approached the topic. We believe that it is time to take a more serious look at the role of ethics in the preparation of educational practitioners, but that what is needed most at this point is reflection that serves to set an agenda. Thus our chief purpose in this volume is to provide a set of articles that we hope will serve to generate debate and to acquaint readers with a range of reasonable options. Although both editors clearly have views on the topic, our intent has not been to provide a collection that is subservient to these views. Instead, we have tried to identify a sample of topics and issues and have invited people to think about them and to say what seems sensible to them. No doubt the editors' views have been reflected in the issues and the authors chosen. Nevertheless, we have tried to represent a range of views as well as to cover a range of topics.

This book does not advance an approach to professional ethics for educators. Instead it lays out positions to be evaluated, problems to be overcome, and strategies to be considered. Notwithstanding, we have devised a plan that structures the kinds of articles we have sought, which cover three broad areas.

First, we wanted to introduce the reader to some issues that concern the nature of ethics itself. Here we have elected to represent a liberal view, an Aristotelian view, and a feminist view. Modern liberalism is a view of ethics that sees justice as the central moral concept and emphasizes the attempt to describe moral principles that allow persons who may have quite different views of their lives to enter into a just scheme of social cooperation. Modern versions of Aristotelian ethics, by contrast, have emphasized the importance of membership in communities of common purpose and the development of virtue and character as the central moral concerns. Finally, some recent feminist writers have attempted to describe a view of ethics that emphasizes relationships over principles of justice and that sees caring as the central ethical concept.

These views by no means exhaust the options we might have chosen to represent. We have chosen them in part because they have the potential to speak to the issues of professional ethics and also because they are currently the focus of a variety of fruitful exchanges about some basic issues in ethics. Thus they give the reader access to some fundamental considerations that must be addressed by any attempt to include ethics in the training of educational practitioners.

We do not assume that these views are mutually exclusive. Indeed, one final reason we have had for using them to represent some basic options about ethics is that each seems to make central a theme that should have a place in an adequate conception of ethics.

Second, we wanted to explore the practical matters of developing a curriculum and instructional problems and strategies dealing with ethics.

The final section of the book contributes to considering approaches to professional ethics by looking at the place of ethics in educational institutions. Here authors consider the place of ethics in a genuine profession of education, the way in which ethics is currently treated in the law, and the way other public institutions deal with ethics. Other authors seek to consider ethics from a normative view of schooling. In each case they describe institutional considerations that will need to be thought about if ethical considerations are to be introduced in the training of professional educators in a way that adequately reflects institutional realities and possibilities.

What the reader has a right to expect from this volume is a set of papers that discuss various views, issues, and problems that must be considered if professional ethics is to be effectively introduced into the training of educational professionals. The reader should not, however, expect a collective approach to emerge. We did not think it appropriate at this early stage in the endeavor to do more than ask the most able people we could find to write on a representative range of topics. We have not attempted to constrain them by our views any more than was required to sketch a range of topics for the book. Our only instructions to the authors have been to do their best work, to make it accessible to a broad audience, and to respect the division of labor involved in the selected topics. If themes emerge, they will do so by serendipity. Our chief hope is that this volume will initiate a productive debate about how ethics should be dealt with in the education of educational professionals.

REFERENCE

Strike, K. A., & Soltis, J. (1985). *The ethics of teaching*. New York: Teachers College Press.

Part I

PHILOSOPHICAL PERSPECTIVES

1 Character and Moral Reasoning

An Aristotelian Perspective

DAVID C. BRICKER
Oakland University

The distinction between how people act and the kinds of persons they are is a familiar one, making it possible for educators to deplore behavior while acknowledging the underlying integrity of a person who acts badly. An associated distinction is that between the way a person reasons and the character of a person. We put this distinction to use when we think of a bad person doing well as a problem solver in, for example, a math or physics course.

In this chapter I argue that character can affect moral rationality through the perceptual preoccupations persons bring to reasoning. Moral reasoning is not a disembodied activity, disconnected from people's habits of seeing. Bear in mind that in part we characterize persons on the basis of what they typically see: Consider, for example, what we make of someone who sees good in virtually everyone, or someone else who sees sexual innuendo in most small talk. Individuals may find that they cannot agree when their character-based perceptual preoccupations influence their reasoning.

I look upon this chapter as a "cautionary note" placed among other accounts of moral rationality that may ascribe too much to the power of reason. Accounts inspired by the work of Lawrence Kohlberg make this mistake: They treat moral reasoning as if it were a disembodied activity, unaffected by character. In support of my view of the connection between character and reasoning I draw upon Aristotle, for Aristotle has much to say about the contribution made by our ability to see the defining, or salient, feature of a situation to our effort to reason out the right thing to do.

I am not a moral relativist, although I do believe that reasonable persons can come to different conclusions. Moral relativists dismiss moral debate as no more than idle rationalizing, in which what people think is driven by the cultural ideals inculcated in them from birth. On the contrary, I believe that Kantian (could the action I contemplate be done by everyone?) and utilitarian (how might I accomplish the greatest good for the greatest number?) modes of moral reasoning can be effective, and I endorse the impartiality and objectivity invoked by these modes as important forms of cognitive accountability.

Nevertheless, in the spirit of a "cautionary note" I stress that in specific instances of moral debate, sometimes different judgments arise from differences between what people see, and sometimes what people see is inarguable for them because it is provided by an ability to grasp the salient feature that is partly constitutive of the kind of person they are. I find that both Kantians and utilitarians do not appreciate enough the contribution made by seeing to judging and thereby give us an account of moral debate that is too rational. I am trying to correct that here. Sometimes what catches the eye as the morally salient feature of a situation is a reflection of the kind of person one is—and one's own rational review of the kind of person he or she is may not suffice as a way of developing into another kind of person. Even though in the minds of others there may be a host of reasons for change, there are limits to the kind of person one can reason oneself into becoming. Perhaps attention to Sophocles' play *Antigone* will help me make plausible what I am saying about the way our moral reasoning can be affected by our ability to see the salient features of situations that perplex us.

SITUATIONAL APPRECIATION IN *ANTIGONE*

The way a person's judgment of the right thing to do can be directed by her ability to pick out the morally salient feature of her situation is illustrated by the confrontation between Creon and Antigone in Sophocles' play. Creon has become King of Thebes, and Polynices, his nephew, has been slain by Creon's men for treacherously turning upon Thebes. Antigone, a sister of Polynices and betrothed to Haemon, Creon's son, must decide whether she will obey the order of her King by leaving Polynices' body unburied (a disgrace fit for a traitor) or the order of her religion by burying the body. To Antigone the most salient feature of the situation is that the body lies before everyone disgraced. She remarks to Ismene, her sister, "Is he not my brother, and yours, whether you like it/Or not? I shall never desert him, never" (Sophocles, 1947, p. 128).

Antigone's reasoning is the practical syllogism:

> Pious people bury their own family members
> Polynices is my brother, and he is unburied
> ____________________________________
> Out of piety I should bury Polynices

In contrast, Creon's ability for situational appreciation causes him to see something different:

> And no less damned is he who puts a friend
> Above his country; I have no good word for him.
> As God above is my witness, who sees all,
> When I see any danger threatening my people,
> Whatever it may be, I shall declare it.
> No man who is his country's enemy
> Shall call himself my friend. (p. 131)

To Creon it is Polynices' treachery that is most salient. He is unable to see, as Antigone does, that disgrace of Polynices' body before God disgraces him as well, so he reasons differently:

> Kings should dishonor traitors to their kingdom
> Polynices is a traitor
> ———
> The right thing to do is to dishonor Polynices
> by forbidding his burial

Although syllogisms can be used to represent the way Antigone and Creon reason, in truth neither of them start with a first premise and reason downward. Instead, they start their reasoning by finding a second premise, and this comes from seeing the salient feature of the situation. They then select from their overarching conceptions of living rightly the major premise that addresses the salient feature as they each see it, and proceed to draw their conclusions.

The ability of situational appreciation exercised in the making of a second premise is not itself a form of reasoning; rather, it is a way of seeing. Admittedly, reasoning can direct seeing. One might look into the trunk of a car to find the cause of a bothersome rattle. But being situationally appreciative is not like being a detective who hypothesizes about a cause on the basis of evidence. Instead, it is much like aesthetic appreciation; that is, it is a matter of letting the most striking feature of a situation catch one's eye much as we let the aesthetically prominent features of a painting capture our attention when we perceive beauty. A visual ability is at work here, not an ability to reason. Creon simply cannot see that the fact that Polynices is an unburied nephew could possibly outweigh the fact that Polynices is a traitor, so he cannot be tolerant of Antigone's reasoning. Similarly, Antigone cannot be tolerant of Creon's reasoning because she does not see what Creon sees.

What people look for in situations may reflect their overarching ideal of the person they would like to be, but the activity of looking is itself not a form of reasoning. Suppose I have decided that I want to be a person of good cheer so that in the situations in which I find myself I look for the positive. To the degree that I become the kind of person endorsed by my ideal, my focusing on the positive features of situations is not something I deliberately do, instance by instance. Rather, it is something I do spontaneously as a result of my being the kind of person I aspired to become. Earlier, it might have been unnatural for me to focus on the positive; now, I cannot do otherwise. An Antigone could, after reflective consideration, decide that a pious life is, overall, best for her, and thus set about training herself to pick out the features of her situations that are pertinent to piety. As a result, in the play, having become the kind of person she wanted to be, it is the disgrace to Polynices' body that strikes her as being the most salient feature of her situation. This is how she sees things.

It is important for my analysis of the nature of the conflict between Antigone and Creon that they both confront the same situation but that what each sees in the situation is different. If they were not confronting the same situation, their determinations of the right thing to do could be interpreted as reflecting the difference between the situations. On the other hand, I want to stress that the determinations reflect what each of them sees, and that they see differently even though the same things are before them to be seen.

Additionally, the conflict between these two figures would be trivialized if it were attributed to their occupying different social roles. Granted, Creon is King, and it is the duty of kings to defend their kingdoms from traitors. But, if Creon were prohibiting Polynices' burial out of a sense of fidelity to his role, he could appreciate the social contingency of his thinking (that were he in another role he might reason differently). Sophocles is careful to avoid suggesting that the protagonists have any sense that they might do otherwise were they in different roles. Their conclusions emanate from who they are as persons, not from the roles they occupy. We must make a distinction between occupying the role of king (I could do that) and being a king (I could not be that). To be a king I must not only act like a king, with regal bearing and so forth; additionally, I must be incapable of acting in any other way. Sometimes, when people play an assumed role long enough, they become the person behind the role. Afterwards, when they speak, they are doing far more than playing a part because the part has become constitutive of who they are as a person. If the part originally called for seeing as salient the political features in situations, now they must see the political features because it has become second nature for them to do so, and they cannot see anything else with equal interest.

People are marked off from each other in part by what they are able to see, and what they are able to see has bearing on what they find it fitting to do.

ARISTOTLE'S THEORY OF SITUATIONAL APPRECIATION

Aristotle's *Nichomachean Ethics* gives attention to the contribution made by our ability for situational appreciation to the determination of what is right. Aristotle explains that living a moral life is a matter of doing well (he calls doing well *eudaimonia*), and doing well is a matter of applying appropriate guidelines (the moral virtues) to instances that require them. The identification of such instances is done through the exercise of "practical reasoning," and the product of practical reasoning is a syllogism, like the ones I used to represent Creon's and Antigone's thinking. An illustrative syllogism provided by Aristotle is:

> Light meats are digestible and wholesome
> That sort of meat (e.g., chicken) is light
> ___
> That sort of meat is digestible and wholesome

Aristotle appreciates that in order to maintain good health people must not only know that light meats are healthy but also must have the ability to see which meats are light and which are not:

> Nor is practical wisdom concerned with universals only—it must also recognize the particulars; for it is practical, and practice is concerned with particulars. This is why some who do not know, and especially those who have experience, are more practical than others who know; for if a man knew that light meats are digestible and wholesome, but did not know which sorts of meat are light, he would not produce health, but the man who knows that chicken is wholesome is more likely to produce health. (Aristotle, *Nichomachean Ethics*, 1141b 15–20)

Aristotle is proposing here that practicing the overarching ideal of "doing well" has much to do with "particulars," that is, with recognizing the features of a situation that are salient to a way of living that gives witness, situation after situation, action after action, to one's devotion to the ideal of doing well. The challenge that people face is not to identify actions that might be casually efficacious toward some future goal; rather, the challenge is, situation after situation, to be true to an overarching ideal by examining the situation in order to see what would qualify as a suitable, achievable instantiation of the ideal at that moment. Seeing the salient features of a situation in order to know how to instantiate an ideal involves the perceptual ability of "intuitive reason" (i.e., nous):

> Now all things which have to be done are included among particulars or ultimates; for not only must the man of practical wisdom know particular facts, but understanding and judgment are also concerned with things to be done, and these are ultimates. And intuitive reason is concerned with the ultimates in both directions; for both the first terms and the last are objects of intuitive reason and not of argument, and the intuitive reason which is presupposed by demonstrations grasps the unchangeable and first terms, while the intuitive reason involved in practical reasonings grasps the last and variable fact, i.e., the minor premiss. For these variable facts are the starting-points for the apprehension of the end, since the universals are reached from the particulars; of these therefore we must have perception, and this perception is intuitive reason. (Aristotle, *Nichomachean Ethics*, 1143a, 31–1143b 6)

Facts serve as the "starting points" for determining the major premise, Aristotle explains, and the facts are identified by exercising a form of "intuitive reason" that is likened to "perception." When they "perceive" the facts that will direct their determination of the major premise, people are functioning nonargumentatively. They are not determining what the facts must be on the basis of reasoning; rather, they determine the facts on the basis of what they simply see before them.

Two of the virtues that win Aristotle's endorsement and serve as ingredients of his conception of living well are "high-mindedness" and "righteous indignation." The high-minded are disposed to shrug off the petty things in life, while those committed to righteous indignation are disposed to treat serious matters seriously. Persons who are committed to both virtues must determine, on the basis of what they perceive to be the facts of a situation, whether they are confronted with something serious or something petty. They will then know which major premise to employ, the one recommending righteous indignation or the one supporting high-mindedness. Suppose, for instance, that I continue to be troubled by what someone said to me last night, and I wonder whether I should let it go or address it. The person said it is often hard to know how to take my jokes. Was she simply saying that I make bad jokes, or was she saying that I use jokes to veil criticisms of people and, perhaps, some hostility toward them? I can't determine how best to respond to the incident by looking at the guidelines endorsing high-mindedness and righteous indignation; I have to determine whether to take what I heard as petty or serious. That determination is not to be arrived at by reasoning. The issue is, "How do I see the incident, as petty or as serious?" I must review from memory what was said, how it was said, and the context in which it was said, and then pick out the salient feature of the incident as I recall it. Having done all that, I now see that something important was said to me, so on the basis of this fact I judge that the right thing to do is, in the spirit of righteous indignation, to bring up the incident and to ask my friend directly if she meant to say something more to me than that I produce bad jokes. Next, I go to my wife and tell her about what I heard, how it was said, and the context. She perceives the whole thing as petty and advises me not to bring up the topic again. There is no disagreement between us concerning what was said, how it was said, or the context; we agree about all that, but we disagree about the importance of what happened. We conclude, after we have talked over the incident at length, that I am simply inclined to be a more serious person than she is, and therefore inclined to see things as important and deserving of being treated in the spirit of righteous indignation. This inclination is one of the things that distinguishes me from her. We are just different kinds of persons in this respect.

Because my wife and I are different in this respect, there are no formal criteria by which we can test the competing conclusions we arrrive at in our effort to decide the right thing to do. There are no rational procedures for determining whether what I heard said to me is important or petty. If my wife and I were to continue to reason about the incident we still could not move toward agreement because we see different things in the situation, and what we see guides our determination of the right way to treat the incident. We simply must live with the fact that we disagree.

It is natural for people to see, but the preoccupations reflected in what adults see are not natural because they evolve through learning and self-examination. Aristotle explains that the guidelines (the moral virtues) that are respected within one's community can be analyzed in order to expose what they have in common (he concludes that they all endorse forms of moderation). People can subject the guidelines to reflective consideration in order that they may become clearer about the kind of person they would be if they were to implement them, and having become clearer they can revise the guidelines if they find reason to do so. Nevertheless, Aristotle disagrees with Plato's belief that those who engage in reflective consideration of guidelines can be imaginatively removed from their culture and community and review the guidelines from afar. Aristotle holds that we cannot seriously consider adopting guidelines that are foreign to the way we have been living our lives all along; people are not that malleable. For example, I can't be serious about the possibility of living a good life as it is typically understood by the Inuit or the Japanese because I have no acquaintance with such ways of living. They are just not possibilities for a person like me. Even reading about foreign ways of living cannot make them available to me as realistic options because no reading can convey all the subtle practices that make up a distinctive way of life from the point of view of those inside it. To learn about some of the things that Inuit or Japanese people do in certain kinds of situations is quite different from living as they do moment by moment. No reading can convey all that is involved in daily living. If I were to try to live as the Inuit or Japanese do it would be my trying to live as someone else, not my living as me. Even my appreciation of the integrity of another way of living does not make the way accessible to me personally.

Through the voice of Haemon, Creon's son, Sophocles gives advice on the wise thing to do when profound differences divide persons because their ability for situational appreciation is different:

> Father, there is nothing I can prize above
> Your happiness and well-being. What greater good
> Can any son desire? Can any father
> Desire more from his son? Therefore I say,
> Let not your first thought be your only thought.
> Think if there cannot be some other way.
> Surely, to think your own the only wisdom,
> And yours the only word, the only will,
> Betrays a shallow spirit, an empty heart.
> It is no weakness for the wisest man
> To learn when he is wrong, know when to yield.
> So, on the margin of a flooded river
> Trees bending to the torrent live unbroken,
> While those that strain against it are snapped off.
> A sailor has to tack and slacken sheets
> Before the gale, or find himself capsized. (Sophocles, p. 145)

Sophocles' advice is that those who confront each other because they perceive different things to be salient should be as tolerant as possible of their opponent's position. Wisdom requires them to yield before the force of each other's position, much as trees that bend with the force of rushing water. Sophocles seems to understand that the perceptual preoccupations people bring to situations do not form a single, closed system. Instead, the preoccupations evoke competing and inconsistent perceptions. As a consequence, there is an unfinished, indeterminant character to the conclusions people draw concerning what is required of them in particular cases in order that they may live a way of life that they aspire to overall.

After Antigone buries Polynices in violation of Creon's edict, she and Creon discuss their respective positions:

CREON: You are wrong. None of my subjects thinks as you do.
ANTIGONE: Yes, sir, they do; but dare not tell you so.
CREON: And you are not only alone, but unashamed.
ANTIGONE: There is no shame in honouring my brother.
CREON: Was not his enemy, who died with him, your brother?
ANTIGONE: Yes, both were brothers, both of the same parents.
CREON: You honour one, and so insult the other.
ANTIGONE: He that is dead will not accuse me of that.
CREON: He will, if you honour him no more than the traitor.
ANTIGONE: It was not a slave, but his brother, that died with him.
CREON: Attacking his country, while the other defended it.
ANTIGONE: Even so, we have a duty to the dead.
CREON: Not to give equal honour to good and bad.
ANTIGONE: Who knows? In the country of the dead that may be the law.
CREON: An enemy can't be a friend, even when dead.
ANTIGONE: My way is to share my love, not share my hate.
CREON: Go then, and share your love among the dead. We'll have no woman's law here, while I live. (p. 140)

This exchange has none of the toleration of diverse thinking and displays none of the appreciation of indeterminacy recommended by Haemon. Unlike trees bending before an onrushing torrent, the exchange is a face-off between two intransigent persons who cannot grasp that the opponent's thinking also has worth. Are Creon and Antigone being willfully obstinate? I don't think so.

Obstinacy occurs when people willfully refuse to free their intellect so that they can entertain their opponent's way of thinking. They are free to do so, but they choose not to. But Creon and Antigone both perceive their situation in the only way their preoccupations make it possible for them to perceive it. They are not free to do otherwise. It is not what they choose that is behind what they are saying; it is what they see. It is because they are giving vent to what they as persons each see that they are not moved by the spirit of compromise to some appreciation of the worthiness of their opponent's view. When the stand people take is rooted in who they are as persons, that is, in what they are able to see given the kinds of people they are, people are not open to negotiation and revision of their positions. Knowing full well what they each see before them and each seeing something different, they are unable to use reasoning to bridge the gulf between them.

Haemon's recommendation that differences be accepted in a spirit of toleration foreshadows the principle of contemporary liberal democracy that no particular conception of what constitutes a good life should enjoy an advantaged position in public policy debates. The principle, called the liberal "neutrality" principle, presumes toleration of diversity and a commitment to arbitration under the principle of fairness. But toleration of diversity is possible only when the issues under debate do not relate to what people see of necessity because of who they are. People can be tolerant only when their disposition to see things in a certain way does not prevent them from grasping the legitimacy of their opponent's position, and that is not what is happening between Creon and Antigone.

We have tragedy when, in order to be true to what they see, people confront one another in Sophoclean conflict because they are unable to do otherwise. Today there are a number of conflicts occurring in the United States (abortion is an example) that do not seem to be yielding before the application of reason. Is this because people are not reasoning competently enough, not being logical enough, or is it because rationality itself is constrained by the different results that people get when they exercise their ability for situational appreciation? I don't know, but it is possible that sometimes it is the ability at work that causes the irresolution. People who do not want to deny what they see before them and who see different things cannot easily be brought together in the spirit of compromise. What can be done in schools to help persons prepare for these confrontations?

EDUCATING THE ABILITY FOR SITUATIONAL APPRECIATION

Most people have a natural disposition to respond to the beauty they see around them, but the beauty that they see as educated adults is quite different from the beauty seen by children. The education of the ability to see beauty is a long process involving, among other things, description of what one thinks one sees, analysis of the relationships between elements within a perceptual field, and comparison of one's aesthetic perceptions with the perceptions of others. Gradually viewers become better at seeing the saliency of the features before them, whether they are the features of a painting or a musical composition, and better at verbalizing what they see so that others may know how things look to them.

Educating the ability to appreciate the morally salient features of a situation is much like educating the ability of aesthetic perception. First of all, those who are educating future teachers and school administrators would do well to become self-aware about the things that are likely to strike them as salient when they look at situations. They cannot help other persons become more perceptive until they know their own preoccupations and the way that those preoccupations are reflected in what they see.

Earlier I observed that today the two most widely accepted models of moral deliberation are the Kantian and the utilitarian. The Kantian model calls upon persons to be attentive to the equality of all persons whereas the utilitarian model calls upon persons to be attentive to the way in which situations can be exploited for the greatest amount of good overall. In some situations (examples of which are given in any introductory level ethics book) being true to the equality of all persons would not be acting for the greatest amount of good overall. What people decide to do in these situations will depend upon what they see to be salient, and they will see differently. All may agree that being true to equality and working for the greatest amount of good overall are part of their overarching conception of living a moral life, but each must determine, situation by situation, which alternative is most fitting.

The customs of a particular culture will influence what people see in their situations. For example, it is customary in our culture to see justice (an ideal that is dependent upon the notion that all are equal) as most salient in situations where professors are grading students' work, and it is customary to think that friendship (which makes it possible to weigh persons unequally as subjects for consideration) between professors and students should be reserved until after course work has been completed.

Educators cannot teach forms of perception that are unfamiliar to them personally. This is why their self-awareness is so important. For example, they should become aware of customary ways of distinguishing between professional and nonprofessional situations and how to respond to conflicting versions of professionalism. I explain in my book *Classroom Life as Civic Education* (1989) that it is customary in our culture to think that professional treatment of students as equals involves trying to motivate them all to do schoolwork and reporting back to them the merit of the work they have produced. These two practices sometimes conflict with each other in actuality because reports of the merit of work can cause students to lose motivation to continue working. When this happens, teachers find that they must cope with conflict between two of their professional practices, neither of which can be abandoned without becoming perceived as unfair. They cope with the conflict by determining what is the most salient, situation by situation. Is the need to motivate most important, or is it the student's need to hear something about the merit of her or his work? For example, what should a teacher who is talking to students about rough drafts do with a student who is easily discouraged by the truth? Which should the teacher address first, the rough draft or the need for encouragement? It would be nice if students were always motivated by hearing the truth, but sometimes that is not the case, leaving the teacher with the task of determining what it is right to do, and that will depend upon how the situation looks to him or her.

Equality and utility are only two of the ideals that might be part of a person's overarching conception of living well. Loyalty and industriousness might be adopted as well. In Wendell Berry's (1986) short story "Thicker Than Liquor," Wheeler Catlett helps his father, Marce, haul water in barrels from a spring to the livestock during a drouth. One evening, as father and son sit side by side on a wagon bed after a long day of hauling, Wheeler sees his father in a new way:

> It was a moment that would live with Wheeler for the rest of his life, for he saw his father then as he had at last grown old enough to see him, not only as he declared himself, but as he was. And in that seeing Wheeler became aware of a pattern, that his father both embodied and was embodied in, that also contained the drouth and made light of it, that contained other hardships also and made light of them. For his father's good work was on that place in a way that granted and collaborated in its own endurance, that had carried them thus far, and would carry them on. Looking at his father, Wheeler knew, and would not forget, that though they were surrounded by the marks and leavings of a bad year, they were surrounded also by the marks and leavings of good work, which for that year and any other proposed an end and a new beginning. (pp. 11–12)

Educators of future teachers and administrators might use literature to bring to their students' attention the way one's ability for situational appreciation works in human relationships. Not only must educators give thought to their own ability for situational appreciation and their overarching conception of living well, they must also help students become similarly self-aware, and this can be done in part by calling their attention to episodes in literature like the one involving Wheeler and his father.

Another thing teachers might do is to give their students situations upon which they may exercise their abilities. What I have in mind is the development of ability by actually making perceptions of the morally salient features of situations, situations that may be provided by literature as well as by life. For example, in the same short story Wheeler is asked to drive into the city to fetch his Uncle Peach. Peach is described by the narrator as a loveable ne'er-do-well who works fitfully as a carpenter between drunken binges that inevitably lead to helplessness in a Louisville hotel. Before he went off to law school Wheeler sought to "oppose" Peach because he was "affronted" by his uncle's sloth and lack of self-control. Later, after graduation, Wheeler sees his Uncle differently:

> Wheeler, who loved his father and liked his ways, assumed that he thought and felt as his father did. But when he returned home, Uncle Peach devolved upon him. He was perhaps made eligible to come into this inheritance by the

> ownership of an automobile, which, as it turned out, proved the finest windfall of Uncle Peach's entire drinking career. It meant that he could get drunk in complete peace of mind. He could go clear to Louisville, spend all his money, exhaust his credit, ruin his health—and then Wheeler would come and take him home in the car, paying off whatever creditors might stand in the way. It was a grand improvement over the horse-and-buggy days. (Berry, 1986, pp. 13–14)

Of course, students would not be related to Peach as Wheeler is, but they could determine whether Peach "devolves" upon them in the same way he does upon Wheeler, and in doing so they might practice instantiating their own overarching conception of living well. What weight do they give to loyalty and industriousness in a situation where these values conflict? What would they see as most salient?

Additionally, educators might consider asking students to give some attention to their conceptions of the values necessary to live a morally admirable life. I have suggested that equality, utility, loyalty, and industriousness might be considered as possibilities. Civic-mindedness and reverence might also be considered. The goal of such considerations would be to arrive at an overarching conception that calls upon a person to bring to situations a large but manageable number of pertinent concerns.

CONCLUSION

I have explained that the moral education of future teachers and school administrators should include development of the perceptual ability to pick out the salient feature of a situation. This is because seeing enters into judging: the better prepared people are to see, the better they may judge. And although there are limits, within a short space of time, to how well people can revise their own ability to see, over a period of years they can be helped to develop comprehensive ideals of living rightly that call for sensitive and thorough inspection of situations. In short, seeing is natural but *how* people see is subject to education, and moral education should have as one of its objectives the enhancement of the way persons see what is most important in the situations that perplex them.

REFERENCES

Aristotle (1941). Nichomachean ethics. In R. McKeon (Ed.), *The basic works of Aristotle*. New York: Random House.

Berry, W. (1986). Thicker than liquor. In *The wild birds: Six stories of the Port William Membership*. San Francisco: North Point Press.
Bricker, D. (1989). *Classroom life as civic education: Individual achievement and student cooperation in schools*. New York: Teachers College Press.
Sophocles (1947). Antigone. In E. F. Watling (Trans.), *The Theban plays*. London: Penguin.

2 The Liberal Democratic Tradition and Educational Ethics

KENNETH R. HOWE
University of Colorado

The preamble to the Code of Ethics of the Education Profession begins with the following two sentences:

> The educator, believing in the worth and dignity of each human being, recognizes the supreme importance of the pursuit of truth, devotion to excellence, and the nurture of democratic principles. Essential to these goals is the protection of freedom to learn and to teach and the guarantee of equal educational opportunity for all. (in Strike & Soltis, 1985, p. xiii)

The "dignity of each human being," the "nurture of democratic principles," "freedom to learn and to teach," and "equal educational opportunity for all" all find their natural homes in the liberal democratic tradition, and their prominent mention in the articulated ethical mission of the teaching profession shows its implicit commitment to this tradition.

Taking this commitment as my point of departure, I will first describe in greater detail just what the liberal democratic tradition is, with the aim of explicating how it undergirds the kind of perspective on educational ethics embodied in the passage above. My aims here will be largely expository, although I will argue that of the strands of the tradition I consider, what I call "liberal egalitarianism" is the most defensible. Using this framework, I will then address some of the current challenges to the tradition that have been developed over the last several decades — namely, that it is inherently biased against women and minorities. My aims here will be to further elucidate the liberal democratic tradition and bring it up to date by illustrating how it is responding to these current challenges.

THREE PROMINENT PHILOSOPHICAL VIEWS IN THE LIBERAL DEMOCRATIC TRADITION

Nowadays the term *liberal* is typically used to describe the end of the political spectrum opposite *conservative*. Liberals endorse, whereas conservatives oppose, governmental intervention to solve social problems, schemes to redistribute income from the rich to the poor, scrupulous protection of civil liberties, a woman's right to an abortion, and a host of other positions. However, the term *liberal* also has a long history in political theory, in which it is used to describe a broad political tradition that encompasses both liberals *and* conservatives (as these terms are used above). What makes views that can otherwise diverge quite dramatically "liberal" in this sense is a shared commitment to the fundamental liberal values of liberty and equality; they differ regarding how to interpret and balance these values.

The liberal democratic tradition is a complex amalgam of philosophy, law, economics, political science, sociology, and so forth. Thus, a focused perspective is needed to make a discussion of the tradition manageable. I will therefore explicate and evaluate three major philosophical competitors in the liberal democratic tradition—utilitarianism, libertarianism, and liberal egalitarianism—using how each interprets and balances the liberal values of liberty and equality as the unifying thread. I have chosen a philosophical perspective both because it is the one I know and because of philosophy's historical effort to provide political theory with an ethical foundation.

Utilitarianism

Utilitarianism is an ethical theory that judges the rightness of actions and policies in terms of their consequences. In particular, an action or policy is right if, from among the available alternatives, it is the one that maximizes total benefit, or, more technically, satisfies the "Principle of Utility." For example, consider the policy debate that is now raging over "schools of choice" plans. For a utilitarian, whether implementing schools of choice plans is morally the best policy will depend on whether such an educational policy shift would result in the best overall consequences. If, all things being equal, schools of choice plans would result in higher student achievement, increased economic competitiveness, and the other things for which they are touted than the alternatives, then they would be endorsed by utilitarianism.

In making their calculations, utilitarians incorporate the principle of equality by insisting that everyone (and some utilitarians would include animals) benefits equally. John Stuart Mill, probably the most well-known utilitarian of all, takes it as a given that "the interests of all are to be regarded equally" (1961b, p. 435). Thus, like any theory in the liberal democratic tradition, utilitarianism precludes providing special privileges to individuals on the basis of considerations such as birthright, social rank, and the like.

As all liberal theorists must, utilitarians also incorporate the liberal value of liberty. In a much cited passage from *On Liberty* (1961a), Mill voices his commitment to liberty, which is unusually strong:

> [T]he sole end for which mankind are warranted, individually or collectively, in interfering with the liberty of action of any of their number is self protection . . . the only purpose for which power can be rightfully exercised over any member of a civilized community, against his will, is to prevent harm to others. . . . He cannot rightfully be compelled to do or forbear because it will be better for him to do so, because it will make him happier, because, in the opinion of others, to do so would be wise, or even right. (p. 484)

Mill was one of the earliest and most influential utilitarians. Since his time, utilitarianism has dominated the liberal democratic tradition (Rawls, 1971), and continues to exert considerable influence. It has come under increasing criticism, however, for the manner in which it construes both liberty and equality—not surprisingly, libertarians focus their criticisms on a perceived compromise of liberty; egalitarians focus theirs on a perceived compromise of equality. These criticisms will be described in greater detail later in a way that will help explicate libertarianism and egalitarianism in addition to utilitarianism. There is an additional criticism, however, that may be most fruitfully introduced here: It is by no means clear, much less uncontroversial, what the benefit (or good) to be maximized should be.

Historically, the most common criterion of the good has been happiness. But this criterion needs to be operationalized in some fashion if it is to permit utilitarian calculations. Individual preferences, as determined by polls, for example, is one modern suggestion. But relying on mere preferences obliterates the distinction between what is legitimate or worthwhile for people to value and what is not. A vulgar, hedonistic society—for instance, one that valued only money and the pleasures it can buy—would be judged morally best if this is what served to maximize the satisfaction of preferences among its members. To take a more extreme case, one could imagine a society in which the satisfaction of preferences was maximized by sanctioning the practices of slavery and fights to the death between gladiators.

This is an unwelcome conclusion, but trying to avoid it (e.g., as Mill did in *Utilitarianism*, 1961b)—by somehow ranking certain preferences as worthwhile or "progressive" and others as vulgar—leads to the difficult problem of determining who is to decide and how they are to justify foisting their judgment on others, particularly in a liberal democracy where people are presumably afforded the freedom to decide for themselves which vision of happiness to pursue.

This problem is perhaps the most fundamental one for utilitarianism because it calls into question the feasibility of utilitarianism's brand of "consequentialism"—relying solely on the consequences for the Principle of Utility to determine whether an action or policy is morally right. Utilitarianism appears to be unable to capture, in its own terms, the difference between *mere preferences* and *legitimate claims*. What seems to be required to capture this distinction is a nonconsequentialist theory that appeals to principles, rights, and other such notions, that apply independent of the consequences for the Principle of Utility, for example, the rights not to be enslaved or forced to engage in fights to the death. Though they differ quite substantially in other ways, libertarians and liberal egalitarians alike reject utilitarianism in favor of nonconsequentialist theories.

Libertarianism

For libertarians (e.g., Nozick, 1974), liberty is the overriding value, and maximizing it is the best way to avoid showing disrespect for persons' dignity by treating them paternalistically (as if they were children or incompetent to judge for themselves what is in their own best interests). According to Nozick, only a "minimalist" or "nightwatchman" state can be justified, in which the state's power to infringe on individual liberty is limited to protecting the rights of citizens to be free from crime, foreign aggression, and interference in freely executing agreements and transferring goods. Thus, unlike utilitarians, libertarians have no difficulty defining what the criterion of benefit should be, for they object in principle to interference by government in the freely chosen activities of citizens in order to distribute society's benefits for the purpose of achieving some "end state" such as maximum total benefit.

Because libertarianism is thus a nonconsequentialist view, it is not the patterns of results that determine the rightness of policies and actions, but the procedures that govern exchanges and agreements among free citizens. Libertarians would endorse Mill's stance on liberty but would reject his stance on the Principle of Utility as the overriding principle for distinguishing right from wrong. In terms of the example of schools of choice plans, Mill might very well endorse them on the grounds that the liberty to choose would result in maximizing total benefit. However, if schools of choice plans did not maximize overall benefit, and if Mill nonetheless remained true to the Principle of Utility as the overriding ethical principle, then he would be required to endorse some other policy on public education. A thoroughgoing libertarian, on the other hand, would object to rendering liberty an *extrinsic value* that is held hostage to producing the right kind of results. Such a libertarian would defend a schools of choice plan solely on the basis of the *intrinsic value* of granting liberty to students (or, more likely, their parents) to choose the kind of education they judged best. Whether such a policy led to bad results, such as a large difference in achievement among identifiable groups, for instance, would be moot.

Just as libertarians take a different view from utilitarians regarding the liberal value of liberty, they take a different view regarding the liberal value of equality. Libertarians also rule out things such as birthright and social rank as justifying inequality, but it is only legitimate interests—interests tied to maximizing liberty versus interests in being given an equal claim to the overall benefits produced by others—that must be given equal protection. In this way, a libertarian conception of equality is formal rather than substantive, and this conception of equality renders it illegitimate for governments to do anything more in the name of equality than play the "nightwatchman" role described above.

Liberal Egalitarianism

I have chosen the term *liberal egalitarianism* (a term also employed independently by Kymlicka, 1990) to refer to the third view in the liberal democratic tradition that I wish to describe. This view is liberal insofar as it is committed to the two liberal values of liberty and equality. It may be distinguished from a strict version of egalitarianism, however, because like all liberal theories it does not hold that inequality must always be eliminated. It holds instead that inequality is only prima facie objectionable, and therefore may be justified. I will explicate this view in terms of the criticisms it advances against utilitarianism and libertarianism, respectively.

It is important to observe that the kind of equality endorsed by utilitarianism does not entail that a policy cannot be right if its result is that different individuals and groups enjoy different levels of benefits. Imagine that a schools of choice plan resulted in a nation composed of 10% rich entrepreneurs, scientists, and engineers, and 90% poor service workers and homeless people—and that this result maximized benefits. Given this result—and setting aside how benefits might be measured (the gross national product is one measure that is implicitly endorsed these days in popular arguments lauding "competitiveness" and the like)—it is consistent with utilitarianism (indeed, it is required by the Principle of Utility as described earlier), to endorse a schools of choice plan. For it is the total benefits, not how evenly they might be distributed, that forms the basis of utilitarian calculations.

Liberal egalitarians find this consequence of utilitarianism unacceptable. Although they do not preclude employing the Principle of Utility, they contend that it can be superseded or "trumped" by rights (e.g., Dworkin,

1979), as well as by principles of justice (e.g., Rawls, 1971). Such liberal egalitarians would object to the above scenario regarding schools of choice plans on the grounds that they are inconsistent with a correct interpretation of equality.

Dworkin (1979), for instance, distinguishes "equal treatment" from "treatment as an equal." *Equal treatment* is the interpretation of equality implicit in utilitarianism, in which everyone's interests are given equal weight. The problem with this interpretation is that it cannot protect essential interests, or rights, which should outweigh or "trump" those that are less essential, or, indeed, illegitimate. For example, if a schools of choice plan were to maximize overall benefit but also result in racial discrimination, the essential interest in, and right to, nondiscrimination would "trump" the Principle of Utility for a thinker such as Dworkin. He would be willing to accept, indeed would insist on, foregoing the Principle of Utility in order to respect rights.

In contrast to the equal treatment interpretation of equality, the *treatment as an equal* interpretation is sensitive to the relative legitimacy of different interests and is closely tied to the concept of "equal respect." Under this interpretation it is difficult to imagine how a society composed of 10% haves and 90% have-nots could show equal respect for its members and thus be ethically defensible, particularly if it failed to do all it could to ensure that those most in need were given the opportunity to share in its goods.

This point leads rather naturally to the principle of equal opportunity and to the views of John Rawls (1971), the foremost twentieth-century philosopher of what I have called "liberal egalitarianism." For utilitarians, equal opportunity, like any other principle, is subordinate to the Principle of Utility. Thus, although utilitarians can (and most no doubt do) endorse equal opportunity, because it ultimately must be sanctioned by the Principle of Utility, its existence is precarious. For example, consider the rapid increase in government support for social programs in general and educational programs in particular following the riots of the late sixties. Such programs can be (and, in fact, often were) justified on the utilitarian grounds that equalizing opportunity leads to a reduction of violence, an increased quality of life for all, identifying and developing talent that would otherwise be wasted, and so forth. Of course, support for such programs has since eroded, and the problem for utilitarianism is that it has been (perhaps unwillingly) an accomplice in this erosion. Nowadays, the perception of many citizens and policy makers is that such programs do not work, or even worse, may be counterproductive (e.g., Murray, 1984), and thus should be abandoned because they do not maximize benefit.

Rawls is able to avoid such waffling on a commitment to the principle of equal opportunity because his theory exempts the requirements of social justice, of which equal opportunity forms a part, from utilitarian calculations. For him, equal opportunity is required for individuals to have a fair chance to enjoy a reasonable amount of society's goods, for example, employment, income, health care, education, and self-respect. And he requires more than equal opportunity in the "formal" sense described in connection with libertarianism's conception of equality; he requires it in a "substantive" sense that he calls "*fair* equality of opportunity" (emphasis added). This conception is based on Rawls's belief that people are not responsible for disadvantages that arise from natural and social contingencies and over which they have no control—who their parents are, how talented they are, whether they are handicapped—and that justice requires social institutions and practices that mitigate these disadvantaging contingencies (to the degree possible) prior to, and sometimes in opposition to, satisfying the Principle of Utility.

Like libertarianism, then, liberal egalitarianism is nonconsequentialist in the sense that it subordinates the Principle of Utility to rights and to justice. Unlike libertarianism, however, it rejects a merely formal interpretation of equality that tends to render liberty hollow. Dworkin (1979) and Kymlicka (1990), in particular, contend that equality is the fundamental value in liberalism, and that rather than existing in tension with liberty such that trade-offs have to be made, liberty requires equality. Liberal egalitarians in general hold that liberty, like equality, must be substantive, or "worth wanting," (Dennett, 1984) rather than merely formal. For this reason, liberal egalitarians, as opposed to libertarians, are disposed to advocate intervening in social activities in order not only to insure equality but, and what for them often amounts to the same thing, to insure that citizens are empowered with a kind of liberty which, as Dewey says, "is found in the interaction which maintains an environment in which *human desire and choice count for something*" (1930, p. 10, emphasis added).

Consider once again the example of a schools of choice plan, and recall that a utilitarian would endorse a schools of choice plan if it maximized benefit and a libertarian would endorse it if it maximized liberty (in the libertarian's formal sense). Liberal egalitarians tend to be much more suspicious and dismissive of such a policy than either utilitarians or libertarians. Amy Gutmann (1987), for instance, contends that the first obligation of public schooling is to ensure that as many children as possible reach the "democratic threshold"—a level of educational success that prepares them to engage as equals in the political processes that shape their lives—and uses this criterion as the standard against which to judge educational policy. A schools of choice plan is thus required to pass a stiffer test than those policies associated with either utilitarian or libertarian reasoning because the requirement of as many children as possible attaining the threshold—attaining the requisites of equality—must be figured in, and this requirement supersedes the values of maximizing benefit and of maximizing liberty.

I have devoted a fair amount of space to the difficulties that beset utilitarianism and libertarianism, and it is thus fitting that I say something about the difficulties that beset liberal egalitarianism. Gutmann's "democratic threshold" provides a clue to the general kinds of difficulties involved. Whereas utilitarians may appeal to the Principle of Utility to set policy, and libertarians may appeal to minimally constrained choice, liberal egalitarianism is more complex and more difficult to apply insofar as it must give some account of what counts as the criterion of a "fair share" (e.g., Kymlicka, 1990) of society's goods and resources. This criterion must blunt both these other forms of reasoning but nonetheless permit justified inequalities. For example, how far should public schools go to ensure that a child with severe emotional disturbances attains the "democratic threshold," and receives his or her "fair share" of educational resources, before it gives up? What is the "democratic threshold" anyway?

The kind of detailed analysis required to meet these difficulties would be out of place in this chapter. (Libertarianism and utilitarianism could be examined in much greater detail as well. See especially Kymlicka, 1990, for an illuminating comparison of the three liberal views I am considering.) Instead, I will simply make explicit my view that, on balance, the difficulties of liberal egalitarianism are less serious than those associated with utilitarianism and libertarianism, particularly regarding what equality requires. Thus it is my view that liberal egalitarianism represents the liberal democratic tradition at its best and most defensible.

LIBERAL DEMOCRATIC THEORY AND EDUCATIONAL ETHICS

Perspectives on educational ethics have both external and internal aims, by which I mean that they concern themselves both with what kind of citizens education should develop and with what kinds of methods should be employed to educate these citizens. Of course, these two aims are intimately related, and how they are fleshed out will depend on the political tradition within which they are formed. In Plato's *Republic*, for instance, the external aim depends on what class of citizens education is being provided for—the leaders, the military, or the producers—and the internal aims—education for knowledge, for courage and loyalty to the state, or for production, respectively—are adjusted accordingly.

In the case of educational ethics rooted in the liberal democratic tradition, the external aim is to develop citizens who are capable of exercising their liberty as equals in a democratic society, and, unlike in Plato's aristocratic form of government, this aim is common to all students. The internal aim is to insure that educational practices as far as possible not only serve this external aim but also exemplify it. Thus, although educational theorists in the liberal democratic tradition certainly have their disagreements (recall the schools-of-choice policy example), they nonetheless agree on certain fundamentals, for example, that public education must produce citizens who can think for themselves and who are thus self-determining. Accordingly, thinkers in this tradition have a long history of criticizing doctrinaire educational practices that suppress, distort, or refuse to entertain questions about truth and about what kinds of lives are worth leading, and that consequently deny students the opportunity to develop their own well-considered views—the kind of educational practice, incidentally, that a nonliberal thinker like Plato openly endorses (at least for certain groups).

By virtue of its commitments to liberty and equality, liberal educational theory is committed to some form of neutrality vis-à-vis the good and virtuous life, and it is just such a commitment that engenders the central problem for a liberal theory of educational ethics (e.g., Strike, 1982), namely, how a system of public education can both be guided by liberal democratic principles and remain neutral regarding what vision of the good it should promote. This general problem has practical and theoretical variants. Practically, particular problematic situations often challenge educators to reason and act in ways that are consistent with liberal principles; for example, should a teacher permit a ninth grader to don a swastika in the name of freedom of expression? Theoretically, broad social and historical realities often challenge the coherence and workability of liberal educational theory per se; for example, is the principle of equality of educational opportunity merely a sham that serves to marginalize groups that reject the received standards of what schooling should promote?

I will devote my attention in the remainder of this chapter to two such theoretical challenges found in the alleged gender and cultural biases inherent in liberal theory. By considering these two issues, I hope to further explicate liberal educational theory, particularly the variety rooted in liberal egalitarianism, as well as to broach several timely and important issues in educational ethics from the perspective of a liberal. I will forestall considering the practical perspective until the case discussion that concludes Part I of this book. There I will be presupposing a liberal approach, rather than explicating and defending it.

Increasingly over the last several decades, liberal political theory in general, and liberal educational theory in particular, have been charged with gender and cultural bias, both of which are inconsistent with the tradition's avowed commitment to equality. These criticisms often take the form of documenting the various and overlapping disparities that exist in educational opportunities and achievement for girls versus boys, men versus women, minority cultures versus white culture, the working class versus the middle class, and so forth. Where criticisms of liberal educational theory take these kinds of disparities as the basis for calls to achieve much greater equality across groups by equalizing educational opportunities, they do not fundamentally challenge the liberal tradition. Instead, they demand that it live up to its promise.

There is a deeper form of criticism, however, that not only goes beyond, but is often at odds with, the type of criticism just described. In particular, liberalism is characterized as being through and through a product and reflection of the historical dominance of white males, particularly those possessing economic power. Although these critics may substantially disagree on other issues, they all seem to agree on the following general conclusion: The liberal quest for equality is a sham because it merely serves to ensconce the status quo, rendering white males the standard of comparison and requiring disempowered groups such as minorities and women to play by existing rules that they had no part in formulating and whose interests such rules do not serve.

In the case of women, for instance, various scholars (e.g., Bellenky, Clinchy, Goldberger, & Tarule, 1986; Gilligan, 1982; Noddings, 1984) have claimed that there are certain ways of thinking and relating to others, as well as certain interests, that are peculiar to women's experience, but that an appreciation of these differences is rarely reflected in society's institutions (e.g., Okin, 1989; Noddings, 1990; Salamone, 1986). For its part, the educational system in particular tends to implicitly embrace the gendered attitudes and practices of society at large and to respond to girls and women accordingly, both in their roles as educators and as students (e.g., Apple, 1988; Kelly & Nihlen, 1982; Oakes, 1990; Sadker & Sadker, 1986; Shakeshaft, 1986; Weiler, 1988; Weis, 1988). Moreover, women are faced with a double bind, insofar as they must pay a price when they *do* play by the existing rules because certain traits are "genderized" (see, e.g., Martin, 1982) such that women are judged differently from men for exhibiting the same behavior.

Similar problems confront certain minorities. "Castelike" minorities—minorities that have involuntarily become a part of the political-economic system, for example, certain Hispanics and African Americans (Ogbu & Matute-Bianchi, 1986)—are faced with the dilemma of either playing by the rules of the dominant culture and compromising their cultural identity or refusing to play and paying a price for preserving it. African Americans, for instance, can either embrace the practice of "acting white" to succeed in school or take an "oppositional" stance that often dooms them to poor performance. A related set of problems faces indigenous peoples such as North American aboriginals (Kymlicka, 1991).

Having briefly characterized these two fundamental criticisms of liberalism, I now return to the overarching question for liberal educational theory—how a system of public education can both be guided by liberal democratic principles and remain neutral regarding what vision of the good it should promote—and address it in the context of these criticisms. It is important, in answering this question, not to confuse and conflate views grounded in liberal egalitarianism with other views that may be advanced within the general liberal democratic tradition. I will thus begin with the now well-known view of E.D. Hirsch (1988) and use it as a foil against which to compare a liberal egalitarian view.

Hirsch does not fit neatly into the three-way division of utilitarianism versus libertarianism versus liberal egalitarianism introduced earlier. As is common in the arena of real-world political and educational argument, he combines elements of several of these philosophical theories, particularly the first two. Hirsch so heavily stresses tradition, however, that it is probably most accurate to simply label his views "conservative." On the other hand, he makes free use of the principles and rhetoric of the liberal democratic tradition, contending that it is only by acquiring "cultural literacy" that the disadvantaged can participate in democratic processes and enjoy equality of opportunity. Hirsch's solution to the challenge posed by multiculturalism is thus to eliminate it by using public education to promote cultural uniformity based on the existing dominant beliefs and practices. According to him, extending cultural literacy to minorities not only benefits them in particular, but is required to preserve democracy. Although Hirsch himself doesn't extend his arguments to include girls and women, his arguments can easily be applied to them. Such an argument would hold that girls and women should become equal to men in various areas of literacy, for example, mathematics and science, where they have traditionally fared poorly.

Hirsch advocates precisely the kind of view within the liberal democratic tradition that is vulnerable to the types of criticisms regarding women and cultural minorities discussed above. In particular, critics charge that because the game is rigged in a way that favors the historically dominant group or groups, particularly white males, equality in achievement of what the dominant group has determined is worthwhile may be quite hollow. In this way, Hirsch's liberal educational ideal incorporates a significant gender and cultural bias, and therefore his version of liberal education fails to adequately resolve the fundamental tension between the requirement of neutrality regarding what public education promotes as the good and the liberal principles of liberty and equality.

Although I think it is a mistake to attempt to formulate a liberal educational ideal that is *completely* neutral (and I will have more to say about this later), it is nonetheless possible to imagine how a theory might be considerably more neutral than Hirsch's concept of cultural literacy. The key to an adequate conception, and what Hirsch seems to so completely miss, is a recognition of the importance of self-respect to persons. Self-respect is in large measure determined by a person's culture and gender, and, intimately related to this, by the degree to which his or her opinions and interests are respected by others.

In his recent defenses of the liberal democratic tradition, Will Kymlicka (1990,1991) concedes to the critics that the liberal democratic tradition has been largely oblivious to the special difficulties presented by cultural and gender differences. He believes, however, that an adequate response to these difficulties is implicit in the writings of prominent liberal egalitarians such as Rawls and Dworkin. (See also Okin, 1989, who advances arguments similar to Kymlicka's, though she focuses exclusively on gender issues.) Specifically, Kymlicka ties the issue of affording self-respect to women and minorities to the principle of granting them equality. He argues that granting women and minorities equality requires giving them a voice in political decision making that is sensitive to their peculiar histories and perspectives. He observes in this connection:

> [I]t only makes sense to invite people to participate in politics (or for people to accept that invitation) if they will be treated as equals. . . . And that is incompatible with defining people in terms of roles they did not shape or endorse. (1991, p. 89)

Extending Kymlicka's argument to address public education, his observation may be slightly reformulated to read as follows:

> [I]t only makes sense to invite people to participate in *schooling* (or for people to accept that invitation) if they will be treated as equals. . . . And that is incompatible with defining people in terms of roles they did not shape or endorse.

In contrast to Hirsch's vision of the liberal educational ideal, which merely explicates and entrenches (or re-entrenches) the status quo, the vision that grows out of a view like Kymlicka's affords everyone, including minorities and women, equal respect, and ensures that their interests will be protected in a process of negotiating educational ideals.

This tack embraces the heart of liberalism, particularly the commitment to equality, but attempts to eliminate the gender and cultural biases that infect it (like those implicit in Hirsch's ideal of "cultural literacy") and stand in the way of realizing true equality. As I intimated above, however, eliminating such biases does not entail embracing a *completely* neutral mission for public education. Liberal educational theorists of all types remain committed to the aim of educating individuals to become competent citizens in a liberal democratic society. The trick is not to eliminate the commitment to the liberal educational ideal, but to define it in such a way that it does not threaten certain identifiable groups like women and minorities with being excluded from enjoying genuine equality.

Amy Gutmann makes a very useful contribution to this line of argument in *Democratic Education* (1987). She asserts that the general aim of public education in a liberal democratic society is to achieve for all students a "democratic threshold" of knowledge, skills, and attitudes that will prepare them to participate as equals in "*conscious* social reproduction." This requires, in turn, that public education be conducted in accord with, and engender in students a commitment to, liberal principles such as nondiscrimination, nonrepression, and tolerance for different ways of life. The application of this general framework to particular educational problems—for example, sexism in education, educating the disadvantaged, integration, vouchers—I will leave to Gutmann's own discussions in *Democratic Education*. The crux of her position is that, in general, far from being neutral, the commitment to a liberal educational theory requires circumscribing democratic negotiations in terms of liberal principles. Similar to Kymlicka's position, however, the correct interpretation and application of such principles vis-à-vis the formulation of educational ideals requires much greater attention to voices that have been historically muted or not heard at all.

CONCLUSION

I have endeavored to provide an overview of the liberal democratic tradition and the kind of theory of educational ethics that grows out of it, as well as to illustrate the tack that liberal educational theorists might take in response to the current controversies surrounding multiculturalism and gender. In the first section I discussed the three predominant kinds of ethical theories in the liberal democratic tradition: utilitarianism, libertarianism, and liberal egalitarianism. Briefly, utilitarianism judges the rightness of actions and policies solely in terms of consequences vis-à-vis the Principle of Utility, and embraces governmental intervention to ensure the principle is satisfied. Libertarianism, a nonconsequentialist view, rejects utilitarianism on the grounds that it entails an unjustified level of governmental interference in individual liberty; it rejects liberal egalitarianism for the same reason. Finally, liberal egalitarianism, also a nonconsequentialist view, rejects utilitarianism on the grounds that it misconstrues the principle of equality and, as a consequence, fails to protect fundamental rights and principles of justice; it rejects libertarianism on the grounds that it misconstrues equality in another way, and, as a consequence, protects only a very hollow kind of liberty for those who are disadvantaged. I concluded that from among these theories, only liberal egalitarianism provides an adequate conception of equality and thus that only it lives up to the promise of liberalism.

In the second section, I employed a liberal egalitarian framework to show how the liberal democratic tradition might be successfully defended against the charge that it is inherently biased against women and minorities. My argument conceded that various thinkers within the liberal tradition are indeed vulnerable to this charge; my specific example was E. D. Hirsch. I argued that other thinkers, however, such as Kymlicka and Gutmann, who emphasize the complex relationships between equality, liberty, gender, and cultural identity, point in the direction of a tenable response.

My discussion was admittedly limited in at least three respects. First, it generally proceeded at a relatively abstract level, linking up to education only in terms of broad issues of educational policy (e.g., schools of choice) quite removed from the day-to-day ethical difficulties that confront educators. I hope to at least partially remedy this deficiency in my discussion of the case to follow in Chapter 4, in which I will address a concrete problem in educational ethics from the perspective of a liberal educational theorist. Second, I neglected or left underdeveloped difficulties with the liberal democratic tradition that certain critics believe are acute, if not fatal. These problems are addressed by David Bricker (in Chapter 1) and Nel Noddings (in Chapter 3). Finally, my arguments defending the liberal democratic tradition against the charge that it is inherently biased against women and minorities obviously require a good deal more development to be convincing. This is a difficulty that has no remedy in the present context. Leaving them in such a sketchy state is unavoidable given the task I set for myself.

On the other hand, this is probably the best place to leave a general discussion of the liberal democratic tradition in education. For it is precisely these kinds of fundamental difficulties that are presently spurring liberal thinkers to refine and adapt it, and the responses that have been, and are being, developed illustrate its vibrant and dynamic nature. It should be observed that far from being apologists for the status quo, the liberal egalitarians have called for transformations of society's institutions in general, as well as its educational institutions in particular, that are nothing short of radical by comparison to what typically passes for "liberal" in the current political arena.

REFERENCES

Apple, M. (1988). *Teachers and texts: Political economy of class and gender relations in education*. New York: Routledge, Chapman & Hall.

Bellenky, M., Clinchy, B., Goldberger, N., & Tarule, J. (1986). *Women's ways of knowing*. New York: Basic Books.

Dennett, D. (1984). *Elbow room: The varieties of free will worth wanting*. Cambridge, MA: MIT Press.

Dewey, J. (1930). *Human nature and conduct*. New York: Random House.

Dworkin, R. (1979). *Taking rights seriously*. Cambridge, MA: Harvard University Press.

Gilligan, C. (1982). *In a different voice: Psychological theory and women's development*. Cambridge, MA: Harvard University Press.

Gutmann, A. (1987). *Democratic education*. Princeton, NJ: Princeton University Press.

Hirsch, E. D. (1988). *Cultural literacy*. New York: Vintage Books.

Kelly, G., & Nihlen, A. (1982). Schooling and the reproduction of patriarchy: Unequal workloads, unequal rewards. In M. Apple (Ed.), *Cultural and economic reproduction in education*. Boston: Routledge & Kegan Paul.

Kymlicka, W. (1990). *Contemporary political theory: An introduction*. New York: Clarendon Press.

Kymlicka, W. (1991). *Liberalism, community and culture*. New York: Clarendon Press.

Martin, J. R. (1982). The ideal of the educated person. In D. DeNicola (Ed.), *Proceedings of the Thirty-seventh Annual Meeting of the Philosophy of Education Society* (pp. 3–20). Normal, IL: Philosophy of Education Society.

Mill, J. S. (1961a). On liberty. In J. S. Mill & J. Bentham, *The Utilitarians* (pp. 475–600). Garden City, NY: Doubleday. (Original work published 1863)

Mill, J. S. (1961b). Utilitarianism. In J. S. Mill & J. Bentham, *The Utilitarians* (pp. 402–472). Garden City, NY: Doubleday. (Original work published 1849)

Murray, C. (1984). *Losing ground: American social policy 1950–1980*. New York: Basic Books.

Noddings, N. (1984). *Caring: A feminist approach to ethics and moral education*. Berkeley: University of California Press.

Noddings, N. (1990). Feminist critiques in the professions. In C. Cadzen (Ed.), *Review of research in education* (Vol. 16, pp. 393–424). Washington DC: American Educational Research Association.

Nozick, R. (1974). *Anarchy, state, and utopia*. New York: Basic Books.
Oakes, J. (1990). Opportunities, achievement, and choice: Women and minorities in science and mathematics. In C. Cadzen (Ed.), *Review of research in education* (Vol. 16, pp. 153–222). Washington DC: American Educational Research Association.
Ogbu, J., & Matute-Bianchi, M. (1986). Understanding sociocultural factors: Knowledge, identity, and school adjustment. In *Beyond language: Social and cultural factors in schooling language minority students* (pp. 73–142). Los Angeles: Evaluation, Dissemination, and Assessment Center, California State University.
Okin, S. M. (1989). *Justice, gender, and the family*. New York: Basic Books.
Rawls, J. (1971). *A theory of justice*. Cambridge, MA: Harvard University Press.
Sadker, M., & Sadker, D. (1986). Sexism in the classroom: From grade school to graduate school. *Phi Delta Kappan, 67*, 512–516.
Salamone, R. (1986). *Equal education under the law*. New York: St. Martin's Press.
Shakeshaft, C. (1986). A gender at risk. *Phi Delta Kappan, 67*, 499–503.
Strike, K. A. (1982). *Educational policy and the just society*. Chicago: University of Illinois Press.
Strike, K. A., & Soltis, J. (1985). *The ethics of teaching*. New York: Teachers College Press.
Weiler, K. (1988). *Women teaching for change*. South Hadley, MA: Bergin & Garvey.
Weis, L. (Ed.). (1988). *Class, race, and gender in American education*. Albany, NY: State University of New York Press.

3 Caring
A Feminist Perspective

NEL NODDINGS
Stanford University

Feminists have raised important objections to traditional ethics (Kittay & Meyers, 1987). At the same time, they have begun to develop an ethical orientation that arises from female experience in such activities as child rearing, nursing, teaching, and homemaking (Noddings, 1984). Although the moral orientation referred to as "care and response" seems to be observed more frequently in women than in men (Gilligan, 1982), feminists do not usually claim that caring is an exclusively female ethic. On the contrary, our claim is that, if caring is a desirable moral orientation, both females and males should engage in the sort of work that induces it—work that Sara Ruddick (1980, 1989) calls the "work of attentive love."

In this chapter I will look first at the objections feminists have raised against traditional ethics. Next, I will give a brief summary of current analyses of caring. Finally, I will discuss caring in its relation to teaching.

OBJECTIONS TO TRADITIONAL ETHICS

Feminists have criticized traditional ethics for devaluing the role of emotions and personal life. The two great comprehensive ethical systems—Kant's ethics of duty, and utilitarianism—put enormous emphasis on human rationality. Kant explicitly banishes emotion from ethical judgment, although he allows the moral agent to "feel good" after he or she has acted appropriately out of duty. Kant and his followers argue that the emotions cannot be trusted to guide moral life because the best emotions (e.g., compassion, joy, generosity of spirit) cannot always be summoned. In times of moral indecision, a person may be dominated by anger, jealousy, or fear. Those who espouse an ethics of duty point to a capacity for detached, principled reasoning shared by all persons. Using this capacity, agents should judge the rightness of their proposed acts by asking: Can I logically will that what I propose to do should become binding on all other agents in similar situations?

Feminists, along with other contemporary critics (MacIntyre, 1981; Williams, 1985), argue that such an ethical orientation strips human life of its humanity—its personal attachments, projects, and sense of community. Contemporary liberal theories of justice, they argue, suffer from the same defect. They call upon us to do what is "right" without regard for any particular person's whole situation. Seyla Benhabib (1987) has argued that these ethics prepare us to deal with a "generalized" other but not with the particular, concrete others we meet in real life.

Similarly, utilitarianism expects us to treat others (and even ourselves) impartially. But in some ways utilitarianism is more intuitively appealing than Kantian ethics. It recognizes that human beings seek happiness and define it in a variety of ways. It admits that we all prefer to optimize the ratio of happiness to pain in our own lives. But, in formulating the utilitarian principle (that we should act to optimize this ratio in whatever arena our judgments are made), it asks us to regard every individual as "one" without regard to personal histories, attachments, or preestablished commitments. (Utilitarians do allow us to consider those characteristics of individuals that might be called "utilities." In making a judgment about the allocation of scarce resources, for example, we may compare people on their likely contributions to the common good.) An even greater fault, many critics argue, is that minority groups may suffer greatly as the ratio of happiness to pain grows impressively in the larger society. Feminists point to situations in contemporary American life where this seems to be true; for example, a substantial minority of workers are paid poverty wages to strengthen the general economy and increase the happiness of the majority. Readers can no doubt think of many other examples.

Some critics—communitarians, for example—agree with feminists that liberalism (the legacy of Kant) and utilitarianism are both badly flawed (Bellah, Madsen, Sullivan, Swidler, & Tipton, 1985; MacIntyre, 1981; Sandel, 1982; Taylor, 1979). They recommend that moral theory incorporate a fuller and more realistic description of persons, that attention be given to the rights of communities as well as individuals, and that we recognize the traditional bonds that guide our moral behavior.

Although feminists and communitarians often agree in their criticisms of liberalism and utilitarianism, those feminists who associate themselves with an ethic of caring find worrisome features in communitarianism, too. For example, when a group or community becomes exclusive, it may begin to act very much like an individual (Noddings, 1989). It may, that is, act to protect its own rights and interests at the expense of other groups, it may erode the individuality of its members beyond a desirable level, and it may begin to justify its acts in terms of affiliation (the "good guys" are those on our side).

Some feminists are, of course, liberals, utilitarians, or communitarians. These feminists believe that the defects in those theories can be remedied and that feminist thought can contribute to their satisfactory revision. Care theorists, however, believe that more than revision is required. They suggest an alternative vision of what it means to live morally. Whether such an ethic can stand on its own is an open question. Its main insights may, for example, need to be combined with a concept of justice (Okin, 1989). That possibility will not be explored here, but thoughtful readers should keep it in mind.

CURRENT ANALYSES OF CARING

An ethic of care starts with a study of relation. It is fundamentally concerned with how human beings meet and treat one another. It is not unconcerned with individual rights, the common good, or community traditions, but it de-emphasizes these concepts and recasts them in terms of relation. One way to start the conversation on caring is to ask: How might ethics have developed if it had arisen from the sort of experience traditionally associated with women rather than with men? Suppose, that is, that the people who have been responsible for child rearing, homemaking, nursing, and, in general, the maintenance of relationships had written about moral life. What sort of moral theory might have emerged?

The connection between experience and worldview or moral orientation cannot be described exactly, but it seems to be a powerful one. (Even Aristotle recognized the connection.) Consider, for example, our use of expressions such as "military mind," "business mentality," and "police mentality." Although some of what we mean when we use these terms is clearly the product of stereotyping, much of what remains is well documented. Institutions that prepare military officers, business executives, police officers, lawyers, and other professionals admit—even insist—that they are shaping minds or worldviews, not just imparting information and training skills. In teacher education, many educators claim that they are shaping "reflective teachers" or "inquiry-oriented teachers." Exactly what they mean by these terms differs, but the basic belief is clear; they believe a form of experience can be provided that will induce reflection and an orientation toward inquiry and critical thinking. Thoughtful people in all of these institutions know that the desired result is not inevitable, but there is often enough evidence of success to maintain faith in the link between experience and worldview or mental outlook. And sometimes we hang onto the faith with very little evidence!

It is not farfetched, then, to suppose that experience requiring close connection to, and intimate responsibility for the physical and emotional well-being of, particular others induces a distinctive moral orientation. Sara Ruddick (1980, 1989), for example, has described a mental outlook that grows out of experience in raising children. She calls this mental outlook "maternal thinking," because it is a direct outgrowth of the continual demands of children and the responses these demands call forth in their caregivers. Traditionally, caregivers (mothers) have been women; hence, Ruddick names the thinking that arises from caregiving "maternal" thinking. Ruddick is careful to say that anyone—male or female—can be a maternal thinker. What is required is that a person engage in the special work of attentive love. Attentive love involves more than monetary support and authority over the lives of others. It involves responsibility for direct care: the physical care of infants, the bodily affection needed for emotional growth in children, and a holistic concern for the physical, emotional, and spiritual well-being of particular others. The experience of caring directly for others, of taking responsibility for meeting their needs and for the maintenance of healthy relations, gives rise to maternal thinking or, in a broader context, caring.

A lively debate has arisen in psychology over whether females, more often than males, really do exhibit the "care and responsibility" orientation in their moral lives. Carol Gilligan (1982) has described this orientation as a "different voice" in moral deliberation and she recorded this different voice in interviews with women. In Gilligan's work, the care orientation presents a challenge to Lawrence Kohlberg's cognitive-developmental theory on how moral reasoning develops. Gilligan's "different voice" differs from the traditional voice of justice and rights described by Kohlberg. It is not surprising, given our earlier discussion of the connection between experience and mental outlook, that this different voice would be heard more often among women than men. It is also not surprising that highly educated women—whose experience sometimes closely resembles that of men—often use the traditional voice. Similarly, some investigators now report hearing the voice of care and responsibility in men whose experience has paralleled that of women.

Interesting as these gender debates are, they are not the focus of attention for moral theorists and ethicists. In moral theory, we are concerned with the logic and phenomenology of a moral orientation, with the concepts it employs and their interrelations, and with its implication for actual moral life.

Some of the concepts used by care theorists play an important part in other theories and have appeared in nonfeminist writing. The emphasis on relation, for example, is found in the work of Martin Buber. (See Buber, 1970 for a history of the "principle of relatedness.") Buber distinguishes between two modes of meeting, or ways of encountering, other entities. We can meet the other in the I-Thou mode, which is the way of relation. Or we can meet another in the I-It mode; in this mode, we observe others or listen to what they say by assimilating it to preselected schemata. In the I-It mode we glean from others material to be used for our own purposes. Such encounters are instrumental. Many, if not most, of life's encounters are necessarily and properly I-It, but ethical and spiritual life require I-Thou encounters.

Care theorists, too, put great emphasis on relation. Saying the relational word "I-Thou" is, for Buber, an act that relates one person to God through another. Care theorists usually write of the direct relation between human beings without reference to God, but the ideas of engrossment (a form of nonselective attention) and motivational displacement (taking responsibility for helping another) are very close to Buber's description of the I-Thou relation.

Attention (or engrossment) is central to an ethic of caring. Iris Murdoch (1970), well before contemporary care theorists were writing, put great emphasis on attention, naming it as essential to moral life. She traced her use of the concept to Simone Weil (1951). Weil wrote:

> In the first legend of the Grail, it is said that the Grail . . . belongs to the first comer who asks the guardian of the vessel, a king three quarters paralyzed by the most painful wound, "What are you going through?"
>
> The love of our neighbor in all its fullness simply means being able to say to him: "What are you going through?" It is a recognition that the sufferer exists, not only as a unit in a collective, or a specimen from the social category labeled "unfortunate," but as a man, exactly like us. (p. 115)

Weil goes on to say:

> This way of looking is first of all attentive. The soul empties itself of all its own contents in order to receive into itself the being it is looking at, just as he is, in all his truth. Only he who is capable of attention can do this. (p. 115)

The concepts of relation and attention thus have histories prefiguring their use in the ethics of caring. The idea of putting one's motive energy at the disposal of another has also appeared widely in ethics that emphasize *agape* or altruism. Writing on caring in 1971, Milton Mayeroff described caring as taking responsibility for the growth of another. Similarly, Buber described love as "responsibility of an I for a Thou" (1970, p. 66).

These concepts and a few others are captured in the following brief summary of recent analyses of care.

1. *Caring* is used to describe both a relation that has certain characteristics, and the behavior, thinking, and attitude of the carer in the relation. In the former use, it is necessary to discuss the contribution of the recipient of care (or cared-for) and the conditions in which the relation is embedded.

2. A carer attends to the cared-for in a special act of receptivity (nonselective attention or engrossment). In this act, a carer hears, sees, and feels what is there in the other.

3. A carer is disposed to help—often with direct involvement in the other's project, but sometimes with advice or even admonition. The carer's thinking and action are often guided by interests in the preservation, growth, and acceptability of those cared for (Mayeroff, 1971; Ruddick, 1980). Carers want to preserve the lives and well-being of cared-fors; promote their growth; and support them in acceptable behavior. (All of these concepts require separate analyses, for which see Mayeroff, 1971; Ruddick, 1980, 1989; and Noddings, 1992.)

4. Carers are guided by a thoroughgoing consideration of care; that is, attention and the desire to help are directed not only at the particular cared-for but also outward across the entire web of relations. This is necessary because the well-being of both carers and cared-fors depends on the health of their relationships.

5. The contribution of the cared-for is vital to the relation; not only does the response of the cared-for sustain carers in their efforts but it is the essential material by which carers monitor the quality and effects of their caring, in continuous cycles of attention and response.

6. Carers, because they care, strive for competence in whatever reactions or arenas their efforts are applied.

The last two points need a bit of elaboration. All ethics are concerned with how we treat others, but most do not consider the contribution of the second party in relations. In an ethic of care, the cared-for plays a significant role. In mature relationships, of course, both parties have the capacity to be either carers or recipients of care, and they change places as the need arises. But in unequal relations such as parenting and teaching, the role of carer falls steadily to one party.

What does the cared-for contribute in these relations? Every parent of a normal infant knows that the baby contributes much to the caring relation. The smiles, wriggles, coos, babblings, and cuddlings of the baby sustain the parents in their caregiving. Even in the middle of the night, when a mother responds to a fretful child, a smiling response from the infant restores her energy and induces reciprocal smiles. Health care workers know how greatly parents suffer when they have a child who is incapable of these normal responses.

In teaching, too, cared-fors contribute to the relation by responding to their teachers. The response need not be one of spoken gratitude. If students show growth as an obvious result of their teacher's efforts, the teacher's caring is completed. Hands raised, eyes alight with curiosity, honest questions, and passionate debates are all teacher-sustaining responses. Teachers who are deprived of these responses are in danger of burnout.

Because the contribution of students is vital to the caring relation in teaching, we need to talk to students about their part. It is not necessary to scold or preach, but just to convey in words and actions that students are important. In some communities today, many students have never learned how to be cared for, and they need to learn how to distinguish genuine caring from cruelty or neglect and how to respond to it. One of the great strengths of caring as an ethic is that it does not assume that all students should be treated by some impartial standard of fairness. Some students need much more attention than others, and some will respond to one teacher's attention whereas others may need a different teacher's care.

Caregivers therefore respond in different ways to the different needs presented by cared-fors. Because they care, carers strive continuously toward greater competence in whatever work they do. Often critics of caring make the mistake of supposing that caring is inherently soft and sweet. In reality, caring requires heightened moral sensitivity. Carers respond with deference and respect to those who are cool and aloof by nature and with hugs and warm smiles to those who need a more affectionate response. Further, carers learn how to read people and respond appropriately. It is often said that women are better at reading people than are men. If this is true, we might attribute women's greater skill to their greater experience. If we, as educators and parents, give boys experience similar to that long enjoyed by girls, and if we expect them to take responsibility for appropriate responses, they may well gain competence in caring.

Finally, carers do not seek growth only in the *attitude* of care. They strive to become competent in the particular work they do. One who sympathizes with another's needs but has no idea how to meet the need cannot provide adequate care. Parents who feed their hungry children junk food, respond tenderly to illness but fail to have their children immunized, or play roughhouse but never read to their children are not adequate as carers. They could do better. Similarly, caring teachers have an obligation to become competent at whatever they teach and to reflect on their own competence with an eye toward continuous improvement.

CARING AND TEACHING

How can an ethic of care guide teaching? There are two broad ways of answering this question. First, an ethic of care can be used as a critical theory; that is, it can be used to analyze and criticize the structures in which teaching is conducted. It can reveal the struggles and aborted wishes of both teachers and students in today's schools. But caring is more than a critical theory; it suggests positive remedies for the abuses it reveals. Second, carers can be guided in their individual attempts to care as teachers. Both ways of describing how an ethic of care can guide teaching require far more discussion than we can give them here. It may be useful, however, to explore them both briefly.

As carers,

> teachers, like mothers, want to produce acceptable persons—persons who will support worthy institutions, live compassionately, work productively but not obsessively, care for older and younger generations, be admired, trusted, and respected. To shape such persons, teachers need not only intellectual capabilities but also a fund of knowledge about the particular persons with whom they are working. (Noddings, 1988, p. 221)

There are people who disagree with this statement at its most basic level; that is, they disagree that teachers should try to shape acceptable people. They think instead that teachers should transmit, or (in some ethically acceptable way) get students to learn, particular subjects. From this perspective, the ethics of teaching should concentrate on how the acquisition of knowledge can be ethically facilitated by teaching. Ethicists who begin with this view of teaching are concerned with equal access to knowledge, fairness in grading and other procedures, and evaluation of teaching methods for their long-range efficacy. In this last category, for example, they might question techniques that produce correct answers quickly but leave students without powerful methods to continue learning.

Care theorists share many of these concerns, but they are as deeply concerned with the moral and social development of students as with their intellectual development. Shaping moral people requires the development of caring relations. Teachers must know their students well enough to be able to make suggestions fitted to the needs of particular students. When a student cheats, for example, the teacher needs to be concerned with the student's motive and what this behavior means for his or her growth as a person. Caring teachers do not confine themselves to stopping undesirable behavior and meting out fair or impartial punishments. They begin with the best possible motive, consonant with reality, and help the student to understand and evaluate his or her own thinking and behavior. One student may be impelled by a desire for some promised reward, another by fear, still another by the wish to help a friend. In dialogue, both teacher and student may come to see that some motives are more desirable than others and, together, they may find a way to construct new motives as well as to eliminate the initial undesirable behavior.

This way of working with students requires the time to build relations of care and trust. Jaime Escalante, the real-life teacher-hero of *Stand and Deliver*, has insisted that he needs three years—not just one—to work with his students. Not only are intellectual needs better met by such extended contact but, perhaps more importantly, the entire range of developmental needs can be more responsibly addressed as well. Caring teachers do not want to treat their students by formula, as though who they are, to whom they are related, and what their special projects are do not matter. Teaching, from the perspective of caring, is very much like parenting.

Caring as a critical theory is activated when we are challenged to justify our recommendations in light of the practicalities of contemporary schooling. Critics ask: How can any teacher do what caring requires? For care theorists, this challenge does not force retreat. Instead, it triggers a deep and devastating critique of the present structures of schooling. We must not convert caring into a manageable, formal, "professional" set of behaviors. Rather, we must transform the conditions of schooling so that teachers and students can adequately care for one another.

Smaller classes, extended contact, and more numerous opportunities for dialogue are among the recommendations we might make. By extended contact we mean finding ways for teachers to work more closely with the same group of students. This might be accomplished in one of several ways: A teacher might stay with the same group of students for three or more years (with mutual consent, of course), one teacher might teach two or more subjects to 30 students instead of one subject to 60 students (Sizer, 1984), or a team of teachers might work together with a group of students for several years. Any of these arrangements would increase opportunities for teachers to develop the relations of trust and care required for fully competent teaching. This is just one example of how an ethic care can function as a critical moral theory.

When we adopt caring as a moral orientation, we are also led to examine our own practices as teachers. Suppose there is a rule (as there was in my school when I was a secondary mathematics teacher) that students who have unexcused absences should not be allowed to make up the work they have missed; that is, these students are to receive zeroes for the days they missed. Should a teacher obey such a rule? Frankly, I ignored the rule. It seemed to me that if we wanted all students to learn the subject at hand, we should encourage them to do the necessary work. Penalties discourage students—especially those students who doubt the worth of what is presented anyway. Because my students knew that I would insist they do the work and that I would credit them for having done it, there was little incentive to cut class. It was easier for students to attend class and do things on time.

There are moral as well as pedagogical reasons for disobeying such a rule. We want our students to know that they—like the prodigal son—will be welcomed enthusiastically when they return to the classroom. We assume the best possible reason, consonant with reality, for their absence. Our message is consistent: We care for you, and because we care, we will persist in helping you to master the material that is our common responsibility.

Is it not unethical—or at least professionally reprehensible—to ignore a school rule? Not always. Indeed, we might argue that sometimes it is morally unacceptable to follow a rule. Advocates of many different ethical theories would agree with this. But some would insist that one must break the rule openly, accept whatever penalty comes with the violation, and thereby demonstrate to the community that one's moral sense challenges the law. This course of action requires a form of moral heroism. Acting within an ethic of care, teachers might behave this way—if, for example, the rule was tremendously important and strictly enforced—but more often, caring teachers just do what they judge best for their students.

There is a caution to be observed here, and its mention should lead to lively discussion. It is always risky to ignore the rules of the group to which we are accountable. If disobeying the rule might lead to chaos or harm, carers would probably do better to follow the rule. But one must remember that following rules and orders can lead to dreadfully immoral behavior. How do we decide? There is no foolproof answer to this question, but from the perspective of care, we ask: What is best for this student? Will doing what is best for her or him hurt other students? What effect will my decision have on the network of relations on which we all depend? Asking such questions, we are led sometimes to follow the given rule, and sometimes to fight it publicly, even at the risk of considerable personal sacrifice. Often, however, we simply ignore it, knowing that we cannot fight pitched battles over every bit of bureaucratic nonsense, but that we can lose our moral sensitivity by acquiescing to rules instead of caring for each student in each situation.

REFERENCES

Bellah, R. N., Madsen, R., Sullivan, W. M., Swidler, A., & Tipton, S. M. (1985). *Habits of the heart*. Berkeley: University of California Press.

Benhabib, S. (1987). The generalized and the concrete other. In S. Benhabib & D. Cornell (Eds.), *Feminism as critique* (pp. 77–95). Minneapolis, MN: University of Minnesota Press.

Buber, M. (1970). *I and Thou* (W. Kaufmann, Trans.). New York: Charles Scribner's Sons. (Original work published 1923)

Gilligan, C. (1982). *In a different voice*. Cambridge, MA: Harvard University Press.

Kittay, E. F., & Meyers, D. T. (Eds.). (1987). *Women and moral theory*. Totowa, NJ: Rowman & Littlefield.

Kohlberg, L. (1981). *The philosophy of moral development*. San Francisco: Harper & Row.

MacIntyre, A. (1981). *After virtue*. Notre Dame, IN: University of Notre Dame Press.

Mayeroff, M. (1971). *On caring*. New York: Harper & Row.

Murdoch, I. (1970). *The sovereignty of good*. London: Routledge & Kegan Paul.

Noddings, N. (1984). *Caring: A feminine approach to ethics and moral education*. Berkeley: University of California Press.

Noddings, N. (1988). An ethic of caring and its implications for instructional arrangements. *American Journal of Education*, *96*(2), 215–230.

Noddings, N. (1989). *Women and evil*. Berkeley, CA: University of California Press.

Noddings, N. (1992). Shaping an acceptable child. In A. Garrod (Ed.), *Learning for life: Moral education theory and practice*. New York: Praeger.

Okin, S. M. (1989). Reason and feeling in thinking about justice. *Ethics*, *99*(2), 229–249.

Ruddick, S. (1980). Maternal thinking. *Feminist Studies*, *6*(2), 342–367.

Ruddick, S. (1989). *Maternal thinking: Towards a politics of peace*. Boston: Beacon Press.

Sandel, M. (1982). *Liberalism and the limits of justice*. Cambridge, MA: Cambridge University Press.

Sizer, T. R. (1984). *Horace's compromise: The dilemma of the American high school*. Boston: Houghton Mifflin.

Taylor, C. (1979). *Hegel and modern society*. New York: Cambridge University Press.

Weil, S. (1951). *Waiting for God*. New York: G. P. Putnam's Sons.

Williams, B. (1985). *Ethics and the limits of philosophy*. Cambridge, MA: Harvard University Press.

4 Comparing the Perspectives
A Case Analysis

DAVID BRICKER
KENNETH R. HOWE
NEL NODDINGS
KENNETH A. STRIKE
P. LANCE TERNASKY

The preceding chapters have described three ways of viewing ethics. The perspectives selected reflect the most promising conversations currently taking place in philosophical circles. But, as we mentioned in the introduction, we envision this book as more than a theoretical offering. If preservice educators are to view it as having relevance for their lives, then we must show how the often abstract ideas found in the theories function in the real world.

Consequently, we asked David Bricker, Kenneth Howe, and Nel Noddings to apply their respective orientations to Kenneth Strike's "I Dream of Jennie and the Great Blue Cloud." We selected this case for three reasons. First, philosophers are understandably inclined to use examples that best fit their theories while eschewing those that make for difficult application. Our choice of a uniform case should place the writers on an equal footing and permit readers to compare equivalents. Second, the case is intentionally open-textured: it was not designed to elicit a particular response or to give an advantage to one of the perspectives over the others. And third, the case displays the simultaneously mundane and ethically disturbing type of problem educators regularly encounter. The proposed solutions and the thought behind them may therefore help educators to respond ethically to the difficulties they face daily.

The following pages contain the case, the responses to it from our three philosophers, and a brief analysis of their comments by the editors.

"I DREAM OF JENNIE AND THE GREAT BLUE CLOUD"

Morris Phillips, the principal of Salem High, found it hard not to be amused when Jennie Spare, a senior and an honors student, stood before him with a petition. Perhaps best described as sweet, Jennie just was not the rabble rousing type. And here she was trying to appear indignant while being undone by her own inherent niceness. It was hard for Mr. Phillips not to chuckle.

Nevertheless, it was clear that she was serious, and Mr. Phillips supposed that he should read the petition and try to get Jennie out of his office gently.

The petition read:

> We, the nonsmoking students of Salem High, wish to request that Salem High reopen the smoking room for students.
>
> Since the smoking room was canceled, students who smoke have been smoking in the rest rooms. The amount of smoking in the rest rooms is so great that nonsmoking students can barely stand to use them. Also, the rest rooms are too crowded between classes and are always dirty and unpleasant. While there is a rule against smoking in the rest rooms, nobody seems to enforce it.
>
> Also, before and after school, smoking students congregate to smoke at the entrances. Now it is hard to enter the building without being jostled, and those of us who don't smoke have to breathe other people's smoke to get into the building.
>
> Since smoking students are going to smoke anyhow, we think that the school should provide them with a place to smoke where nonsmokers don't have to breathe their smoke.
>
> We think it is unfair that teachers have a smoking room and students don't.
>
> We also think the school should consider that smoking in the rest rooms has become a cause of conflict between students.
>
> Thank you.
>
> Signed,

The petition had been signed by nearly 150 students.

Mr. Phillips looked guiltily at his own unpleasantly full ashtray (he had failed to quit smoking again this year), then looked back at Jennie. The petition she'd brought him was certainly right about a couple of things. There had been a lot of fights in the rest rooms this year, and one or two of them had been over smoking. And he suspected that many of the other fights were indirectly related to smoking. The rest rooms were now crowded in between classes with defiant kids. Moreover, it was clear to Mr. Phillips that teachers were reluctant to enforce no-smoking rules in the rest rooms. And he didn't really blame them.

What should he say? He looked at Jennie and said, "Thank you, Jennie, for your concern. I'll give it some thought." He added, "Have you considered that one reason we got rid of the smoking room was that we didn't want to show approval for students' smoking. We have to be careful to send kids the right messages."

Jennie was ready for this. She said, "So we've been told. But we have a hard time believing it. If you were really concerned about the messages you send us, you'd stop teachers from smoking. When you do that, we'll believe you."

Mr. Phillips was beginning to feel uncomfortable. It was time to move on. He said, "I want to thank you for being such a good citizen, Jennie, but now I have to go to an important meeting, so I can't talk about this with you any more. I'll see you around."

Mr. Phillips thought that Jennie looked a little crestfallen at this dismissal, but he soon found that he was wrong. As she opened the door and stepped into the outer office, she turned and said, "I'm glad you approve of our exercising our rights as citizens, Mr. Phillips, because we sent the petition to the newspaper." Then she flounced triumphantly into the hall.

COMMENTARY by David Bricker

In Chapter 1 I explained that our ability to see the salient feature of a situation can influence our judgment of the right thing to do. The "I Dream of Jennie" case presents us with a number of situational features, among which are:

1. Morris Phillips, the principal, is somewhat condescending toward Jennie.
2. Because Jennie is fundamentally a sweet person, she must to some degree be feigning an air of righteous indignation.
3. The teachers have access to a smoking room, whereas the students do not.
4. Smoking, wherever it occurs (indoors or outdoors), is hazardous to the health of smoker and nonsmoker alike.
5. Student rest rooms are presently unpleasant places to visit because they are crowded with smokers.
6. Although there is a ban against smoking by students in the school, teachers are not enforcing the ban in student rest rooms.
7. Nearly 150 students have signed the petition asking Mr. Phillips to reopen the smoking room for students.
8. Jennie has sent a copy of the petition to the newspaper.

Now, which of these eight situational features is salient, that is, most representative of the problem that needs to be solved? Is it, for example, that the teachers have access to a smoking room whereas the students have no room of their own? Or, are we confronted, most importantly, by insincerity in an exchange between principal and student in which the principal is trying hard to take a student initiative seriously and a sweet student is trying hard to be serious? Or, is the dominant feature of the situation the fact that smoking is always hazardous? In short, what do we see as the feature of the situation that most needs to be addressed?

The unfair distribution, between teachers and students, of space for smoking, the acting out of attitudes that are not truly felt, the danger to health of smoking—these and other features of the situation that confront us in the "I Dream of Jennie" story strike us as possibilities for our moral attention. But we cannot address all of the features at the same time. For example, if we perceive that we are primarily confronting a problem of unfairness, then a recommendation that the smoking room for students be reopened would not address the fact that smoking, whether or not it is done in a sanctioned room, is a hazard to health. Conversely, if we see the hazard to health as the salient feature, we cannot conclude that the situation calls upon us to redress the unfair distribution of rooms for smoking. Furthermore, it would be hard to know how to address some of the features of the situation that are of concern. How, for example, would one go about changing Mr. Phillips's way of talking to students so that he would be less condescending, or how would one change Jennie's sweet nature so that righteous indignation might become easier for her? These features are bothersome, but I doubt there is a way to address them immediately. Mr. Phillips's condescension is part of the kind of person he is, and Jennie's sweetness is part of who she is as a person. As I explained in Chapter 1, changing character traits is possible, but it takes years, openness to change, and assistance from others who already have the traits being sought. So what do we each see as the feature of the situation that we should address in our effort to make an appropriate moral response?

The feature that strikes me as being most salient is the hazard that smoking poses to health. Others may see the situation differently, but that is what I see. Accordingly, to me it looks like the reasonable thing to do would be to prohibit everyone—teachers and students alike—from smoking anywhere on the school premises. The school premises should be declared a smoke-free zone, I reason. I can't believe that some students and teachers have a "right to smoke" that would override the responsibility of school officials to protect the health of all of the teachers and students, so to me it looks like the most reasonable thing to do would be to ban smoking everywhere, both within the school building and on the grounds that surround it. Students and staff should be reminded that smoking is a serious public health hazard by the ban on smoking in and around their public school.

Now, do you, the reader, see the salient feature of the situation differently? If you do, do you think we could come to some sort of compromise? I would hope that any difference between us would not have the weight of Sophoclean tragedy, and I would do my best to heed Haemon's advice to "bend to the torrent" provided by what you see, but if what each of us sees in this situation (however mundane it may be) is caused by a preoccupation that is part of the kind of person each of us is, such bending may not be an option for us. Let's hope not. Who wants to spill blood over smoke?

COMMENTARY by Kenneth R. Howe

This case raises a great many issues that deserve comment—Morris Phillips's condescending attitude toward Jennie Spare, his need now to "save face," the importance of maintaining a sense of community and tolerance among students, and broader questions about the aims and nature of education in a liberal democratic society. In a brief commentary such as this, I can hardly tackle all of these questions. I have thus elected to focus on three issues that complement and extend my discussion in Chapter 2: justified paternalism, arguments from consequences, and fair decision procedures. In each case, Mr Phillips's action will be the object of scrutiny and questioning.

Paternalism

Paternalism (sometimes, and perhaps more accurately, termed "parentalism" [Benjamin & Curtis, 1986]) occurs when an individual or group uses the criterion of best interests to override the choices of another individual or group. By way of illustration, parents behave paternalistically when they insist that their children brush their teeth and do their homework; states behave paternalistically when they pass seat-belt and helmet laws.

In liberal democratic societies such as ours, paternalism is *prima facie* objectionable and thus requires justification. Of course, paternalism toward children is much easier to justify than paternalism toward adults. This is so because adults are presumed to be competent to make decisions for themselves—even decisions to risk their health and their lives by engaging in activities like boxing, skydiving, mountain climbing, and, of course, smoking—especially if their actions do not harm others. Children, by contrast, are typically considered to be incompetent to make a great many decisions that adults are ordinarily permitted to make. Parents and other adult authorities (including, of course, teachers, principals, and counselors) are accordingly granted substantial latitude to make decisions on children's behalf.

The elimination of the smoking room at Salem exemplifies paternalism directed specifically at the students. For, unlike seat-belt and helmet laws, which apply to everyone who operates a vehicle, the students at Salem are denied a privilege extended to the adults: They no longer have a smoking room, whereas the teachers continue to have theirs and Morris Phillips smokes in his office. An underlying assumption for this differential smoking policy, it would seem, is that students are not competent to decide for themselves whether to smoke.

The assumption that high school students, who typically range from ages 14 to 19, must be denied the same privileges as adults vis-à-vis smoking is problematic because they (unlike kindergartners, for instance) stand at the threshold of adult competency and responsibility. An important feature of this threshold is that no single criterion can be applied to settle all questions regarding individuals' competence to make particular kinds of decisions. This fact is reflected in the legal system, which establishes no uniform age for competency. Instead, whether an individual is competent depends on the nature of the activity: compare voting, drinking, driving, obtaining contraceptives, and standing trial as an adult.

These observations imply that denying Salem students smoking privileges requires some justification that is sensitive to the nature of the particular issue and context. Mr. Phillips apparently offers such a justification when he suggests that the student smoking room was eliminated because its existence gave the impression that the school approves of students smoking. But this argument is suspect, for at least three reasons. First, as Ms. Spare is quick to point out, it applies as much to adult as to student smoking at Salem. (One might even argue that it applies even more to teachers, who are supposed to be mature adult role-models.) Second, it is relevant that nonsmoking students are responsible for the petition. Apparently the existence of smoking rooms—for teachers or students—does not encourage them to smoke. Indeed they wish to return to the situation in which smoking is segregated. Third, because a distinction can be made between what is *permitted* and what is *endorsed* by the school, the existence of a student smoking room need not entail that the school approves of smoking. (A somewhat analogous situation exists regarding sex education. In particular, schools need not endorse premarital sex among high school students in order to provide them with information about how to avoid pregnancy.)

Arguments From Consequences

If there is a good justification—a justification, that is, that does not simply assert adult prerogative and power—for denying students a smoking room while permitting teachers to have one, Mr. Phillips has failed to provide it. His action may also be criticized because of its probably altogether foreseeable consequences: Closing the student smoking room resulted in smoky, dirty, and crowded bathrooms; congestion and smoke at the school entrances; and conflict between smoking and nonsmoking students. Furthermore, support among the faculty for the new policy and plans to enforce it seem altogether lacking, which suggests that it was ill-considered and shortsighted.

A likely response to this appeal to consequences is to dismiss it as crude utilitarianism, which indiscriminately responds to whatever pleases people and is convenient—that just because closing the smoking room has prompted smoking students to violate other no-smoking rules that are not being enforced, resulting in a significant amount of annoyance, inconvenience, and conflict, this is no reason to capitulate. By parity of reasoning, or so this argument would go, laws against theft are not abolished just because certain individuals will steal in any case.

On analysis, this response is far too facile, and one need not be a utilitarian (especially a crude one) to hold that consequences are relevant to ethical deliberation, especially when what should be permissible is seriously in dispute. (Recall that what makes a theory utilitarian is the view that maximizing utility is the *overriding* criterion, not merely a relevant one.) Unlike theft, there is nothing approaching unanimity regarding the prohibition of smoking. Whether smoking should be permitted is subject to reasonable disagreement among well-intentioned individuals. The fact that many students will continue to smoke and will break other rules to do so is more akin to the issue of dispensing contraceptives to teens than it is to theft. In particular, teens will engage in extramarital sex when contraceptives are not readily available—and with bad consequences—and whether teenage sex is good, or at least not deserving of sanctions, is an object of serious disagreement.

Fair Decision Procedures

Again, taking consequences seriously does not entail embracing utilitarianism, particularly when what is good or desirable is the object of disagreements. Indeed the existence of such disagreements leads rather naturally to an issue that is of central importance in nonutilitarian theory: the question of how to attain fair (or just) resolutions.

Regarding the case at hand, Ms. Spare claims that closing the student smoking room was unfair to students because the teachers were allowed to keep theirs. She apparently has the *outcome* of Mr. Phillips's decision in mind. But fairness is often determined by the *procedures* by which decisions are made, particularly when the question of what would be a fair outcome is in dispute (see, e.g., Rawls, 1971). Indeed, insofar as liberal democracies afford equal respect and tolerance for competing views, fair procedures are the hallmark of democratic deliberation and negotiation.

For various reasons, schools need not (should not) be fully democratic (see, e.g., Gutmann, 1987), particularly if this is understood to mean that students should have an equal voice in *all* decisions. On the other hand, if schools are to promote democratic skills, they must allow and encourage students to practice them when possible. This is especially important for high-schoolers, who are approaching adulthood.

Although we are given little of the details of how Mr. Phillips's decision to close the student smoking room was actually reached, it appears quite clear that the students at Salem, smoking and nonsmoking alike, had little or no say. This model of decision making is not conducive to preparing students to engage in democratic deliberation and negotiation. On the contrary, as Ms. Spare's remarks about the unfairness of the continued existence of the teachers' smoking room and about her being a "good citizen" suggest, Mr. Phillips's model serves to encourage sarcasm, defiance, and charges of hypocrisy. Thus, Mr. Phillips's action may be criticized on educational grounds, namely, for failing to foster skills in democratic deliberation and negotiation.

Conclusion

This discussion is admittedly far from conclusive regarding whether the *outcome* of Mr. Phillips's decision procedure, closing the student smoking room, was the correct one. Paternalism may indeed be justified in the case, or there may be other considerations that supported closing the student smoking room. In my estimation, however, the correctness of the outcome cannot be divorced from the correctness of the *procedure*. Students should have been afforded a much greater opportunity to be heard, and, if Mr. Phillips was under constraint in some way (e.g., owing to parental pressure or a local ordinance), students at least should have been provided with this information so as to enable them to take their grievance to those ultimately responsible for the decision. As Justice William Brennan observed:

> Schools cannot expect their students to learn the lessons of good citizenship when the school authorities themselves disregard the fundamental principles underpinning our constitutional freedoms. (in Johnson & Crowley, 1986, p. 223)

References

Benjamin, M., & Curtis, J. (1986). *Ethics in nursing* (2nd. ed.). New York: Oxford University Press.
Gutmann, A. (1987). *Democratic education*. Princeton: Princeton University Press.
Johnson, J., & Crowley, D. (1986). T.L.O. and the student's right to privacy. *Educational Theory, 36*(3), 211–224.
Rawls, J. (1971). *A theory of justice*. Cambridge, MA: Harvard University Press.

COMMENTARY by Nel Noddings

From the perspective of care, we might begin by gently chiding Mr. Phillips for his condescension toward Jennie. He may be a nice man and, perhaps, a good principal, but he is a sexist, and he should reflect on his attitude.

When we approach moral life through an ethic of care, we are concerned with the preservation, growth, and acceptability of those we care for. Clearly, the nonsmoking students need to be protected from unwanted smoke, and the school should respond to this need. There are, theoretically, two ways to do this: we can provide a separate space for the smokers so that their habit doesn't affect the nonsmokers, or we can try to put a stop to smoking altogether.

As we consider these alternatives, we have to look at the whole web of caring. We care about the smokers, too. What is best for them? From a health perspective, they should quit smoking. But we probably can't force this. We could, as many places in California have already done, declare the building smoke-free and insist that everyone—teachers included—go outside to smoke. We could even apologize, as I do in my own home, for causing discomfort to smokers on chilly days, but we keep to the rule for the sake of inhabitants who can't tolerate smoke. With so many teenagers, however, this probably would not work. And if Salem High is in New England or the midwest, an outside smoking area is impractical for much of the year.

How about instituting severe penalties to eliminate smoking? If we care for the smokers, we will probably reject this strategy. We want them to grow ethically and socially. They have to accept responsibility for what they are doing. Besides, rules and penalties are too often interesting challenges to teenagers.

Mr. Phillips should call a school meeting—or a series of class meetings. He should get suggestions from both faculty and students. Perhaps the best alternative (one that may emerge in dialogue) is a dual one: provide a smoking room for students but discourage its use through a continuous and intensive education program. Provide a very attractive place for nonsmokers. Provide help for those who are addicted. Encourage nonsmokers to support smokers who are trying to quit. Study advertising and its evil techniques. Make the problem a community problem to be solved cooperatively.

Finally, faculty and administration should set the tone for continued dialogue. Getting up petitions ought not to be equated with rabble rousing but with responsible citizenship. The presence of a young woman serious about her civic responsibility and personal comfort ought not to be an occasion on which it is "hard not to be amused." One can be both nice and indignant. There is much more to this story than the ethical solution of a smoking problem.

EDITORS' OBSERVATIONS

We have heard from three theorists. Each has offered a different view of the situation and, not surprisingly, a different solution. What can their responses tell us about a more coherent role for ethics in educational settings? The reader undoubtedly noted the care taken by all three theorists in making responses to the case a reasonable extension of the argument developed in their respective chapters. The philosophers analyzed the case using the vocabulary and standards of appraisal intrinsic to their theories. Other than a shared concern for students and schools, their proposals seem at odds. Is permanent disagreement the most we can expect?

Such an outcome could hardly be desirable given our stated intentions. We suggested earlier that the study of ethics might connect to education in three broad ways: it may aid in the development and analysis of educational policy, it may help in evaluating the school's role as moral educator, and it may suggest the kinds of values and principles that should guide professional conduct. If we approach this task as philosophers, and the philosophers we have chosen to lay the foundation disagree, then it might seem that we are pursuing a failed project.

We have two responses to this. The first questions the level of disagreement. The second considers the role and importance of dialogue.

Theoretical differences exist. For instance, in contrast to Bricker and Noddings, Howe approached the case procedurally. His perspective placed greater emphasis on how decisions are made rather than on whether the outcomes conformed to a specific vision of the good. Despite such differences, the issues raised by all three theorists point to a highly intersecting set of concerns. And while their theoretical thinking diverges, they display considerable agreement at the level of intuition.

All three concurred that the principal's actions were troublesome, that students had reason to complain, and that the recognized dangers of smoking justified concern. One possible reason for such agreement is that if ethical intuitions are part of the data of ethical theories, then any adequate theory will need to address them, and a theory unable to cope with basic intuitions is of limited value for persons concerned with ethical application. The similarity between proposals is what one would expect from approaches that "work." Typically, it is when we near the margins and consider cases that are peculiar or purely hypothetical that the distinctive features of the individual theories become evident.

The critic might ask whether we have not overstated the case for agreement and if the theoretical commitments of our philosophers could not result in irresoluble disagreement regarding the appropriate actions in the "Jennie" case. Although this is possible, we think it less likely where real dialogue occurs. Is there reason to believe that dialogue could diminish the potential for marked disagreement among our philosophers?

Our faith in dialogue has much to do with the fact that our philosophers have carefully considered opposing points of view. Each knows the others' basic stance and further knows how these differing viewpoints may prompt criticism of one's own position. We are suggesting not just that each theorist knows the opposition, but more importantly, that the substantive challenges raised by antagonists prod the philosopher to modify or replace those notions that are indefensible. Consider these examples.

In his introduction David Bricker is quick to note that he is not a moral relativist, and further that he recognizes the value of the Kantian and utilitarian approaches. This is a weighty admission, for although he correctly argues that rationality has its limits, it is also clear that much of what we now see as ethical has as its foundation Kantian or utilitarian thought. The contributions of these rationality-based systems make it unlikely that we will ever again view enslavement or ceremonial human sacrifice as forms of right conduct.

The things we see have origins. If we accept that tolerance and fairness are features of living rightly, it is reasonable to ask what is the source of these ideals. And even if we know the ethical by seeing and living it rather than by rationally choosing it, it is probable that Bricker's understanding of ethical life works conjointly with the raw material generated by the prominent ethical theories of our time rather than in lieu of it.

Kenneth Howe notes potentially fatal weaknesses of liberal theory. He concurs with many of the indictments of utilitarianism and libertarianism.

He goes to great length, however, to defend liberal egalitarianism against charges of gender and cultural bias, and the nature of the defense is worth noting. Howe does not argue that the critics have somehow misunderstood liberal theory or the consequences likely to follow from it, nor does he assert that the criticism is unworthy of serious consideration. Instead he describes how one variant of liberalism is actually guilty of the charges and consequently illiberal. That the application of liberal principles might disadvantage certain groups seems not only theoretically untenable but personally offensive for him, and his acceptance of the validity of the criticism serves to distance liberal egalitarianism from its illiberal relatives. His comments speak less of the appeasement of one's adversaries than of his having listened carefully to their complaints.

When the caring perspective was first discussed in traditional circles it was thought to suffer from several weaknesses. Some charged that the absence of impartiality could lead to widespread discrimination against those outside the caring relationship. But in her analysis of traditional ethics Nel Noddings tells us that it is still an open question as to whether an ethic of caring can stand on its own or whether it must be joined, as in her example, to the concept of justice.

With its increased valuation of "the role of emotions and personal life," caring was sometimes viewed as being an ethical system without teeth, which simultaneously called upon caregivers to practice a compulsive selflessness. Noddings rejects any characterization of caring that limits it to endearment. As a critical theory, caring demands that schools be transformed.

Mr. Phillips is gently chided for his sexist attitude, but he is chided just the same. Caring is not a system where the ethical mistakes of responsible persons are glorified or ignored. And rather than calling for selflessness, the image Noddings offers is one of reciprocity of care, by which caregivers also receive—for all ethical sainthood guarantees is teacher burnout and moral desensitivity.

Bricker, Howe, and Noddings's openness to the opposition could be dismissed as self-serving, but it is more reasonable and more generous to think that ongoing conversations with non-like-minded persons reveal lacunae that demand reflection. The willingness to engage in dialogue with one's interlocutors holds the promise of personal ethical clarity and the potential for substantial agreement at the level of policy among those who theoretically disagree.

Because most educators will not have a professional philosopher on hand when making difficult ethical decisions, what suggestions for school settings can we extract from the responses to the case? We propose three. First, there is the need for ethical judgment and wisdom. Judgment permits us to list and balance the relevant ethical considerations by asking, What is happening here and what is at stake?

But this is not a simple task, for real issues are typically ambiguous and unstructured, and none of the philosophers offered a simple, foolproof strategy for ethical problem solving. It is here that wisdom is required. Wisdom operates when one determines the salient features of a situation and the relevant principles that must be brought to bear. The choosing is not capricious but a subtle form of discernment that permits the moral person to distinguish apparent similarities from actual differences.

Although the fundamentals of judgment can be learned in the classroom, wisdom is neither taught nor inherited. It comes from the serious study of pressing moral issues and of the chief ways that people have approached their resolution. Wisdom is less a template for problem solving than an intimate familiarity with a characteristic human endeavor.

Second, the dialogue that philosophers find invaluable is also essential for educators. The chapters that follow suggest practical ways educators may approach ethical problems. One theme that repeatedly surfaces is that teachers benefit from substantive ethical conversation with colleagues. Potentially, such discourse exposes all the relevant considerations. This is critical in situations where it is unlikely that there is "one right answer," for educators may then draw on the collective wisdom of the group and may ultimately legitimate a decision by consensus when certainty cannot be assured.

Finally, Bricker, Howe, and Noddings's openness to their critics suggests that favored theories are always subject to revision and clarification. Two obvious benefits follow. Revisability checks the notion that policy decisions born of consensus via dialogue are perfect and permanent. The dialogue described above is instead characterized by an ongoing cycle of exploration, reflection, and correction. Second, openness to revision should cause prospective teachers and administrators to question the popular notion that ethical autonomy means that ethics is a solitary affair—best accomplished alone with a mind uninfluenced by the ideas and concerns of others. In actuality the preceding chapters and the responses to the case suggest that insight may effectively come from wrestling with the disconcerting ideas of others, and of equal importance, that the ensuing encounters need not cause us to fear the spilling of "blood over smoke" but may offer instead compromise over coffee.

Part II

ETHICS IN PRESERVICE EDUCATION

5 Ethics in the Preservice Curriculum

BARRY L. BULL
Indiana University

Over the past decade there has been increased professional interest in the ethical dimension of teaching and subsequently in the place of ethics in the preparation of new teachers. Probably the surest sign that ethics is becoming a subject for serious consideration in the education of teachers is the role it plays in John Goodlad's (1990) recent large-scale study of teacher education in the United States:

> We [Goodlad and his research team] came to see with increasing clarity the degree to which teaching in schools, public or private, carries with it moral imperatives—more in the public schools, however, because they are not schools of choice in a system requiring compulsory schooling. At first we viewed these moral imperatives as composing one leg of the chair on which rests teaching as a profession. Collectively, they pointed to a body of subject matter to be synthesized into part of the teacher education curriculum. We soon abandoned this view, however, in favor of one in which the moral imperatives in schoolteaching were seen to characterize *each* of the four legs—indeed, the entire chair. (p. 47)

It is, of course, much too early to tell just what the results of the renewed interest in the ethics of teaching in general and Goodlad's analyses of, and recommendations for, teacher education in particular will be. However, it is likely that some faculties of teacher education will over the next few years be wrestling with whether, why, and how to include ethics in their programs of professional preparation for new teachers. Indeed, that the *Journal of Teacher Education* (Lasley, 1986; Ashton, 1991), a publication of the American Association of Colleges for Teacher Education, the nation's largest organization of teacher education institutions, has published two theme issues in the past five years on the ethics of teaching is a clear sign that this rethinking of the role of ethics in teacher education is well under way.

This chapter considers, first, some of the reasons why ethics has become a part of the current reconceptualization of teacher education, and some of the social and institutional realities with which contemporary efforts to change teacher education must cope. Combined, the rationales for ethics in the teacher education curriculum and the contexts in which that curriculum operates produce a number of difficulties in designing the content and procedures for teaching ethics in preservice programs for teachers. Next, this chapter explains how these difficulties arise and ponders the prospects for overcoming them. These difficulties, I argue, turn out to be too severe to be overlooked in our current enthusiasm for including ethics in the preservice curriculum. As someone who has been involved with the issue of ethics in teacher education for over a decade, this is not a message that I am happy to deliver. Nevertheless, any lasting success our teacher education programs may achieve in this regard depends on our facing these difficulties honestly.

WHY ETHICS SHOULD BE PART OF TEACHER EDUCATION

As the statement of John Goodlad quoted above makes clear, the basic rationale for including ethics in the preservice curriculum lies with a renewed conviction that teaching itself has an inherent moral dimension. Contemporary, as well as classical, discussions of the nature of this moral dimension usually take one of two different, but sometimes related, forms. The first, the political perspective, notes that public education involves the exercise of governmental power over citizens and observes that any such exercise, including that in which teachers engage, must meet appropriate moral standards. The second, the interpersonal perspective, notes that teachers and students are involved in a particular kind of personal relationship that imposes moral responsibilities upon its participants. Let us examine these two perspectives on the moral dimension of teaching in greater detail.

The Moral Dimension of Teaching as Political

Teaching, at least within a public school system, and perhaps under any circumstances, is a political act. Teachers in the United States work under the auspices of a wide variety of formal political authorities, including legislatures, school boards, and state and local bureaucracies. They also work within informal social structures that regulate and distribute power, ranging from large-scale economic systems and traditions that assign social positions according to race and gender to the unwritten rules that govern social relationships in particular schools. As a result, the acts of individual teachers inevitably involve the exercise of political power, either their own or that of those who—explicitly or implicitly, by law or by custom—direct their activities.

Now, not every exercise of power is morally justified; might does not necessarily make right. Thus, the political actions of teachers must adhere to appropriate standards of political morality. In the most general terms, teachers have two sorts of moral obligations, the duty to be conscious of, and to resist, efforts to exercise power illegitimately and the duty to comply with, and carry out, legitimate efforts. From this perspective, then, the ethics of teaching is defined within a justified theory of political obligation.

But just what standards of political morality are most justified, and when is an exercise of power legitimate? In the West, and increasingly around the world, a deceptively simple answer to this question is emerging: Democracy is the most morally justifiable political system. And the ethics of teaching, therefore, is simply teachers' obligations to govern their actions according to democratic political theory.

Although democratic theory rules out many political systems—dictatorship, totalitarianism, hereditary aristocracy—just what it should include is, unfortunately, a matter of profound controversy both in the United States and around the world. Some more traditional versions of democratic theory, like that propounded by Amy Gutmann (1987), argue that all political decisions in which all citizens have had a chance to air their views and participate are morally legitimate. Others, like Bruce Ackerman (1980), hold that the moral purpose of a democracy is to enhance and protect the personal autonomy of its citizens. Some theorists, like Allan Bloom (1987), hark back to the thinking of Thomas Jefferson, in which the purpose of democracy is to permit the best ideas to flourish and to guide the society. Still others, like Jürgen Habermas (1987), believe that democracy demands a universal critical awareness of existing social constraints and a consensus about social decisions that can emerge only from an unconstrained dialogue among citizens.

These approaches to democracy define the ethics of teaching in significantly different ways. The traditionalist, for example, believes that teachers should promote in all children the skills and values of negotiation and collective deliberation. The Jeffersonian asks teachers, among other things, to select out the most talented students and to provide them with the intellectual skills and attitudes necessary for moral leadership. As we shall see, this plurality of interpretations of democracy makes clear specification of the content of the ethical curriculum for prospective teachers difficult.

The Moral Dimension of Teaching as Interpersonal

Teachers have a personal relationship with each of their students, a relationship that is substantially different from most relationships among adults. From the perspective of students, this relationship is compulsory; it is a given in their lives, and there is very little they can do to escape it. The relationship is intimate, for teachers become privy to a detailed knowledge of the character, talents, failures, dreams, and fears of their students. It is also asymmetrical because teachers' knowledge of, and responsibility for, their students is not reciprocated by students. Finally, the relationship is pervasive in the students' present and, to some extent, future lives; teachers have a comprehensive and sustained influence on the actions, beliefs, aspirations, and motivations of their students. From the interpersonal perspective, this unusual combination of the compulsory, intimate, asymmetrical, and pervasive in the relationship between teachers and students implies that students are particularly vulnerable to their teachers' actions and motivations and, therefore, that teachers have special moral responsibilities toward their students.

Just what standards should this relationship meet? Most people would agree that the relationship is to be nonexploitive and humane, that it is to be for the benefit of the child. Thus a number of models for this relationship are ruled out, for instance, the child is not the servant of the teacher nor is he or she the teacher's property. And it is increasingly accepted that the child is not simply raw material to be shaped into a desired product by the teacher. Nevertheless, precisely what the appropriate model for this relationship should be is still a matter of great controversy.

Some, like Nel Noddings (1984, 1986), propose that the appropriate model for the teacher-student relationship is that of parent and child, that is, the teacher is to care for and nurture the student. Others, like R. S. Peters (1966), argue that the master-apprentice model is more fitting; the teacher is to induct the child into the roles and practices of adulthood in his or her society. Some, like Carl Rogers (1980), see the relationship of teacher to student like that of therapist to client; the teacher is to assist the student to realize his or her real self and in the process to overcome the barriers to self-realization imposed upon the student by the social, emotional, and material environment. Recently, some proponents of choice, like John Chubb and Terry Moe (1990), compare the student-teacher relationship to that between a customer and a business; the responsibility of the teacher is to serve the express wishes of the student (and his or her parents).

From the interpersonal perspective, too, we have many possibilities, such as the caring, induction, therapeutic, and commercial models of the teacher-student relationship, all of which imply significantly different ethics of teaching. Here, again, this plurality of conceptions of beneficial interpersonal relations will pose difficulties for the coherent specification of the content of the teacher education curriculum.

In brief, we have found that there are many good reasons for including ethics in teacher education, as many reasons as there are plausible conceptions of democracy and beneficial teacher-student relationships. But before we consider the implications of these multiple sources of justification for ethics in the preservice curriculum, let us briefly examine some facts about the social and institutional context of preservice teacher education programs that will further complicate the effort to define the content of, and procedures for including, ethics in teacher education.

SOME REALITIES OF PRESERVICE TEACHER EDUCATION

The interest of education reformers in the quality of teaching in public schools has begun to produce a literature that describes the current state of the occupation of teaching and of the programs in which college students prepare to become teachers. To date, the two most wide-ranging studies of teacher education are a review of recent research on teacher preparation faculties, students, and programs (Lanier & Little, 1986), and a detailed examination of 29 schools or departments of education throughout the country (Goodlad, 1990).

Both studies remind us of the scale of the teacher education enterprise. Over 2 million teachers are employed in the public schools, and about 150,000 teachers enter service every year (Lanier & Little, 1986). Although hundreds of colleges and universities prepare teachers, the enormous demand for teachers means that most are prepared in relatively large state and regional public institutions. The students who prepare to be teachers and the schools for which they prepare are diverse in ability and motivation. The large number of new teachers needed means that teaching candidates must be drawn from the full achievement range of students; teacher education is not and probably cannot be particularly exclusive (Lanier & Little, 1986; Goodlad, 1990). The motivations of students to enter teacher education programs also vary widely, from a clear focus on a career in teaching to a desire to supplement a liberal arts education with an immediately salable skill (Goodlad, 1990; Lanier & Little, 1986). Goodlad (1990) notes the local character of teacher education; by and large, teaching candidates come from the geographic area of their college or university and wish to teach in that area when they have completed their studies. Thus students do not see themselves as preparing to be members of the mobile workforce of a nationwide profession, but as preparing for service in a concrete and familiar context. Despite this parochial focus, Goodlad (1990), and Lanier and Little (1986), found an overwhelming uniformity in teacher education programs. On the whole, these programs are large, impersonal, and fragmented. They consist of a traditional pattern of background courses, methods courses, and fieldwork experiences. Explanations of this uniformity include the large size of the programs, the rapid expansion of public schools in the past 50 years, the limited funding of programs, and the increased pressure on education faculty members to emphasize research rather than teaching.

In summary, teacher education is a vast enterprise conducted in large part by the nation's public colleges and universities. It is populated by students of diverse abilities, motivations, and aspirations. And it is conducted in large, impersonal programs consisting of conventional course work that is more often than not only weakly sequenced and articulated. According to Goodlad (1990), one consequence of these realities is that prospective teachers develop little sense of the ethical character of teaching during their education: "The idea of moral imperatives for teachers was virtually foreign in concept and strange in language for most of the future teachers we interviewed" (p. 264).

THE CONTENT OF ETHICS IN THE PRESERVICE CURRICULUM

Against this background of diverse conceptions of the moral role of teachers and the existing context of teacher preparation programs, what should be the substance of the ethical curriculum for teaching candidates? In this section I will consider four different approaches to answering this question. In assessing these alternatives I will have in mind what seems to me the typical institutional context for teacher education—the relatively large state or private university in which teacher education represents a significant proportion of the undergraduate or graduate program, and in which faculty and other resources are relatively limited. All of these approaches, I will argue, pose various difficulties.

Facultywide Agreement on the Moral Basis of Teaching

John Goodlad's (1990) solution to the absence of definite moral content in teacher education programs is for the appropriate members of each institution's faculty to:

> have a comprehensive understanding of the aims of education and the role of schools in our society and be fully committed to selecting and preparing

> teachers to assume the full range of educational responsibilities required. (p. 282)

The first step in developing a good teacher education program, according to Goodlad, is for the faculty to fashion at least a rough consensus about the public purposes of education at the elementary and secondary levels. The advantages of this approach are obvious. If the involved faculty members fundamentally and explicitly agree on the moral justification of public schools, the ethical content of the program will naturally and spontaneously emerge from such agreement. Just as important is that ethical content become an organizing principle for the program as a whole. The pedagogical skills, subject matter knowledge, and contextual knowledge to be taught in the program will be selected on the basis of this agreement, and there will therefore emerge a coherence in the total program content now almost entirely missing in teacher education programs.

The difficulties with this approach are, I believe, partly practical and partly moral. From the practical perspective, it is implausible to suppose that a fairly large faculty—one of 20 to 70 university professors, and perhaps an even greater number of public school teachers and administrators who are involved in the program's field components—would be able to reach substantial agreement about the moral justification of teaching. As we have noted, there are many competing justifications for schooling and teaching currently available in our society, each of which provides a significantly different prescription for practice. Although it might be possible to develop a consensus among the faculty members of a small liberal arts college, for instance, the faculty members of the large institutions in which most of the nation's teachers are educated would be unlikely to reach such agreement.

From the moral perspective it is not clear that such an agreement is justified. As we have noted, the competing justifications are interpretations of two broad and widely accepted principles—that public schools should serve a democratic polity and that the relationship between teachers and students should be for the benefit of the students. The members of this society are engaged in a healthy debate over the most reasonable meaning of these principles. That this debate should also take place *within* a university program in teacher education seems not just practical but also desirable.

Facultywide Agreement on What the Ethics of Teaching Forbids

Perhaps the agreement on which a teacher education program depends can be narrower than the sort of full-scale faculty consensus that

Goodlad recommends. As we have noted, a commitment to democracy rules out a number of forms of political organization, but does not imply that some particular form of organization is the best interpretation of democracy. Similarly, a commitment to humane and beneficial relationships between teachers and students rules out certain types of relationships, namely, ownership, servitude, and production. Thus it might be possible for a relatively large faculty to agree upon a code of ethics for teaching that specifies what teachers should not do and that leaves open to debate precisely what teachers should do. In effect, such a code is a series of "thou shalt nots" for prospective teachers (Bull, 1990, and, perhaps, Sockett, 1990, propose something like this).

An agreement of this sort has at least some of the advantages of Goodlad's proposal. It brings the moral content of teacher education into conscious focus, and the theoretical basis for the agreement can therefore serve as a partial principle for the coherent organization of a teacher preparation program. And to create such an agreement is also to avoid the practical and moral difficulties of achieving a detailed facultywide consensus on the aims of public schooling.

Nevertheless, there are at least two problems with this approach. First, it may assume more agreement between the political and interpersonal perspectives on the moral content of teaching than actually exists. And second, it is radically incomplete.

Morality, at least in part, concerns how human beings should treat one another. In Western philosophy, there have been two primary ways of thinking about the origin and nature of moral values. The first, exemplified in the philosophy of Plato, argues that justice is the result of the operation of universal principles and large-scale social arrangements that govern particular human interactions. The second, exemplified by Plato's philosophical opponents, the Sophists, argues that what is right depends upon the particular context in which individuals happen to find themselves. This ancient debate between moral universalists and moral contextualists is reflected in the contemporary distinction between the political and interpersonal perspectives on the ethics of teaching. The argument of the political perspective is that we need to seek general principles for arranging our social institutions, and that the part that teachers play in establishing, maintaining, and operating those institutions defines their ethical obligations (see, e.g., Ackerman, 1980). The interpersonal perspective, by contrast, holds that teachers' responsibilities are defined by the particular relationships that exist between them and their students, and that these relationships and responsibilities can, and should, vary according to the specific needs, aspirations, talents, and contexts of individual students (see, e.g., Noddings, 1984).

Of course, some political theorists, like John Dewey (1966), have expressed the hope that democratic political institutions would make it possible for relationships that are moral in context to flourish. Nevertheless, there continues to be a profound tension between these two perspectives on the morality of teaching. Teachers with a contextual orientation seem baffled, or even offended, by the claim that their relationships with their students are fundamentally political. And those with a political orientation find the contextualists' unwillingness to follow universal rules in the treatment of their students to be irrational or even morally abhorrent. In any case, the supposition that the most plausible political and interpersonal theories of the ethics of teaching substantially agree on what teachers *should not do* even if they do not agree on what teachers *should do* is problematic because of the antiuniversalist character of the interpersonal perspective. This perspective does not absolutely forbid any particular action as long as that action can be represented within the context of a particular teacher-student relationship as in the best interest of the student.

Even assuming that a substantial agreement about what the ethics of teaching forbids is possible, such an agreement is still an insufficient basis for a teacher education program because teaching candidates still want, and need, to know what they *should do* as teachers. And programs necessarily must teach some techniques and subject matter in preference to others; it just is not possible within a year or two to teach or to learn everything that all the plausible theories of the ethics of teaching imply it is necessary to know to be a good teacher. Thus, some selection of appropriate knowledge in ethics seems inevitable.

There are at least two ways in which this selection might be made. First, groups of faculty members who share a particular theory of the ethics of teaching might create small alternative programs among which applicants can choose at the beginning of their preparation as teachers. Second, students might develop their own commitment to a theory of the ethics of teaching in the course of their studies and, individually or with a group of like-minded students, fashion a program of study that matches that conviction. Let us examine each of these approaches to determining the moral content of teacher education programs.

Student Choice among Alternative Programs

As we have noted, it is unlikely that the fairly large faculty typical of the institutions in which most teacher education occurs would be able to agree upon a single theory of the moral basis of teaching. Nevertheless, it might be possible for small groups of faculty members in such an institution to agree on one of the available theories. Each group could then design a program of study around that ethical theory. And students, at the point of entry, would select the program that seems most appropriate for them.

This approach has a number of advantages. Each of the small programs would have the commitment to ethics in education and the resulting curricular coherence that Goodlad seeks. Because of their relatively small size, such programs would deliver the consistent socialization that Goodlad (1990) wants, even more effectively than the campuswide program he describes. These programs avoid the practical problem of getting a large faculty to agree to a single moral theory of teaching. And they also avoid the moral problem of limiting the debate about the moral foundation of teaching on the campus precisely because the programs and their faculties would be engaged in that debate in the most meaningful way—by educating teachers according to particular theories and experiencing the practical consequences of doing so.

Nonetheless, there are several difficulties with this approach. Perhaps the most notable are practical. At relatively large universities most undergraduate programs, especially those with significant enrollments, have the same basic structure as current teacher education programs, that is, self-contained courses that students take in whatever order and student groupings happen to occur. Program incoherence and student anonymity are the rule at such institutions. Considerations of efficiency dictate this structure. The student body at these institutions is relatively fluid. Students transfer in and out frequently; they often drop out of college for personal or economic reasons; and whereas many drop out completely, some return to college after taking several years off to work or start a family. The faculties at these institutions are also fluid. Some faculty members retire, others go on sabbatical or on research leave, and many move to other, more prestigious institutions. Whether we like it or not, these facts of institutional life at state and regional universities make a curriculum of independent and interchangeable parts—whether in English or in teacher education—probable if not absolutely necessary. Under these circumstances, it is difficult to develop and maintain small, carefully sequenced, and coherent programs of any kind. What happens if 20% of the students transfer or drop out each year? What should be done with the students who transfer into the university after completing half of their teacher education program at a sister state institution? How can such programs be maintained if 20% of the faculty resigns or is on leave each year? Although it may not be impossible to resolve these problems, they do present a genuine practical challenge to this approach. It was, in part, problems of this kind that led the Holmes Group (1986) to propose an entirely postbaccalaureate teacher education program and Goodlad (1990) to suggest a fifth year of study for undergraduate teaching candidates.

These programs also present moral difficulties. Goodlad (1990) reports an unwillingness and perhaps an inability among education faculty members he interviewed to speak directly and in detail about the moral dimension of teaching. Lanier and Little (1986) noted that the work of many teacher educators "demand[s] minimal intellectual flexibility and breadth and require[s], instead, conformity and limited analysis" (p. 535). These findings suggest that if education faculty members are willing to design and develop alternative programs at all, those programs are more likely to be conceived on technical rather than moral grounds, as offering, say, more efficient methods of instruction rather than a more morally justifiable conception of the purposes of schooling. If this speculation proves correct, then under this approach some prospective teachers will experience alternative programs as at least as bereft of coherent moral content as current programs, and perhaps even more so.

Finally, this approach may leave many teaching candidates without a sense of the complexity of the contemporary debate over the moral purposes of schooling. If the faculty of an alternative program have a shared moral commitment and if the program is designed to reflect and promote that commitment, students in that program may develop a particular moral perspective without a clear understanding of the alternatives and the arguments for and against it. There is an unavoidable trade-off between a program's effectiveness at moral socialization and its ability to develop critical awareness of the complexities and uncertainties of moral judgment. Socializing teachers to a single view of the ethics of teaching is morally and intellectually problematic, since there are, as we have noted, many plausible alternative views.

It might be supposed that this problem can be overcome by giving students a choice of programs. But that assumes that prospective teachers are already well informed about this debate, that they have the background necessary to make informed judgments about the moral basis of teaching before entering a program. Goodlad's findings seem to belie that claim, however. With the possible exception of the older students he interviewed, most teaching candidates sense that there is a moral dimension of teaching, but they lack the vocabulary and the understanding to express that belief in any depth or detail (Goodlad, 1990). Against this background, it would make sense to offer a program that gives students the necessary background to be able to reach these judgments. This is, in effect, the fourth approach to answering the question of the moral content of teacher education programs.

Enabling Students to Develop Their Own Moral Commitments

In general terms, this approach embodies one of the oldest conceptions of teaching in the Western tradition, namely, Socrates' belief that good teaching enables students to form their own conclusions rather than simply to internalize the conclusions of the teacher. Conceptually, this approach to the moral content of teacher education includes two elements: it provides students with the background and opportunity to develop a reasonable commitment to a theory of the moral basis of teaching, and it enables students to develop the skills and knowledge necessary to teach in accordance with that theory. In practice, however, these two elements are likely to take place simultaneously. As students observe classrooms or engage in teaching informed by particular moral theories, they are acquiring part of the background necessary to judge moral theories. And as students learn about moral theories, they become better able to understand and judge their practical experience.

As a result, this approach need not fall prey to one of the oldest criticisms of teacher education programs—that they are overly theoretical and disconnected from the context of practice. Nevertheless, the intellectual demands of this approach are considerable. Students must become acquainted with a wide range of moral theories of teaching. They must be able to infer the logical and practical consequences of those theories. Students must also learn to interpret their observations, experiences, and activities in schools in light of those theories. And they must engage in the critical reflection, argument, and dialogue necessary to evaluate those theories and their consequences.

Just how might these demands be met? One possibility is to present the theories directly to students and expect them to apply those theories to school and classroom practices. Howe (1986) notes several problems with this strategy, perhaps the most troubling of which is that the theories are, for reasons of convenience, often presented without clear justification and that the theories are too abstract to permit immediate practical application to real situations of practice. As a result of the first problem, students often make intuitive and unreflective commitments to particular theories. As a result of the second, students are unable to reach coherent moral judgments about the actual moral problems of practice.

To meet these difficulties, Howe (1986) proposes, in line with some other thinkers in the field (like Strike & Soltis, 1985), that ethical instruction in teacher education programs be centered on critical reasoning about particular and concrete dilemmas of practice. But this strategy has similar problems. Starting with concrete situations, students are unlikely to develop a knowledge of the moral theories of teaching and are thus unlikely to develop a rigorous and systematic justification for the conclusions they reach about specific cases. Howe thinks it unimportant for students to know about general types of moral theory like utilitarianism and Kantian nonconsequentialism. Perhaps he is right about such extremely abstract theories, but a strong case can be made for prospective teachers' learning about the most plausible contemporary moral theories *of teaching*, theories that, like those identified above, are at the heart of current controversies over education policy and practice. As a result, I see no alternative to both teaching those theories and analyzing particular classroom, school,and policy problems in light of them. I also see no alternative to infusing critical reflection based on these theories into the teacher education curriculum as a whole. All teaching methods, school curricula, and institutional practices need to be understood critically against the background of the current debate over the moral purposes of teaching and schooling.

The intellectual demands of this approach on those involved in teacher education, students and faculty alike, are therefore profound. Ethical instruction cannot be relinquished to a few faculty members in the educational foundations department. Nor can such instruction be limited to a single moral theory of teaching. Nor can the moral theories be presented as just so many alternatives among which students must choose. Instead, teaching candidates, professors, and the school professionals involved in the program must be systematically engaged in the imaginative, sympathetic, and critical development, evaluation, interpretation, and application of the full range of plausible responses to questions regarding the moral basis of teaching.

Unless teacher education instructors are as good as Socrates and teacher education students are as good as Plato, this approach is likely to fall far short of its objectives. The demand for teachers generated by an ideal of universal public education, even if only approximately realized, does not permit teacher education to be an elite enterprise. And the Socratic ideal of fully deliberative ethical judgment in teacher education is therefore an artifact of an elitist intellectual heritage out of step with contemporary political and interpersonal perspectives on teaching.

CONCLUSION

These reflections on the ethical content of teacher education have led to many more questions than answers. Starting with Goodlad's (1990) proposal for a full-scale, facultywide agreement about the ethical basis of teaching, the practical and moral difficulties of each approach to determining this ethical content have led us to consider yet another approach that, unfortunately, has also proved to be inadequate. I suspect that the basic reason for this series of difficulties must lie with a conflict between our ethical and intellectual ideals, a conflict I cannot characterize adequately, let alone resolve. Short of resolving this conflict, we are left with the choice among admittedly only partially satisfactory ways of defining this moral content. And I am not now able to say whether, for example, it is better to try to achieve an unattainable facultywide agreement about that content or to develop an unattainable degree of moral deliberation among prospective teachers. In any case, the task of defining a fully satisfactory approach to that content is one that will take real moral and creative energies.

REFERENCES

Ackerman, B. A. (1980). *Social justice in the liberal state.* New Haven, CT: Yale University Press.

Ashton, P. T. (Ed.). (1991). *Journal of Teacher Education, 42,* 163–215.

Bloom, A. (1987). *The closing of the American mind: How higher education has failed democracy and impoverished the souls of today's students.* New York: Simon & Schuster.

Bull, B. L. (1990). The limits of teacher professionalization. In J. I. Goodlad, R. Soder, & K. S. Sirotnik (Eds.), *The moral dimensions of teaching* (pp. 87–129). San Francisco: Jossey-Bass.

Chubb, J. E., & Moe, T. M. (1990). *Politics, markets, and America's schools.* Washington, DC: Brookings Institution.

Dewey, J. (1966). *Democracy and education.* Chicago: Free Press. (Original work published 1916.)

Goodlad, J. I. (1990). *Teachers for our nation's schools.* San Francisco: Jossey-Bass.

Gutmann, A. (1987). *Democratic education.* Princeton, NJ: Princeton University Press.

Habermas, J. (1987). *The philosophical discourse of modernity* (F. Lawrence, Trans.). Cambridge, MA: MIT Press. (Original work published 1985.)

Holmes Group. (1986). *Tomorrow's teachers.* East Lansing, MI: Author.

Howe, K. R. (1986). The conceptual basis for ethics in teacher education. *Journal of Teacher Education, 37,* 5–12.

Lanier, J. E., & Little, J. W. (1986). Research on teacher education. In M. C. Wittrock (Ed.), *Handbook of Research on Teaching* (3rd ed., pp. 527–569). New York: Macmillan.

Lasley, T. J. (Ed.). (1986). *Journal of Teacher Education, 37,* 2–20.

Noddings, N. (1984). *Caring: A feminine approach to ethics and moral education.* Berkeley, CA: University of California Press.

Noddings, N. (1986). Fidelity in teaching, teacher education, and research for teaching. *Harvard Educational Review, 56*, 496–510.
Peters, R. S. (1966). *Ethics and education*. London: Allen & Unwin.
Rogers, C. R. (1980). *Freedom to learn for the 80s*. Columbus, OH: Merrill.
Strike, K. A., & Soltis, J. F. (1985). *The ethics of teaching*. New York: Teachers College Press.
Sockett, H. (1990). Accountability, trust, and ethical codes of practice. In J. I. Goodlad, R. Soder, & K. S. Sirotnik (Eds.), *The moral dimensions of teaching* (pp. 224–250). San Francisco: Jossey-Bass.

6 Lawrence Kohlberg's Approach and the Moral Education of Education Professionals

DAWN E. SCHRADER
Cornell University

Moral education in school contexts has been student-centered, focused on changes in moral reasoning stage, moral type or orientation, and moral atmosphere in classroom environments, alternative school settings, and curricula (Berkowitz & Oser, 1985; Kohlberg, 1984; Mosher, 1980; Power, Higgins, & Kohlberg, 1989). However, moral education techniques hold promise not only for developing the moral reasoning of young people, but for teacher education as well. This chapter explores the ways in which the education of teachers might utilize a developmental theory such as Kohlberg's life-span cognitive developmental approach as a basis for professional educational programs.

This chapter posits that the goals of Kohlberg's moral theory and education programs, particularly the dilemma discussion technique developed for those programs, are appropriate for the ethical education of teachers. To demonstrate this position, the goals and processes of a cognitive developmental approach to ethics education are contrasted with other approaches, and shown to be particularly appropriate for teacher education. Next, Kohlberg's theories of moral development and education are summarized. Third, research studies that have used the main components of moral education theory are examined in the context of the suitability of this approach for educational professionals.

THE COGNITIVE DEVELOPMENTAL APPROACH TO MORAL EDUCATION

Kohlberg and Mayer (1981) compare three major "streams" of educational ideology to teaching ethics—romanticism, cultural transmission, and progressivism. Romanticism follows the ideals of theorists such as Rousseau, Freud, Gesell, and G. Stanley Hall, and practitioners such as

A. S. Neill. According to Kohlberg and Mayer (1981) romanticism contends that:

> [W]hat comes from within the child is the most important aspect of development; therefore, the pedagogical environment should be permissive enough to allow the inner "good" (abilities and social virtues) to unfold and the inner "bad" to come under control. Thus teaching the child the ideas and attitudes of others through rote or drill would result in meaningless learning and the suppression of inner spontaneous tendencies of positive value. (p. 51)

Kohlberg and Mayer also discuss cultural transmission as a "stream" of educational ideology. This ideology is rooted in Western education, which focuses its tasks on the transmission of the knowledge, skills, and moral values of the past to the current generation, with the hope that the current generation will internalize this information. Educational theories that might represent this ideology include social learning theory, which emphasizes imitation of adult behavior models, or behavioral learning theory, which focuses on contingency reinforcements.

The third stream of thought Kohlberg and Mayer present is the developmental or progressive approach. This ideology follows Dewey's (1938) and Piaget's conceptions that "a core of universal ideas are redefined and reorganized as their implications are played out in experience as they are confronted by their opposites in argument and discourse" (Kohlberg & Mayer, 1981, p. 56) and that "mature thought emerges through a process of development that is neither direct biological maturation nor direct learning, but rather a reorganization of psychological structures resulting from organism-environment interactions" (p. 56). Unlike the romantic view of development as an innate tendency within the individual, the progressive approach views healthy development as the progression through an invariant sequence of stages that is constructed as children actively organize both cognition and emotion through interaction with their environment. The aim of progressive or developmental education, therefore, "requires an educational environment that actively stimulates development through the presentation of resolvable but genuine problems or conflicts" and that "the organizing and developing force in the child's experience is the child's active thinking, and thinking is stimulated by the problematic, by cognitive conflict" (p. 54).

These three ideologies have dominated the field of moral education of both children and professionals. Inherent in the first two of these views is that moral development can and should occur either through the structuring of a free and nourishing environment, or through an autocratic educational experience in which external contingencies or authorities control the experience. The progressive or cognitive developmental perspective takes into account the active agency of the person who progressively constructs an understanding of morality. Thus, this perspective is most suitable to a professional educational program of moral education.

Both the romantic and the cultural transmission approaches have inherent difficulties when applied to professional education. The romantic approach treats the moral development of professionals as an informal occurrence or by-product of the process of professional education, thereby treating it as a part of the "hidden curriculum" of the professional program. This approach has been criticized in the past by the medical profession (GPEP report, 1984), as it has not been successful in developing the kind of moral integrity one might wish to see in the profession. A tenable argument could be made for the cultural transmission approach to professional education, since professionals are accountable to larger professional organizations. Rules of conduct could be developed that would regulate and predict the moral decisions that arise in the profession. This approach has the advantage of specifying moral codes that could lead to consistent practice among members of a profession. However, this approach has been criticized for its limitations, one being that with the changing nature of society and technology, new moral dilemmas arise that have not been explored. Thus the cultural transmission model may provide a guide for moral values when problems are clearly delimited, yet the everyday decisions professionals make are not able to be codified. This is particularly so in teaching where decision making is an ongoing process, and where new theoretical advances are made prior to their institution in the professional organization and its ethical codes. In professional education it is essential to take into account the notion of what it means to be "professional." Professionals, by definition, are self-regulated experts in a particular body of knowledge who act autonomously. Education for professionals, therefore, ought to recognize the nature of professional practice and design educational programs that foster independent, self-regulated moral thought and action. Kohlberg's approach to moral education does just that. The use of hypothetical and real-life moral dilemmas, presented in a developmentally structured, interactive environment such as that advocated by the progressive approach, fosters moral development through critical reflection and moral justification.

Teachers exercise their professional autonomy when they apply their own moral perspectives and judgments to making decisions about specific problems. Kohlberg's approach to moral education enhances education professionals' abilities to make sound moral judgments, and does so in a way that upholds the autonomy of teachers as professionals and as morally responsible decision makers. Kohlberg's theory of moral development provides an underlying structure for the cognitive developmental approach to moral education described above. Specifically, Kohlberg's moral development theory provides the invariant sequence of stages that individuals construct based on experience and social interaction, and his moral education theory provides stimulation for such development.

The next two sections describe Kohlberg's theories of moral development and moral education, which provide the theoretical grounding for using his approach to ethics education for educational professionals.

KOHLBERG'S THEORY OF MORAL DEVELOPMENT

Kohlberg began his work in the moral domain in the 1950s with a cross-sectional study of adolescent boys aged 10 to 16. Using hypothetical moral dilemmas that he constructed based on themes from literature, Kohlberg found that boys exhibited six types of moral reasoning strategies to resolve these moral problems. Kohlberg interviewed these boys every 3 years until the early 1980s. Based on these longitudinal interviews, and subsequent studies that included girls and women, cross-cultural participants, and participants from various social and economic backgrounds, Kohlberg continually modified his theory of six types of morality to a six-stage theory. These six stages have been refined over the last 30 years to distinguish between what Kohlberg referred to as the *content* of moral thinking and the *structure* of moral reasoning. The most current formulation of Kohlberg's theory of moral development stages is reported in Colby and Kohlberg (1987). In this statement, the moral judgment stages are defined according to the six stages, simplified in Table 6.1. This table illustrates the development from an egocentric sociomoral perspective to stages that incorporate multiple perspectives, to stages that coordinate among multiple perspectives.

Embedded within this description is the central point that any particular moral judgment includes not only a decision about what is right, but also the *reasons* for doing right and a *justification* as to why those reasons are important to consider. These three elements, combined with the underlying sociomoral perspective, are the essential components of Kohlberg's moral stage theory.

Moral judgments, according to Colby and Kohlberg (1987), are judgments of value and fact, which makes them distinct from Piagetian cognitive reasoning and judgment. Moral judgments are social judgments and are prescriptive or normative judgments about people's rights, obligations, and responsibilities rather than their preferences. Critics, including Carol Gilligan (1982), have argued that Kohlberg's theory is a theory of "justice

Table 6.1 Six stages of moral judgment

Level and stage	Content of stage		
	What is right	*Reasons for doing right*	*Sociomoral perspective of stage*
Level 1: Preconventional: Stage 1. Heteronomous morality	To avoid breaking rules backed by punishment, obedience for its own sake, and avoiding physical damage to persons and property.	Avoidance of punishment and the superior power of authorities.	Egocentric point of view. Doesn't consider the interests of others or recognize that they differ from the actor's, doesn't relate two points of view. Actions are considered physically rather than in terms of psychological interests of others. Confusion of authority's perspective with one's own.
Stage 2. Individualism, instrumental purpose, and exchange	Following rules only when it is to someone's immediate interest; acting to meet one's own interests and needs and letting others do the same. Right is also what's fair, what's an equal exchange, a deal, an agreement.	To serve one's own needs or interests in a world where you have to recognize that other people have their interests, too.	Concrete individualistic perspective. Aware that everybody has his own interests to pursue and these conflict, so that right is relative (in the concrete individualistic scene).
Level 2: Conventional: Stage 3. Mutual interpersonal expectations, relationships, and interpersonal conformity	Living up to what is expected by people close to you or what people generally expect of people in your role as son, brother, friend, etc. "Being good" is important and means having good motives, showing concern about others. It also means keeping mutual relationships, such as trust, loyalty, respect, and gratitude.	The need to be a good person in your own eyes and those of others. Your caring for others. Belief in the Golden Rule. Desire to maintain rules and authority which support stereotypical good behavior.	Perspective of the individual in relationships with other individuals. Aware of shared feelings, agreements, and expectations which take primacy over individual interests. Relates points of view through the concrete Golden Rule, putting yourself in the other guy's shoes. Does not yet consider generalized system perspective.

Stage 4. Social system and conscience	Fulfilling the actual duties to which you have agreed. Laws are to be upheld except in extreme cases where they conflict with other fixed social duties. Right is also contributing to society, the group, or institution.	To keep the institution going as a whole, to avoid the breakdown in the system "if everyone did it," or the imperative of conscience to meet one's defined obligations.	Differentiates societal point of view from interpersonal agreement or motives. Takes the point of view of the system that defines roles and rules. Considers individual relations in terms of place in the system.
Level 3: Postconventional or principled: Stage 5. Social contract or utility and individual rights	Being aware that people hold a variety of values and opinions, that most values and rules are relative to your group. These relative rules should usually be upheld, however, in the interest of impartiality and because they are the social contract. Some nonrelative values and rights like life and liberty, however, must be upheld in any society and regardless of majority opinion.	A sense of obligation to law because of one's social contract to make and abide by laws for the welfare of all and for the protection of all people's rights. A feeling of contractual commitment, freely entered upon, to family, friendship, trust and work obligations. Concern that laws and duties be based on rational calculation of overall utility, "the greatest good for the greatest number."	Prior-to-society perspective. Perspective of a rational individual aware of values and rights prior to social attachments and contracts. Integrates perspectives by formal mechanisms of agreement, contract, objective impartiality, and due process. Considers moral and legal points of view; recognizes that they sometimes conflict and finds it difficult to integrate them.
Stage 6. Universal ethical principles	Following self-chosen ethical principles. Particular laws or social agreements are usually valid because they rest on such principles. When laws violate these principles, one acts in accordance with the principle. Principles are universal principles of justice: the equality of human rights and respect for the dignity of human beings as individual persons.	The belief as a rational person in the validity of universal moral principles, and a sense of personal commitment to them.	Perspective of a moral point of view from which social agreements derive. Perspective is that of any rational individual recognizing the nature of morality or the fact that persons are ends in themselves and must be treated as such.

Source: Reprinted from Kohlberg (1976), pp. 34–35.

reasoning" rather than a theory of moral judgment; however, Colby and Kohlberg (1987) dispute this, stating that:

> Although it is true that the dilemmas in the Standard Moral Judgment Interview pose conflicts of rights, the actual judgments made by respondents may focus on concern and love for another person, on personal commitments, on the need for sympathy and understanding, on responsibility to humanity and one's fellow human beings as well as rights, rules and duties. As long as these concepts are used prescriptively, as defining what is morally right or good, they fall within the scope of the moral domain as we construe it. In this sense, the scope of the domain we assess is considerably broader than is conveyed by the term *justice reasoning*. (p. 11)

Kohlberg's theory of moral judgment can thus be considered to be widely applicable in discussing moral education in a variety of fields and with a variety of age groups. Kohlberg postulated that all people construct moral reasoning according to this sequence of stages if given opportunities for social interaction and role-taking, and have requisite cognitive developmental reasoning. Cross-cultural longitudinal data have borne this out (Colby & Kohlberg, 1987). Although controversy over gender bias emerged based on an early formulation of Kohlberg's theory (Kohlberg, 1969), gender differences in the stages have been largely unsubstantiated in the current formulation of his developmental theory (Kohlberg, 1984; Walker, 1983; Gibbs, Arnold, & Burkhart, 1983). Kohlberg's moral education theory was designed to enhance role-taking opportunities and cognitive conflict to facilitate progression through his stage sequence.

KOHLBERG'S APPROACH TO MORAL EDUCATION

Lawrence Kohlberg's moral education theory derives, in part, from an experiment designed by one of his students, Moshe Blatt, in 1975. Blatt based his ideas on research by Elliot Turiel (1966) and James Rest (1968), who found that if people were systematically exposed to reasoning one stage higher than their own, they would try to incorporate that reasoning into their own reasoning strategies, and thus develop to the next stage of moral judgment. Blatt hypothesized that peer discussion of hypothetical moral dilemmas would be the "most effective and least artificial way" to expose them to adjacent stages of moral reasoning while at the same time encouraging them to articulate their own reasoning (Power, Higgins, & Kohlberg, 1989; Blatt & Kohlberg, 1975; Kohlberg, 1985). Blatt's original study confirmed his hypotheses, as did his replication. Blatt found that, on the whole, during a one-semester (approximately 12-week) program one fourth to one half of the students would move partially or totally to the next stage of moral judgment, whereas students in control groups demonstrated no such movement. This effect was subsequently replicated by numerous studies (for example, Lockwood, 1978; Leming, 1981; Enright, Lapsley, & Levey, 1983).

Effective dilemma discussions involve two fundamental elements. First, participants are encouraged to examine their moral thoughts about, and reasons for, choosing what they considered to be the morally right or obligatory action in each of the dilemmas. Second, the discussions focus primarily on participants' reasoning. Teachers facilitate these discussions using their knowledge of Kohlberg's theory and a Socratic dialogue in which increasingly more sophisticated sociomoral justice operations (such as reciprocity and reversibility) are constructed by the students. This process is, in Kohlberg's view, both theoretically appropriate and empirically successful; fundamentally it is an elaboration of the processes of Jean Piaget's explanation of cognitive development applied to the moral domain (Kohlberg, 1985).

Based on this pioneering research, Kohlberg elaborated what he called the "cognitive developmental approach to moral education," exemplifying the progressive approach discussed earlier. Kohlberg viewed dilemma discussion as being consonant with the goals of a developmental approach to education, which is "to promote the development of students' capacities in areas of cognitive, social, moral and emotional functioning" (Power, Higgins, & Kohlberg, 1989, p. 16). Kohlberg, like Piaget, cautioned that such development is not designed simply for accelerating individuals through stages of development, but rather to avoid temporizing within a particular stage. Thus, providing educational opportunities is the aim of such a program. Kohlberg looked upon moral dilemma discussion as facilitating *decalage*—a breadth of understanding about various moral, social, and cognitive issues (Power, Higgins, & Kohlberg, 1989).

The Dilemma Discussion

Dilemma discussion plays an important role in assisting participants to make moral decisions. James Rest (1984, 1985) outlined four components of moral decision making:

1. Increasing sensitivity to and identifying moral issues
2. Identifying possible alternative action choices
3. Selecting from among available action choices
4. Implementing choices into action

Rest states that moral education programs should target these processes and attempt to help people develop proficiency in each of them. Dilemma discussions encourage participants in their development of at least the first three of these components. Dilemma discussion also provides the means by which individuals can increase their role-taking ability so that they begin to see the points of view of others involved in the dilemma, as well as a larger societal viewpoint of a dilemma's resolution. In other words, participants learn to play what Kohlberg whimsically called "moral musical chairs," a technique that encourages participants to see a dilemma from many perspectives. The limits of the perspectives taken in dilemma discussions hinge on the developmental role-taking abilities of the participants involved. The active dialogue of dilemma discussions encourages discourse between people who are ideally at adjacent stages of moral development. This provides a rich context in which discussion can be guided to encourage those with more elaborated sociomoral perspectives to articulate those perspectives, and persuade others to reevaluate their arguments. This is called a "plus-one" condition. The facilitator of the discussion should be cognizant of moral theory and encourage a plus-one discussion so that even those with the more elaborated sociomoral perspectives of the group are challenged in their role-taking and moral justifications.

Classical and Real-Life Dilemmas

Dilemma discussions may use classical hypothetical dilemmas or real-life moral dilemmas. Real dilemmas may be either personal dilemmas faced by participants in a group, or case examples. Classical hypothetical dilemmas involve a conflict between two moral rights or goods, for example, saving a life versus obeying a law—the fundamental moral conflict in Kohlberg's classic "Heinz Dilemma" (Colby & Kohlberg, 1987). Such dilemmas are based on the notion that when two conflicting goods are juxtaposed, a reasonable number of people may reasonably disagree on the good chosen. Dilemma discussions work best with a morally heterogeneous, small group of peers (Berkowitz, 1985). The success of a dilemma discussion is based on one fundamental idea that was originally put forth by Piaget: disequilibration. Stage development is due to the reequilibration processes necessitated by individuals experiencing cognitive conflict. Small groups are essential to this process because they facilitate the interactions necessary for cognitive conflict, whereas large groups would not. In dilemma discussions, participants must explain and justify their reasoning about a dilemma, and smaller, more diverse groups facilitate the active participation of all of their members, thus creating the cognitive conflict that promotes stage change. The groups should be heterogeneous rather than homogeneous because, as a number of studies indicate, such groupings result in greater development (Colby, Kohlberg, Fenton, Speicher-Dubin, & Lieberman, 1977; Berkowitz, Gibbs, & Broughton, 1980). Some have indicated that a plus-one condition, in which a teacher presents moral reasoning one stage above that of the students in the group, can promote moral development. Berkowitz (1985) questions the necessity of such a situation, noting that in a heterogeneous grouping, the plus-one condition is provided by the peer group itself. In professions where peer review is the standard, dilemma discussion techniques provide an optimal form of interaction that not only develops professionals morally, but provides socialization for professional interaction.

Real-life dilemma discussions differ from the classical hypothetical dilemmas discussed above in several respects. First, there may not be two goods in conflict, such as saving a life versus upholding the law. Real-life conflicts may involve only one moral issue, or not knowing what would be the right or most responsible thing to do in a moral situation (Gilligan, 1982). Real-life dilemmas tend to be more personal, and/or constrained by contexts (practical considerations, personality factors, professional codes of conduct, and so forth), than classical hypothetical dilemmas. Hypothetical dilemmas tend to be abstract, allowing the individual to construct the moral ideal, whereas real-life dilemmas tend to be profoundly real, requiring practical as well as normative reasoning. Both types of dilemma discussions, however, involve the process of small group discussion and are based on the concept of creating cognitive conflict to promote moral stage development.

Limitations of Dilemma Discussions

Kohlberg recognized the limitations of the dilemma discussion approach. For example, hypothetical dilemma discussions do not fully address everyday issues faced by discussion participants, or the impact of such discussions on behavior or on the overall sociomoral climate within which people live and work. Because of this deficit, Kohlberg elaborated a more complete moral education program called the "Just Community" approach, which incorporated dilemma discussion and its developmental-psychological underpinnings with the sociological aspects of education based on the work of Dewey (1960), Durkheim (1973), Dreeben (1968), Jackson (1968), and Royce (1982). Although the Just Community approach is not the focus of this chapter, it is important to note that a moral education program that uses dilemma discussion is only part of what is useful for educating educational professionals. Ethical education must permeate not only educators' reasoning about hypothetical situations, but also the everyday moral issues in professional educators' environments.

While the Just Community approach may not be feasible for all professional education programs, the use of real life cases for dilemma discussion is a reasonable start toward improved moral education of educational professionals. This method has thus begun to permeate curricula in professional education programs (for example, at Harvard, Yale, and Case Western Reserve medical schools). The education profession might follow their lead. Even though much of Kohlberg's early research on the dilemma discussion method of moral education centers on secondary and late elementary school ages, professional educators have recognized the value of Kohlberg's moral theory as the life-span developmental theory it is. Programs have thus been created that expand the application of the dilemma discussion method to case studies (Self et al., 1991) and clinical experience (Candee, 1985; Sheehan, Husted, Cook, & Bargen, 1980) and incorporate the types of ethical judgments required for making difficult moral decisions in complex professional ethical situations.

Although the strength of dilemma discussion is its grounding in formal moral and psychological theory, it is not a panacea for moral education. Discussion of either type of dilemma—hypothetical or real-life—presents the same weakness: dilemma discussions are only discussions. Discussions of neither type of dilemma can predict action. In addition, dilemmas used for discussion can neither include all possible moral issues in conflict nor prescribe clear cut moral solutions to problems. Thus it is important to recognize that dilemma discussion is only a part of a concerted effort toward ethics education, and that effort should include components of the moral decision making process itself in addition to the elaboration of more complex forms of moral reasoning.

INTERVENTIONS USING KOHLBERG'S APPROACH

Schläfli, Rest, and Thoma (1985) reviewed 55 moral education interventions published between 1972 and 1983 that utilized the Defining Issues Test to assess moral stage reasoning. The interventions reported in the meta-analysis might be classified into three types: (1) Dilemma Discussion—interventions that follow the methods suggested by Blatt and Kohlberg, 1975; (2) Personality Development—interventions that use the experiential activity and self-reflection suggested by Mosher and Sprinthall (1970); and (3) Academic Courses—interventions that use academic course content in humanities or social studies. As examples of the types of ethical education interventions that have been conducted, two interventions will be briefly reviewed.

Boyd (1976) conducted two ethics-related academic courses using dilemma discussion techniques as outlined by Blatt and Kohlberg (1975). Although Schläfli, Rest, and Thoma (1985) concluded that academic courses generally do not have a significant effect on moral judgment development, Boyd's studies demonstrated that if academic courses combine dilemma discussion and personal reflection with didactic course content, moral development will take place. What we do not precisely know, however, is whether the discussion technique or the personal reflection accounted for such development.

In 1973 an intervention was instituted at Alverno College (Earley, Mentkowski, & Schafer, 1980) that made moral decision making and development an integral part of all students' coursework. Research teams, panel presentations, small-group seminars, moral dilemma discussions, role-taking exercises, real-life simulations, forced-choice inventories, values clarification exercises, and analytic journals were all used. One conclusion Mentkowski (1984) drew from the first seven years of the longitudinal study was that Alverno students "became increasingly sophisticated in their use of principled reasoning in resolving moral dilemmas"[1] (p. 22). Again, this study does not reveal *which* of the many techniques used were most effective in creating the change in students' ethical reasoning. Such discernment is essential because many educational institutions and many educators are unable to make the significant economic or personal investments made in programs such as the Alverno Project. Such varied, wide-ranging programs suggest that moral development is possible to effect, but they do not provide the *reasons* underlying these psychological changes.

Schläfli and colleagues' (1985) meta-analysis demonstrated that dilemma discussion interventions yielded the greatest average increase in subjects' principled moral reasoning; personality development interventions were nearly as successful. Academic course interventions, on average, had no real effect on moral reasoning development. However, they found that when Kohlberg's theory was taught to participants, the effect size was twice as large as in interventions where participants did not learn Kohlberg's theory. Thus, academic exposure to moral theory may facilitate individuals' moral judgment reasoning development (Schläfli, Rest, & Thoma, 1985; Oser & Schläfli, 1985).

---

[1]As measured by the Defining Issues Test. When the Moral Judgment Interview was used, similar trends existed, but the effect was more dramatic.

The findings cited above indicate that requiring courses in ethics as part of the curriculum is not enough to effect moral development in students. Including components of moral dilemma discussion, case studies, personal reflection, or analytic journals in professional training programs for future educators can provide the support needed to facilitate moral stage development.

IMPLICATIONS FOR PROFESSIONAL EDUCATION PROGRAMS

This chapter outlined the theoretical underpinnings and practical components of Kohlberg's approach to moral education. Fundamentally, Kohlberg's cognitive developmental theory and dilemma discussion technique exemplify the progressive approach to moral education. By using dilemma discussions, especially those of real-life situations, Kohlberg's theories of development and education demonstrate the role of disequilibration in moral stage transition, the use of peer interaction for sociomoral development, and the significance of real experiences for understanding moral issues. Case studies used as the basis for dilemma discussions foster an awareness of moral issues in everyday life. This, as Rest indicated in his four-component model, is the first step in moral decision making. Kohlberg's model of moral education also exemplifies the importance of discourse in leading a moral life.

Combining Kohlberg's moral theory with other moral and psychological concepts can contribute to developing effective programs for the education of education professionals. Schläfli, Rest, and Thoma's (1985) meta-analysis demonstrated that the most successful forms of moral education involve dilemma discussion and the teaching of moral theory. Programs for education professionals could be created that use the aforementioned to educate ethical practitioners. (It should be emphasized, however, that intensive and wide-ranging experiences also contributed to the results cited above by Boyd and Mentkowski.)

The research cited above demonstrates the usefulness of Kohlberg's approach to the moral education of education professionals. Future developments in professional education programs might take the cognitive developmental approach one step further and use metacognitive strategies for thinking about moral dilemmas. The literature on metacognition and on reflective educational practice could inform the development of professional education programs because it is consistent with the progressive approach to moral education, and can expand the dilemma discussion technique outlined in this chapter. I contend that metacognitive reflection is essential to moral stage development (Schrader, 1988) and the development of morally responsible professionals. Specifically, there is a dynamic interaction between one's experiences, moral judgments, and metacognitive reflection (Schrader, 1990). Dilemma discussion of real cases that bear on the process of professional education can be an integral part of one's experience. As reported above, Schläfli, Rest, and Thoma (1985) found that some of the studies that used personal analytic journals resulted in moral stage development. Stimulated by Kohlberg's dilemma discussion, metacognitive strategies could be used to direct individuals' moral decision making toward principled morality.

It is important that professionals be responsible for consciously reflecting on the ethical reasoning capabilities and character virtues that are consistent with principled reasoning. Professionals need to use principles to guide ethical choices and cognitive, moral, and social skills to respond to new situations. Professions may influence moral conduct via guidelines and regulations, but they do not inherently possess character virtues—people possess these. The person as professional is the key instrument of both ethical and technological competence. The person must be knowledgeable of ethics *and* of teaching. Dilemma discussion and metacognitive reflection on one's own thinking processes facilitates this competence.

In *The Moral Collapse of the University*, Bruce Wilshire (1990) states that Albert Einstein, William James, John Dewey, and others believed in the "interactive nature" of individuals with the field in which they are involved. Wilshire states,

> Reality is the field of concrete interactivity. The notion of a detached, nearly passive, 'value-free' consciousness or observer must be abandoned. (p. 190)

Wilshire further poses the question of how "a self" could be singled out from the attachments and involvements in a field. After professional training, one is no longer the same moral person one was prior to that educational experience. Experience informs reason, which in turn informs later experience. Professions ought to rely on that interaction and develop programs that assist in the development of ethical individuals and practitioners.

DEVELOPING MORALLY REFLECTIVE EDUCATION PROFESSIONALS

Applying Kohlberg's theories of moral education to the training of professional educators could result in the development of programs that would teach individuals to:

1. Apply the guiding ethical principles of their profession to novel situations
2. Recognize, interpret, and act on moral issues and conflicts that arise in practice
3. Understand how their actions in moral situations relate to both the profession as a whole and their constituents as individuals
4. Develop into reflective professionals; that is, understand how reflection on actions and reflective awareness of one's own moral reasoning influences ethical choices and actions taken in professional practice

These abilities are important for developing persons who are both principled moral thinkers *and* members of a profession. They also exemplify the progressive approach to moral education discussed earlier in this chapter. Kohlberg's approach to moral education, with its use of dilemma discussion and real-life cases, represents a reintegration of the psychology of the individual and the moral and philosophical justifications necessary for ethical practice. By applying this approach, professional training programs encourage professionals to act more "professionally," that is, with autonomy and self-regulation, as well as stimulate the personal growth of these professionals from a moral standpoint.

Rest's ethical decision making components—the ability to identify problems, generate alternatives, reason through outcomes, and act morally—*and* the ability to reflect on moral judgments and experiences, are important for professionals to develop because educators act autonomously in their practice. Kohlberg's approach to moral education provides the theoretical bases for assisting moral stage development as well as for developing these components in future educational professionals.

Although criticisms have been levied against Kohlberg's moral stage theory for not being inclusive of women's moral reasoning (Gilligan, 1982), or of being too "rational" (see Kohlberg, 1984, for a detailed summary of his critics and his response to them), Kohlberg's moral education program has escaped such criticism. Dilemma discussion of real-life cases leaves open the opportunities for responding to dilemmas from either a justice or care orientation, or from universality or particularity; it allows individuals to express their own moral judgments and sentiments about the cases, but without being value-free. Further, it opens the door to dialogue—an essential component of postconventional morality (Habermas, 1991). Although Kohlberg's theory of morality has its critics, his progressive educational approach stands strong in its effectiveness and usefulness in promoting moral stage growth and fostering moral autonomy.

REFERENCES

Berkowitz, M. W. (1985). The role of discussion in moral education. In M. Berkowitz & F. Oser (Eds.), *Moral education: Theory and application* (pp. 197-218). Hillsdale, NJ: Lawrence Erlbaum.

Berkowitz, M. W., Gibbs, J., & Broughton, J. (1980). The relation of moral judgment stage disparity to developmental effects of peer dialogues. *Merrill-Palmer Quarterly, 26*, 341-357.

Berkowitz, M. W., & Oser, F. (1985). *Moral education: Theory and application.* Hillsdale, NJ: Lawrence Erlbaum.

Blatt, M., & Kohlberg, L. (1975). The effects of classroom moral discussion programs upon children's moral judgment. *Journal of Moral Education, 4*, 129-161.

Boyd, D. (1976). *Education toward principled moral judgment: An analysis of an experimental course in Lawrence Kohlberg's theory of moral development.* Unpublished doctoral dissertation, Harvard University, Cambridge, MA.

Candee, D. (1985). Classical ethics and live patient simulations in the moral education of health care professionals. In M. Berkowitz & F. Oser (Eds.), *Moral education: Theory and application* (pp. 297-318). Hillsdale, NJ: Lawrence Erlbaum.

Colby, A., & Kohlberg, L. (1987). *The measurement of moral judgment* (Vol. 1). New York: Cambridge University Press.

Colby, A., Kohlberg, L., Fenton, T., Speicher-Dubin, B., & Lieberman, M. (1977). Secondary school moral discussion programs led by social studies teachers. *Journal of Moral Education, 6*, 90-111.

Dewey, J. (1938). *Experience and education.* New York: Macmillan.

Dewey, J. (1960). *Theory of moral life.* New York: Holt, Rinehart & Winston. (Original work published 1910)

Dreeben, R. (1968). *On what is learned at school.* Reading, MA: Addison-Wesley.

Durkheim, E. (1973). *Moral education: A study in the theory and application of the sociology of education.* New York: Free Press. (Original work published 1925)

Earley, M., Mentkowski, M., & Schafer, J. (1980). *Valuing at Alverno: The valuing process in liberal education.* Milwaukee, WI: Alverno Productions.

Enright, R., Lapsley, D., & Levey, V. (1983). Moral education strategies. In M. Pressley & J. Levin (Eds.), *Cognitive strategy research: Educational application*, (pp. 43-83). New York: Springer-Verlag.

Gibbs, J., Arnold, K., & Burkhart, J. (1983). Sex differences in the expression of moral judgment. *Child Development, 55*, 1040-1043.

Gilligan, C. (1982). *In a different voice: Psychological theory and women's development.* Cambridge, MA: Harvard University Press.

GPEP Report. (1984). *Physicians for the twenty-first century.* Report of the panel on the general professional education of the physician and College Preparation for Medicine. Washington D.C.: Association of American Medical Colleges.

Habermas, J. (1991). *Moral consciousness and communicative action*. New York: Academic Press.

Jackson, P. (1968). *Life in the classroom*. New York: Holt, Rinehart and Winston.

Kohlberg, L. (1969). Stage and sequence: The cognitive developmental approach to socialization. In D. Goslin (Ed.), *Handbook of socialization theory and research* (pp. 347–480). Chicago: Rand McNally.

Kohlberg, L. (1984). *Essays on moral development: Vol. 2. The psychology of moral development*. San Francisco: Harper & Row.

Kohlberg, L. (1985). A just community approach to moral education in theory and practice. In M. W. Berkowitz & F. Oser (Eds.), *Moral education: Theory and practice* (pp. 27–87). Hillsdale, NJ: Lawrence Erlbaum.

Kohlberg, L., & Mayer, R. (1981). Development as the aim of education: The Dewey view. In L. Kohlberg (Ed.), *Essays on moral development: Vol. 1. The philosophy of moral development* (pp. 49–96). New York: Harper & Row.

Leming, J. S. (1981). Curriculum effectiveness in moral/values education: A review of research. *Journal of Moral Education, 10*, 147–164.

Lockwood, A. (1978). The effects of values clarification and moral development curricula on school-age subjects: A critical review of recent research. *Review of Educational Research, 48*, 325–364.

Mentkowski, M. (1984, November). The college as an enabling institution. Keynote address at the annual meeting of the Association of Moral Education, Columbus, OH.

Mosher, R. (1980). *Moral education: A first generation of research and development*. New York: Praeger.

Mosher, R., & Sprinthall, N. (1970). Psychological education in secondary schools: A program to promote individual and human development. *American Psychologist, 25*, 911–924.

Oser, F., & Schläfli, A. (1985). But does it move: The difficulty of gradual change in moral development. In M. W. Berkowitz & F. Oser (Eds.), *Moral education: Theory and application* (pp. 269–296). Hillsdale, NJ: Lawrence Erlbaum.

Power, F. C., Higgins, A., & Kohlberg, L. (1989). *Lawrence Kohlberg's approach to moral education*. New York: Columbia University Press.

Rest, J. (1968). *Developmental hierarchy in preference and comprehension of moral judgment*. Unpublished doctoral dissertation, University of Chicago, Chicago, IL.

Rest, J. (1984). The major components of morality. In W. Kurtines & J. Gewirtz (Eds.), *Morality and moral development*. New York: John Wiley & Sons.

Rest, J. (1985). An interdisciplinary approach to moral education. In M. W. Berkowitz & F. Oser (Eds.), *Moral education: Theory and application* (pp. 9–25). Hillsdale, NJ: Lawrence Erlbaum.

Royce, J. (1982). *The philosophy of Josiah Royce*. J. Roth (Ed.). Indianapolis, IN: Hackett. (Original work published 1908)

Schläfli, A., Rest, J., & Thoma, S. (1985). Does moral education improve moral judgment? A meta-analysis of intervention studies using the DIT. *Review of Educational Research, 55*, 319–352.

Schrader, D. (1988). *Exploring metacognition: A description of levels of metacognition and their relation to moral judgment.* Unpublished doctoral dissertation, Harvard University, Cambridge, MA.

Schrader, D. (1990, November). Action-Judgment-Awareness: A model for consistency and change. Paper presented at the meeting of the Association for Moral Education. Notre Dame, IN.

Self, D., Schrader, D., Baldwin, D., Safford, S., Wolinsky, F., & Shadduck, J. (1991). The influence of veterinary medical education on the moral development of veterinary students. *Journal of the American Veterinary Medical Association, 198*(5), 782–787.

Sheehan, T., Husted, S., Cook, C., & Bargen, M. (1980). Moral judgment as a predictor of clinical performance. *Evaluation and the Health Professions, 3,* 393–404.

Turiel, E. (1966). An experimental test of the sequentiality of developmental stages in the child's moral development. *Journal of Personality and Social Psychology, 3,* 611–618.

Walker, L. (1983). Sex differences in the development of moral reasoning: A critical review. *Child Development, 54,* 1103–1141.

Wilshire, B. (1990). *The moral collapse of the university: Professionalism, purity, and alienation.* Albany, NY: State University of New York Press.

7 Teaching Ethical Reasoning Using Cases

KENNETH A. STRIKE
Cornell University

In this chapter I argue that a central goal in teaching ethics to aspirant educational practitioners is to develop *dialogical competence* in *the public moral language*. In the first section I explain what I mean by dialogical competence in the public moral language. In the second I describe dialogical competence as it relates to ethical reasoning. In the final part I offer suggestions for teaching ethical reasoning, emphasizing the use of cases.

DIALOGICAL COMPETENCE AND THE PUBLIC MORAL LANGUAGE

I often use cases in my teaching. One case goes like this.

> A teacher is called out of the room. When the teacher returns, it is discovered that a student had done something that might have endangered the safety of the class. The teacher thinks it is important to find the perpetrator. However, the perpetrator is unwilling to confess, and no one else will turn in the perpetrator. The teacher decides to put the entire class on detention.

Student responses to this case are varied. Some emphasize the ways in which the teacher can make sure that further incidents do not occur. Others express concern about the effect of the teacher's solution on classroom morale or on the teacher's relationships with the students. Suggestions as to how the teacher might explain the gravity of the situation to the students are commonly offered.

Some students want more information. They believe that the best solution would have to be made against a background of detailed knowledge of how the children would respond to the matter. They want to know whether this classroom has had a history of racial or ethnic conflict, whether the teacher has been perceived as a role model or a representative of some set alien values, or whether some or all of the students in the class might be disadvantaged. They have many ideas about how various student characteristics might affect the appropriateness of a teacher's decision. Many of the students feel that only someone who knew these students well could decide what was best.

Let's consider some observations about these typical discussions. First, the students' initial comments could be characterized as more strategic than ethical or moral. That is, they are dominated by a concern to achieve certain ends, but tend not to appraise the ends sought, address potential conflicts between different ends, or constrain the pursuit of these ends by any moral principles. Typically, students attempt to discover means to secure classroom discipline and ensure safety. Questions as to whether discipline and safety should be the central concerns or whether the means proposed are morally permissible are rare.

Second, while students rarely provide arguments that identify moral principles or seek to appraise ends, they do recognize the importance of such considerations once they are pointed out. One often gets such responses as, "Yes, that's what I meant," or "That's important too." These comments express the recognition of something that was already known, but that was inadequately articulated or did not seem to be what was at issue. Students rarely experience observations about moral principles or ends as though they were encountering unfamiliar ideas.

This second point seems especially important in that the case I described above was developed to allow students to explore moral quandaries that often arise in considerations of student discipline. A teacher who gives detention to an entire class can be said to have violated several ethical principles. One is the principle that people are innocent until proven guilty. Another is that the punishment must fit the "crime." But perhaps the most interesting issue concerns group punishment. The teacher may have violated a norm that prohibits punishing the members of a group for the acts of an individual.

Once these issues are raised, students have much to say about them, and they are often able to come to quite a sophisticated understanding of the issues. For example, some students will argue that each member of the group has committed the "crime" of withholding evidence. Others will wonder whether that is a crime. Some will wonder if it is appropriate to talk about this case using a "crime and punishment" vocabulary. Numerous questions are asked and difficulties expressed. I do much reformulating because students often are not good at saying what they seem to want to say. Thus I frequently ask students, "Is this what you mean?" or "Well, then, how about this?"

There is also a deeper issue. Students often find that once they admit that such moral ideas as those noted above are relevant to judging the case, they must also admit the possibility that there may be a conflict between the right thing to do and the best thing to do. That is, they may discover that they have proposed a strategy that they believe will accomplish some good end, such as safety or a better learning environment, but that there are moral objections to this strategy. Students must then ask themselves whether or when moral considerations should preclude strategies that seem to be the most direct path to a good outcome.

The conversation takes these directions because I am the instructor and I ask some questions and not others. At the same time, the direction of the conversation is not unnatural. Students understand its point and experience as familiar the issues raised during the discussion. They usually regard the questions asked and the direction of the conversation as theirs, not mine.

What I find noteworthy about this kind of classroom discussion is that students find moral ideas familiar even though they are not the kinds of considerations that come to their minds first and they often need help in finding the words to express them. I want to suggest a characterization of the transformation of conversations about cases such as these.

1. There is usually a shift from what I have called strategic language to ethical language. Strategic language is characteristically instrumental language. It is concerned with the means to realize assumed ends. Ethical language is concerned with the appraisal of ends or with decisions about whether a particular course of action is right. At this point, I am not asserting that these two forms of discourse are unrelated or drawing any conclusions at all about their relationship. I am only stating that they are distinguishable from each other. They are distinguished by their purposes and by the concepts that are linked to those purposes.

2. The transformation of language is accompanied by a transformation of perception. Students who are able to conceptualize a problem in a new way are also able to see it in a new way. They will be able to experience detention as a case of (possibly illicit) punishment. This means that a new range of feelings and expectations will be brought into play. Students who previously experienced only difficulty over how to produce a desired result may now experience injustice.

3. The process of discussion, when things go well, involves a move from what students intuitively know or feel to more articulate and explicit formulation of this intuitive knowledge. This is a kind of process that philosophers should find familiar. The idea that coming to know is sometimes a matter of being able to articulate that which is already known is at least as old as Socrates and the Socratic method. This suggests that ethical reasoning begins with knowledge that is intuitive or pretheoretical. I do

not mean to assert either that this knowledge is innate or that it involves "seeing" into some special properties of goodness or "oughtness" that can be observed only with the mind's eye. I presume that this pretheoretical knowledge is a product of prior socialization. We learn the "feel" of ethical concepts in the process of learning the "forms of life" and their associated ways of speaking that constitute human lives. Thus, ethical reflection begins from within a perspective that most competent people are able to adopt with a bit of proper stimulation. Its first task is to formulate what is intuitively known. This is the beginning of ethical reflection.

These points about what is learned through a good discussion support the claim that a central purpose of teaching ethics and ethical reasoning to educational professionals is to enhance *dialogical competence.* Dialogical competence is the ability to talk about, reason about, and experience appropriate phenomena via a certain set of concepts. When students achieve dialogical competence in ethical discourse, what they are doing is learning to do what they already know how to do, but learning to do it in a more sophisticated and conscious way. This learning involves the ability to see the world in a certain way as well as the ability to talk about it in a certain way.

We should emphasize dialogical competence in what I shall call the *public moral language*. In a pluralistic society there will inevitably be various moral discourses in progress. People disagree about ethical matters. There is also disagreement about how ethical judgments and decisions should be made. In our society, which respects pluralism and expresses this respect in such measures as the religion clauses of the First Amendment of the Constitution and elsewhere, we have the right to disagree. Thus, in a pluralistic society people rightfully speak a variety of "primary" moral languages. A primary moral language is the one that an individual is likely to have learned from parents or community and that is used to express that individual's central moral convictions and view of a good life.

Any society in which people speak a variety of primary moral languages will also need a public language with which to discuss public issues. This language will have to be a form of discourse that can be conscientiously spoken by otherwise diverse people, despite the fact that they disagree about much. Thus it is unlikely that this language will have much to say about God or about the nature of a worthwhile life, but it will have something to say about justice, fairness, and legitimate decisions. Topics like God will not be part of the public moral language because we are at odds about them, whereas topics like justice are likely to be part of the public language because they must be. We cannot have a common life apart from shared notions about justice, fairness, and legitimate decisions.

We might think of this public language as a form of discourse that expresses an "overlapping consensus" about public or civic matters among people who may have different and conflicting primary ethical languages (Rawls, 1985). This public moral language should be seen as the product of several centuries of argument that continues to undergo constant re-negotiation and revision. Calling it a consensus does not mean that it is not the object of much squabbling.

Achieving an overlapping consensus involves certain values, one of which is civil peace. One purpose of the public language is to allow people who disagree to live together peaceably. If they are to do so, they must settle disputes and govern their affairs by reason and argument. The alternative is coercion and domination. An overlapping consensus must also achieve some degree of neutrality in relation to the various ethical languages spoken in a society or it cannot be a consensus. This form of neutrality is likely to find expression in doctrines such as tolerance and freedom of the individual to follow the dictates of his or her conscience. Finally, an overlapping consensus must recognize some form of basic equality between people because few people would be likely to enter into such a consensus if they, or their interests, were regarded as less important than others.

A public morality is likely to emphasize concepts that are either important for public decisions or function to define the boundaries of public authority. Among the former will be such notions as due process, equality of opportunity, and democratic decision making. Among the latter will be freedom to follow one's conscience, privacy, and intellectual freedom.

Why emphasize dialogical competence in the public ethical language? Because teachers and administrators work in public institutions and make the kinds of decisions that the public moral language is designed to deal with, they need to be able to employ it with sophistication in their reflection and decision making. Teachers and administrators distribute resources, mete out punishment, grade papers, evaluate performance, make curricular choices, and deal with comparatively naive and vulnerable people. Concepts such as democracy, due process, and privacy regulate such matters. If teachers and administrators rely exclusively on strategic reasoning or if they lack facility with such moral concepts, that is a professional liability and a situation that needs to be rectified.

There are a number of other things that might be of concern to us in teaching ethics to teachers. We might emphasize the development of virtuous or caring people. Or we might emphasize the moral development of aspirant teachers and administrators, including delineation of the path through various stages of development. Others in this volume will, I trust, so argue. And there are complex issues involved in assessing these views.

Here I would note that my suggestion that we emphasize the acquisition of dialogical competence in the public moral language may have the advantage of achievability. It is important that teachers and administrators be virtuous and caring persons. Indeed, I think that popular views of moral education are deficient in their attention to these aspects of moral development. However, as we formulate goals for the curriculum for aspirant teachers and administrators, we need to consider not only what kinds of people we need in schools but also what can be done in a teacher education program. I think it is unlikely that those who teach teachers or administrators can do much in a course, or even in a semester, to make them more virtuous or more caring. Character is the product of years, not credit hours. However, it may be possible to help teachers and administrators to understand the concept of due process as it applies to such concerns as grading or evaluation.

The aspirations we have for including ethics in the curriculum for teachers and administrators must not only meet a legitimate need and make some philosophical sense, they must also be achievable in a relatively brief time, usually by means of formal instruction. I suspect that this means that we should look for caring people of good character to become teachers, and that we should help them to achieve some fairly unambitious cognitive goals. Thus, we should emphasize development of some degree of dialogical competence in the public moral language. Such instruction in ethics will not make students saints or sages, but it can help them to conduct their professional lives in a more responsible way.

DIALOGICAL COMPETENCE AND ETHICAL REASONING

I shall describe moral reasoning as a complex interaction between three kinds of components: moral data, moral principles, and background conceptions. These can be roughly characterized as follows:

Moral data are derived from each individual's intuitive sense of right and wrong. Often the beginning of moral reflection is a sense that something is not right. This impression is often difficult to articulate. Thus the initial task is to explain to ourselves what is wrong.

Moral principles are assertions of some norm of action that expresses the grounds of our moral intuitions and reasons for moral actions. They function to make explicit what we intuitively know. However, learning moral principles can also alter or structure our moral intuitions.

Background conceptions are any ideas that we may have that serve to

> inform or structure moral intuitions, moral principles, or moral deliberations. The term is deliberately vague. This vagueness expresses the connectedness of our cognitive life. No idea can be ruled out in advance as irrelevant to any moral question.

I shall try to illustrate these views with a simple case and then develop the case in a more complex fashion. Imagine that we are rounding a corner and come on a scene where someone is lying on the ground bleeding, still, and apparently dead. A second person is standing over the first with a smoking gun, apparently having shot him. What feelings are we apt to have? We are likely to feel moral indignation: an intuition that something wrong has been done, along with a feeling of anger. We are not likely to think thoughts like, "I am indignant because. . . ." However, if we are asked why, we are apt to say something like "It's wrong to kill people." If we are asked why it is wrong to kill people, we may say a variety of things, depending on our particular beliefs. Thus we might say that God has forbidden killing, that there is an obligation to respect life, or that there is a duty to accord other moral agents equal respect.

Our response began with a moral intuition, a feeling of indignation, followed by the assertion of a moral principle intended to express some of its content. If necessary, we are able to interpret this moral principle against the background of a wider range of convictions. How are these connected?

Suppose Jones, a principal, received an anonymous letter about Smith, a teacher, at the time that Smith was up for promotion. The letter accused Smith of being a child molester. Jones put the letter in Smith's personnel file. Later Jones recommended against Smith's promotion, and Smith was denied tenure.

We will probably feel that Smith was wronged. In trying to explain why, we may appeal to such principles as that Smith was denied the right to confront his accuser or that the letter was hearsay evidence. Both principles seem to be instances of a more general principle that requires us to have adequate evidence for decisions made about the welfare of others, and to have public procedures for obtaining and testing that evidence. But let's suppose Jones replied, "I grant the validity of your concerns, but my first concern is for the welfare of children in this school. It is notoriously difficult to prove cases of child molestation. Moreover, requiring a molested child to give testimony in such a case is often traumatic for the child. Although my case against Smith is weak, child molestation is so serious that I did not think I could risk having Smith in my school in case he's guilty, even though I'm far from certain that this is the case."

Consider what has happened. First, Jones has tried to construct a new way to see the case. He has represented the issue as a conflict between the possibility of wronging Smith and the possibility of risk to children. He has asked us to see his decision as a case of risk management. Thus he has brought additional factors to bear and asked us to see the facts in a different way. He has also suggested the relevance of additional principles. We can express one such principle as follows: *When in conflict, the rights of teachers should be subordinated to the welfare of children.*

Is this a view we are willing to accept? How might we test it? One way is to try to imagine various applications of the principle. Consider a variation of the facts. Suppose that Smith was a convicted child molester who had acquired a college degree and certification while serving time and who was now applying for a job as an elementary school teacher. I suspect that some of us would be willing to apply "Jones's principle" as a reason for not hiring Smith. We might hold that some wrong was done to Smith who had "served his time and paid his debt," but that this was insufficient reason to run the risk that he might again molest a child. But even here there are various things to consider. Is Smith cured? How certain can we be of this? Could we hire Smith for a job that minimized the risk to children? Why might we feel a lesser obligation to this second Smith than to the first Smith? Does the fact that we have already hired the first Smith increase our responsibility to him?

Now imagine a different application of "Jones's principle." Suppose that Jones had discovered that Smith was a member of a religious group that disapproved of the provision of medical services. Jones wished to fire Smith because he believed that Smith might fail to call for medical assistance in an emergency. However, Jones has no evidence for this concern beyond a vague knowledge of Smith's religion. Moreover, Smith had made it clear that he would follow normal institutional procedures in the matter. Jones, however, continues to worry that Smith would fail to respond promptly to a real medical emergency. Are we still willing to apply "Jones's principle" in this case? Here we must notice that we are being asked to balance a conflict between what seems a small risk to children against a significant violation of Smith's religious liberty. Yet "Jones's principle," as stated, seems to require that any risk to children, no matter how small, is sufficient to overrule any right of teachers, no matter how central.

What this thought experiment allows us to notice is that "Jones's principle" is, at best, too broad. Thus we must modify "Jones's principle" to provide a more reasonable balance. The adequacy of this balance might be tested using other possible cases. However, we might also reflect on the nature of an appropriate balance by asking deeper questions about how rights relate to issues of welfare. We might, for example, assert that some rights or all rights are absolute, that is, they do not admit of exceptions.

Thus they always win when mere issues of welfare are threatened. Or we might assert that the real test is whether the right creates "the greatest good for the greatest number." In this case, "rights" themselves would have to be justified by showing that they enhanced the general welfare. The version of "Jones's principle" we would be willing to accept, if any, might be much influenced by our views of such matters. The results of this inquiry would again need to be tested on additional cases.

These examples illustrate some of the ways in which the components of moral reasoning interact. Some general characterizations of this interaction are:

1. The process is dialectical. There is constant motion between the various levels of thought as different kinds of issues are raised. While there are few firm rules that characterize the types of interactions that can occur, two types of interactions should be noted. First, there is the testing of moral principles against moral experience. This may result in the modification of moral principles, but it can also lead us to see moral issues differently. Second, there is the attempt to achieve a deeper understanding and further refinement of moral principles by relating them to a wide range of background considerations.

2. One goal of such reflection should be to seek context-sensitive, but general, moral principles as well as a sense of how they are to be applied to particular cases. The point is to achieve reasoned agreement on what constitutes a principled resolution of an issue. This requires that decisions be justified by reasons based on principles that could regulate conduct in other similar situations. Such principles cannot be formulated in such a context-dependent way that they apply only to single cases. Nor can they be so abstract that nothing clearly follows from them. Asserting such principles often focuses argument on whether different cases are relevantly similar. In this respect, moral reasoning has much in common with legal reasoning.

3. The test of the adequacy of moral reflection is reflective equilibrium. Reflective equilibrium is achieved when we have developed an understanding of a moral phenomenon in which our moral experience, our moral principles, and relevant background conceptions are integrated and consistent. It is a requirement for both individuals and groups. Especially in schools, for an individual to have resolved an issue in her or his own mind is not sufficient unless reflective equilibrium has also been achieved in the group. Reflective equilibrium is always provisional. It is always possible for some new consideration to call into question the adequacy or applicability of principles.

4. This view of moral reflection assumes a participant's view of the

moral life. Its purpose is to reflect on and to organize moral experience "from the inside." Moral experience disappears if we insist on stepping outside of it to demand justification for it.

5. Because the purpose of ethical reflection is to achieve reasoned agreement about the moral norms that should regulate shared life, moral reflection is inherently social. It must involve real conversation between real people. Two considerations lead to this conclusion. First, the reflective equilibrium to be achieved about norms must be collective, otherwise moral principles cannot function adequately to regulate collective life. Second, we cannot treat our individual moral experience as sufficient for moral reflection. Because the purpose of moral reflection is to achieve rational consensus on shared norms, the experience of all relevant participants needs to be included.

6. Because moral reasoning is a form of dialogue intended to achieve rational consensus, it is itself governed by certain moral requirements that regulate rational deliberation. Moral discourse should be open and undominated. Openness means that participants cannot be arbitrarily silenced. An open discourse is one in which all of the relevant evidence and all relevant perspectives are considered. A discourse is undominated when no one in the dialogue is coerced and when the ethos or underlying assumptions of the conversation do not implicitly favor the interests of some over those of others.

7. Insofar as moral conversations are within the public ethic, there are constraints that must be recognized on the kinds of reasons that can be asserted for moral principles. Essentially, the requirements are that no one can assert as public reasons arguments that assume the intrinsic superiority of either the individual's group or primary moral language. Since such claims cannot be accepted by all, their assertion undermines the overlapping consensus that is the basis of the public moral language.

TEACHING THE PUBLIC MORAL LANGUAGE

I have claimed that the emphasis in teaching ethics to teachers and administrators should be on achieving dialogical competence in the public moral language. Achieving competence is a matter of acquiring facility with the concepts that regulate our public life. It involves mastery of a form of discourse that integrates moral intuitions, moral principles, and background conceptions into a dialogically achieved reflective equilibrium. Such conversations should be open, and undominated, and should avoid arguments that cannot be public arguments. How is such dialogical competence achieved?

Instructional Forums

Helping students acquire dialogical competence requires the creation of a suitable forum for discussing ethical issues. The argument in this chapter suggests that for adults the task is not so much to acquire the appropriate concepts as it is to articulate them in a way that allows them to become objects of conscious reflection and enhances the sophistication of their employment. Thus what is required are forums that emphasize the conscious articulation of moral arguments. In creating such opportunities, we are also seeking to help students see the world in a certain way. Finally, in creating suitable opportunities we need to consider how to create an environment conducive to undominated and open discussions and that encourage the assertion of public reasons for beliefs and actions.

Instructional forums that can accomplish these tasks should have some of the following characteristics:

1. They should emphasize the achievement of competence through participation. Dialogical competence, like any skill, requires practice.
2. They should create a structured relationship between a competent speaker and novices. Achieving the ability to articulate moral principles is much assisted by someone who is able to ask the kinds of questions that will help students formulate, test, and reformulate moral principles.
3. Material for discussion should be selected or created to teach specific concepts. While instructors should always be open to insights from students, they should also prepare material that allows students to focus on specific concepts to be learned. Such materials should meet normal pedagogical requirements. For example, they should be engaging and adapted to the student's current capacity.
4. An open and undominated environment should be maintained.
5. Students should be encouraged to emphasize public reasons for beliefs and actions.

Good Cases as Teaching Vehicles

I believe that well-crafted cases can be used effectively to help students achieve dialogical competence. They provide material for discussions of moral principles that can be selected or crafted to serve the purposes of instruction. It is important not to claim too much for cases. They are not the be all and end all of moral learning. What they are is a useful way to teach specific moral concepts to novices in classroom settings.

Ingredients of good cases include the following:

1. Good cases should have inherent interest. Students should find them engaging and realistic. However, sometimes improbable cases are occasions for interesting thought experiments. Moreover, one should be cautious in using cases about highly charged emotional issues. When students are locked into a position, it is difficult to maintain an open, undominated atmosphere. Moreover, highly charged issues can lead students to formulate principles that guarantee predetermined results.

2. A good case should be a vehicle for teaching a particular moral principle. A good case is constructed or selected to exemplify the application of such principles. Instructors should not use cases merely because they seem in some vague way to raise moral issues. They should use cases that require certain principles, and they should structure the facts of these cases to allow discussions of these principles to take place. Note that a case need not be a dilemma. Although using cases that pose hard questions and conflicts of principle is often useful and engaging, it may also be of value to use some cases that are less complex.

3. Good cases contain enough detail to make them realistic and permit a good discussion of the moral principles that apply to them. All of the central facts should be stated clearly. However, be aware that too much detail can be confusing and distracting. Material that is not relevant to the moral principle involved should not be included. Cases are more like diagrams in a science text than literary works. Their point is to simplify the world so as to focus attention on relevant facts and issues. One must grant that the real world is messy. However, it does not follow that good cases must reproduce this messiness. My point is not that we should avoid cases that pose hard choices or moral complexities, but that we focus our cases on the principles we wish to teach and the issues we wish to discuss, and that the facts and details we include be designed to highlight these things.

4. Good cases should hint at directions for analysis without asserting them. One may do this either in the text or in the questions that follow. How subtle these hints should be depends on the difficulty of the issues and the sophistication of the students. When the concept to be taught is difficult, it may be useful to provide the ingredients for an argument in the words of the parties involved. Students can then be asked to formulate these seminal arguments and criticize them.

Teaching Cases

Cases can be fun. Students may be willing to discuss them for hours. However, the point is for students to learn something. A lively discussion may engage and motivate students, but the instructor needs to consider how the discussion can be directed so as to make it most profitable for students. A fun hour of "slinging it" does not mean that anything of educational value has happened. Cases are well suited to a certain form of instructional irresponsibility in which teachers provide material for class discussion and congratulate themselves on a good class solely because students were fully involved for the required period. Using cases responsibly requires both planning and facility with the relevant concepts.

Here are some suggestions for the effective use of cases:

1. The instructor may need to establish some ground rules for discussion. It is important that everyone feel free to talk, that students respect one another's views, and that they feel free to disagree. Sometimes occasional reminders are in order. It is especially important to prevent students from creating an atmosphere of moral intimidation where only the views of a dominant orthodoxy can be aired. The instructor's own openness to diverse arguments is probably the most important factor in maintaining an open atmosphere in which all students are treated with equal respect.

2. The central objective is to help students to see what is at stake in a case and to develop their capacity for ethical reflection. It is therefore important that students try to formulate arguments before they decide what to do. Thus instructors should emphasize the formulation and criticism of principles and arguments, not the assertion of solutions or policies.

3. Sometimes it can be useful to separate students into small groups and let them discuss the case among themselves. Each group might be asked to formulate an argument for each party in the case and to report their conclusions.

4. Sometimes students find it difficult to formulate positions. If so, start by asking them to list some things they might do, but insist that they also justify their choices. When a student says, "Here's what I would do," the best response may be to ask the student why rather than to ask if anyone else would act differently.

5. In the discussion, the instructor has these tasks to perform:

Reflect student statements: Often it is useful for the instructor to reformulate what the student has said. This may involve suggesting a principle that captures what the student seems to want to argue or more clearly stating a principle that the student has suggested. The interpretation should be presented to the student as a hypothesis about what the student meant. Let's consider this example concerning the keeping of promises.

STUDENT: If a person was confused about a promise, then maybe he doesn't have to do what he said he'd do.

INSTRUCTOR: Are you saying that agreements are only binding when they are freely entered into? In that case, that a person didn't understand what he was agreeing to is reason to assert that the agreement wasn't freely entered into. Thus perhaps agreements made when one party is unclear about the terms may not be binding.

Ask leading questions: The instructor will often find it useful to ask questions that test or require qualification of the principle under discussion.

STUDENT: Yes that's right. You can't be held to an agreement that you didn't understand.

INSTRUCTOR: Suppose the individual should have known what he was agreeing to, but didn't take the trouble?

Give counterexamples, suggest alternatives, offer counterarguments: A central role of the instructor is to help students test a viewpoint that is currently being discussed. Suggesting counterexamples, counterarguments, and alternative positions is part of this process.

STUDENT: I don't see why we should be bound by any agreement we didn't understand.

INSTRUCTOR: If you sign a rental agreement, are you excused from its provisions if you fail to read it, even if you're given the opportunity to read it?

Summarize: Conclude the discussion by reviewing the arguments that have been made.

6. Be open to issues and points of view other than those you had in mind. Often students will discover issues that you had not meant to put in the case. These issues are not invalid merely because you did not intend to discuss them.

Once again, the purpose of using cases is to help comparative novices achieve dialogical competence in the public moral language. We should not delude ourselves about what is possible in classroom contexts in professional programs for aspirant teachers and administrators. We need to have achievable goals. Creating a suitable forum for the discussion of moral issues is unlikely to greatly alter people's characters. Discussing cases will not make undergraduates wise. However, this approach to helping students achieve dialogical competence may help them to see moral issues, and to articulate moral principles and arguments more clearly. Students may learn to think more clearly about conflicts of principle. It may help them to acquire the social skills required for moral deliberation. And students may learn to listen better, acquire a sense of moral diversity, and respect differences of opinion.

In such teaching, the basic purpose is not so much to discover moral truth as it is to help students to make principled moral decisions. The idea of a principled moral decision can be expressed as follows: *A moral decision is principled if it can be adequately supported by reasons that appeal to public moral principles that would be accepted after open and undominated discussion by reasonable individuals with potentially conflicting interests and outlooks.* This definition assumes that reasons can be given for ethical decisions and that some reasons are better than others. It also assumes that while there is not always one right answer or one best choice, some answers and some choices are genuinely better than others.

A final caveat. As with any language, skill in ethical reasoning increases with use and declines with disuse. No one who attempts to teach moral reasoning under the time constraints that characterize professional training programs in education can expect to do much more than facilitate an incremental improvement in the ability of students to articulate a moral perspective. What this means is that any hope that sophistication in ethical reasoning will actually characterize the practice of teachers and administrators in schools depends on the existence of forums where the language is commonly spoken. It is not evident that schools are such forums. Teachers work in significant isolation. Decision making is often neither dialogical or collegial, and it is dominated by strategic, not ethical, concerns. If we wish the decisions of educational professionals to be informed by competent ethical reasoning, we will need to attend to constructing social conditions in schools that permit serious moral deliberation to occur. The importance of doing so might be enhanced if we consider that the dialogical competence of teachers and administrators is a significant resource for developing the dialogical competence of students in the public moral language. If teachers and administrators are not competent speakers of the public moral language, it is not likely that students will be.

REFERENCES

Habermas, J. (1990). *Moral consciousness and communicative action*. Cambridge, MA: MIT Press.

Rawls, J. (1985). Justice as fairness: Political, not metaphysical. *Philosophy & Public Affairs, 14*(4), 223–251.

8 Coping with Relativism and Absolutism

P. LANCE TERNASKY
Cornell University

As between Scylla and Charybdis, teachers exploring ethics with their students must contend with certain extreme ethical positions. Two likely positions are extreme relativism and extreme absolutism. The first holds that moral considerations are simply expressions of preference. There are therefore no objective ethical standards, but only those born of convention or desire. The other position, extreme absolutism, asserts that answers to ethical questions have already been provided by an extant code of ethics. Given the existence of such a code, the study of ethics is a diversionary exercise for those unwilling to obey the code's direct command.

Each of these positions presents a formidable challenge for the teacher, and this chapter will suggest how the teacher may meet such a challenge. Specifically, it will address the following questions:

1. Why might students espouse the extreme form of either relativism or absolutism?
2. How might the teacher respond to those who take each of these positions?
3. Does it really matter that students hold such positions?

Before addressing these questions, however, certain features of the forthcoming argument need to be described. First, although I intend to show that both extremes suffer from deficiencies, this is not an attempt to simply dismiss relativism and absolutism. There are coherent and quite sophisticated versions of both, but this chapter is not a response to them. It is, instead, a challenge to the more common and often ill-considered embodiments of these arguments: the ones teachers are most apt to encounter. Second, the argument's length prohibits a full exposition of either position and limits itself instead to questioning the self-evidence of relativism and the practicality of absolutism. Third, I imagine this chapter to have classroom application for those who train teachers as well as for these prospective teachers once they find themselves in their own classrooms. Henceforth, "teacher" suggests those in both groups.

WHY STUDENTS SUBSCRIBE TO COMMON MORAL RELATIVISM

With few exceptions, philosophers reject a simplistic relativistic understanding of ethics.[1] How, then, do we explain the widespread acceptance of common moral relativism in educational circles?

A relativistic understanding of ethics may mean different things to different students. It may refer to a radical skepticism or to an equally radical ethical egoism, but the most prevalent form of relativism derives from differences within and between cultures.[2] This is the form on which this chapter will focus.

A culturally derived relativism argues that there are no universally true moral norms. It suggests instead that conventionally accepted norms are specific to particular times and places. Since the norms apply only to individual cultures or subcultures, when the norms of different periods or cultures conflict, we seemingly cannot determine which of two antagonistic systems is correct. The common relativist view of this is that both systems are simultaneously correct for their respective cultures, and that therefore both moral systems should be exempt from any external criticism. (See Brandt, 1967, for a more detailed account of the levels and evolution of the common forms of moral relativism.)

What support can be offered for this popular version of relativism? For the purpose of this argument, I will use the three themes of moral disagreement, moral diversity, and tolerance to briefly suggest how a relativistic understanding of ethics may be constructed, and then suggest why these various constructions are flawed.[3]

Consider the first theme: moral disagreement. We are faced with the problem that persons disagree not only about right and wrong, but also about how we are to arrive at such decisions. Since the moral opinions of different persons often appear incommensurable when troublesome moral issues arise, students may conclude that only relativism can provide a justification for ethics.

The second theme, moral diversity, suggests that a relativistic understanding best explains the crosscultural diversity that fields such as anthropology have revealed. Practices Americans may deem immoral could in this scenario reflect the highest standards of behavior in another culture. On discovering this the student may ask, "which culture is right and how can we really know?" The student may conclude that there is no single correct answer and that acceptable behavior is simply conformity to the standards of one's immediate culture. From this perspective, it would seem presumptuous, at best, for one culture to condemn another's moral standards.

The fear of condemning a perhaps more fragile or "less advanced" culture than ours contributes to the introduction of tolerance as the third justification of moral relativism. Most Westerners find intolerance offensive. Students have heard countless stories about zealots of various persuasions decimating "primitive" cultures. These stories have contributed to an uneasiness about the claim that "we" are absolutely right while "they" are absolutely wrong. For those troubled by the condemnation of a society's religious, familial, and dietary traditions by outsiders, it may appear that tolerance can only emerge from a relativism that does not elevate one system or culture above all others.

We have now briefly examined popular reasons for accepting common moral relativism. The arguments offered coincide well with many of our considered moral judgments and permit many students to accept the apparent truth of relativism. But we must still ask whether these three themes offer *good* reasons for accepting a relativistic understanding, and if not, what good reasons can be offered for rejecting it?

THE ARGUMENT AGAINST MORAL DISAGREEMENT

The first question we must ask is whether the disagreement is really moral in nature. Suppose that one group held that tomato-eating leads to lasciviousness and therefore avoided it, whereas another group perceived no relationship between tomatoes and behavior and regularly consumed them. Although the belief that tomato-eating leads to lasciviousness may seem farfetched (it, however, was held to be true by many in the New World), one can imagine that tomato-eating could come to be seen as a moral issue. But on closer examination, we discover that lasciviousness is the real moral issue, and while we do not know how the second group regards such behavior, it is probable that they also condemn it. Consequently, the actual dispute is factual rather than moral, and concerns whether there is a real relationship between tomatoes and lewdness. Once the factual issue is definitively answered, the apparent moral disagreement will evaporate.

Now the relativist may reply that while this may be true, it confuses moral judgments with objective facts. She or he might argue that while it is a fact that the earth orbits the sun and a fact that heavy consumption of alcohol contributes to liver disease, nothing comparable exists within the moral realm. But is this reasonable? For the argument for moral disagreement to hold, the relativist must show that facts about the world are of a different nature from moral ones. For instance, while there is clearly progress in science, the relativist would have to claim it is not possible in morality, but the near universal rejection of slavery should cause us to wonder whether this is correct (Irwin, 1989).

To this the relativist might reply that in science facts are universally accepted but that this is not true in morality. Here again, there are still people who believe that rain comes from the gods having pierced the heavens and others who hold that a knife beneath the bed of a laboring mother will "cut" labor pains, but we do not count this as evidence against scientific fact. Why, then, do we hold morality accountable to a more demanding standard?

There is nothing magical about scientific fact. Like their moral equivalents, such facts are sometimes difficult to find, they are highly dependent on the theories from which they were conceived, it may take decades or centuries to establish them as trustworthy indicators of a real world, and they are subject to misinterpretation whenever bias is introduced. I am not asserting that moral and scientific fact are isomorphic, but that disagreement alone cannot justify moral relativism.

THE ARGUMENT AGAINST MORAL DIVERSITY

What about the relativistic argument for moral diversity? The social sciences have revealed culturally divergent practices and preferences, and this revelation has caused many to wonder if there can be any moral standard other than the one operating within a given culture. Let's consider three problems with this thesis.

The first is that the mere fact that societies are not identical does not imply that they are intrinsically different. Consider the oft-cited example of the treatment of the elderly by certain Arctic peoples. It has been noted that in some societies the elderly are set adrift on an ice floe toward certain demise. In contrast, we place our elderly in rest homes. Superficially, this difference is profound, and the initial observation of this situation was followed by the question of which approach was the moral one. A closer look, however, revealed that in both instances concern for one's elders was the motivating factor. In the first instance, setting the elderly adrift on ice floes guarantees them vitality in the afterlife, and in the second instance, placing the elderly in rest homes promises them long life. Apparent diversity sometimes masks fundamental similarity.

A second problem for the moral diversity thesis concerns the potential moral conflict for the person belonging to multiple groups within a pluralistic society such as ours. If I belong to two groups with very different moral norms, then it would seem possible for me to be simultaneously right and wrong in performing a single act, and the problem is compounded if there is no method for adjudicating the disagreement. Although the relativist solution may be for individuals to adhere to the standards of the group they are with or to the standards of the group individuals count as primary in their lives, this does not resolve the issue. Imagine, for example, what this would mean if the groups were composed of either cannibals or the criminally insane. The moral diversity thesis cannot tell us by which standard to abide when we move into a group that is not one of our own.

The third weakness is that if the moral diversity thesis were credible, we could never criticize another culture, and as importantly, we could never claim to truly understand it. These two consequences are inseparable. Criticism and evaluation presume that each party understands what the other is saying, even if they disagree. If we refrain from criticizing another culture out of concern that we may mistake the meaning of, or the motivation behind, certain moral acts, then we must admit our lack of understanding of the other culture. If their moral code or the linguistic system they use to convey it are incommensurable with our own, then they must remain a mystery to us. But it does not stop here, for if the diversity thesis truly holds, then when two distinctly different cultures *agree* we must assume that at some fundamental level they are actually at odds and that the perceived agreement is only in our imaginations (Lyons, 1976).

Moreover, if we cannot critique what we do not fully understand, then can we even critique our own culture? If we do not fully understand it (and this seems likely), then it must be beyond our ability to criticize it. We would be unable to make corrections in our moral course, and the seriousness of this situation would be compounded by our inability to enlist the assistance of an objective observer. If the moral diversity thesis were correct, we could not expect valid insight or analysis about our moral condition from those outside our culture, for they too are prohibited from criticizing what they do not fully understand. And if we do not criticize alien cultures, then surely they must resist criticizing us. Pushed to its inevitable conclusion, the diversity thesis would invalidate moral reasoning because nothing could ever be known sufficiently well to evaluate it (Midgley, 1986).

THE ARGUMENT AGAINST RELATIVISTIC TOLERANCE

The third theme of common moral relativism is tolerance. The argument for relativistic tolerance runs something like this. People who think they possess the absolutely true morality will be intolerant of those who do not, and will try to coerce them to follow this true morality. The relativist, on the other hand, does not hold that there is a single, absolutely true morality and will therefore be tolerant of divergent moral systems. And because tolerance is desirable, we should all be relativists.

There are several serious problems with this argument, but two are pivotal. It assumes that tolerance is dependent upon relativism. To show that this is an erroneous assumption, we need only consider an encounter between two distinct societies. The first is relativistic, tolerant, and believes that moral norms are culture-specific. Because of this, they eschew interference. The second society is also relativistic, and it, too, holds that norms are determined solely by society and convention, but it is intolerant. Because norms are culture-specific there is nothing to prevent the second society from viewing the first society as inferior. Consequently, the second society may behave intolerantly toward the first with impunity, for it need only adhere to its own principles. And if relativism grants that morality is simply agreement with the norms of one's own society, then it must conclude that the second society is behaving morally when it is intolerant. Relativism is therefore incapable of guaranteeing tolerance.

The corresponding flaw in the relativistic tolerance thesis is the claim that absolutism (meaning that there are universal, objective, moral principles) inevitably leads to intolerance. This is *only* true if the absolutist standards possess a directive demanding that it is right to coerce persons to abide by the standards and wrong to tolerate their refusal to do so. While there are and have been such systems, there is no reason to conclude that this connection is ineluctable. If, however, the absolutist believes tolerance to be good in and of itself, she or he will ensure its presence as a standard (Irwin, 1989).

If there is no legitimate connection between relativism and tolerance, then why do we frequently find the former being used to justify the latter? The difficulty may lie in a misunderstood justification for tolerance. Most persons in the West believe that every individual possesses certain inalienable rights. Among these rights are freedom to follow one's conscience, tolerance in the form of freedom from unreasonable interference, and equality. The widespread acceptance of self-evident rights sometimes stands in contrast to our conviction that certain beliefs and practices are misbegotten and dreadfully wrong (e.g., the practices of infibulation and clitoridectomy among certain tribal peoples). The tension between these two convictions is pronounced. We simultaneously feel compelled to interfere and to refrain from interfering.

Our reticence emerges from our liberal ideology and our history. History reveals that loss of life and property accompany conflicts between different groups with strong convictions (Rawls, 1985; Strike, 1990). One accommodation born of this realization is a heightened acceptance of diversity in the guise of pluralism. Liberalism's endorsement of pluralism should not, however, be confused with acceptance of the idea that there are multiple, equally correct, moral systems. Members of a liberal society may be convinced that they have the best system or the correct view of a particular issue, but they may also realize that they are presently unable to persuade their opponents of this. Their pluralistic tendencies come not from the belief that all other views are equal to their own, but from the knowledge that they could only convince their opponents by resorting to violence or coercion.

But what does this really tell us about why relativism and tolerance are popularly seen as inseparable? Pluralism is commonly misunderstood to mean that we must be tolerant and inclusive because people are different and because we cannot assert that one worldview is better than the others. This misunderstanding closely resembles the common view of relativism that because people are different and we cannot know which group is absolutely correct, we must be tolerant. Given this confusion, relativism seems to coincide with, or even to derive from, legitimate liberal thought, and it is but a short step from lay acceptance of a distorted pluralism to its translation as moral relativism with tolerance as a by-product. The mistake in this thinking is obvious. Rather than following from pluralism, tolerance shares with pluralism a common parentage. Both derive from our commitment to an ideology of rights and our avoidance of potentially undesirable consequences (i.e., violence and coercion) that accompany the violation of such rights. The Western argument for tolerance cannot be grounded in diversity and uncertainty. It is, instead, grounded in the belief that all people share the same rights and that the violation of these rights can be costly. Viewed in this way, it is clear that it is not tolerance that derives from common relativism, but the inverse—a misconceived relativism that derives from tolerance.

I have thus far offered philosophical criticism of the common conception of relativism. To conclude this section with criticism of a more pragmatic nature we might ask, What are some of the untoward consequences of an applied relativistic stance?[4] The most serious consequence, of course, is that relativism cannot give us reasons for acting or for refraining from action, and we expect that a moral system will at least give us reasons for choosing right over wrong (Irwin, 1989). Because it lacks such reasons, relativism constrains moral influence in many ways, two of which follow.

Suppose that within a society some people believe that infanticide is evil, whereas others consider it an acceptable practice. The most a relativist could assert is "I personally hold X, but I cannot say what you should believe," and she or he can offer no reasons for or against the practice without forsaking relativism. Given this situation, in a society of tolerant relativists we could not expect moral progress because relativism could offer no grounds for calling for change and no reason for preferring one state of affairs over another. In this respect, relativism is a conservative doctrine that defers to the existing moral structure, regardless of its nature.

Suppose, this time, that in a tolerant, relativistic society there is a distinct and sizable subgroup that is markedly less tolerant. It is not difficult to imagine the majority yielding to this minority and its interests. In the process, the majority might find that a common relativism demands that they subordinate their interests (and potentially society's interests) to those of the minority — despite personal or societal conceptions of morality.

The popular version of relativism is critically flawed. It cannot guarantee tolerance or respect for alien cultures or a workable code that does not give the intolerant the advantage. Despite all this, students will encounter variations of simple relativism throughout their educational careers. In addressing cultural, political, social, and sexual differences some instructors will use relativism to prod unreflective students. If, through trickery, an instructor can "prove" that multiple correct moral codes exist, then she or he can wield relativism as a weapon against smirks, condescension, and ethnic, national, and gender-based ethnocentrism. While this could be accomplished without resorting to relativism, the instructor may willingly trade coherence for expedience. For this reason alone, we can expect students to enter our classrooms with a confused relativism as part of their understanding of ethical discourse.

UNDERSTANDING THE ABSOLUTIST

Absolutists are not a homogeneous group. In our society they are connected by their conviction that morality is not idiosyncratic or culture-specific but universal, and that it is expressed in a coherent code or standard of belief. Beyond this, we can expect great diversity among absolutists, a list of whom might include conservative religious groups, objectivist philosophers, Marxists, and, curiously, even some relativists who view their beliefs as absolute principles. None of these groups represent an explicit challenge to teachers discussing ethics in the classroom. All of them, however, represent a threat to ethical discussion when they become dogmatic and attempt to stop discourse or to limit it so as to exclude certain people from participating in it. Consequently, this portion of the chapter will describe a way to respond when dogmatic absolutism is encountered.[5]

For the purpose of exposition, religious fundamentalism will be used as an example of dogmatic absolutism. This selection is not intended to disparage people of faith nor to suggest that the religious are more apt to be dogmatic. Rather, this group is chosen because the chapter's stated intent was to address the impediments to ethical discussion that the teacher is most likely to encounter, and in our culture the best developed and most prevalent varieties of dogmatic absolutism are those found in religious fundamentalism. It should be noted, however, that much of what is said about this particular worldview will predictably apply to other forms of absolutism.

If we wonder why religious fundamentalists may be dogmatic, we might begin by asking whether their stance is defensive. They may have reason to feel threatened when morality is discussed. For them, morality emerges from revelation and reflects a divine order. It is woven into the fabric of their personal and community life, and the popular notion that persons can "purchase" the ethical system of their choice is simply incomprehensible to them.

We can imagine that there would be considerable conflict for religious fundamentalists when they encounter educational disciplines that question the value and contribution of religion. After exposure to the comparative study of religion and culture and contending with sociology's secularization theory, which presupposes religion's universally waning influence, the fundamentalist is likely to agree with Dostoevski that there can be no morality without God.

What religious fundamentalists sense as a direct assault on their faith is compounded by the compartmentalization of knowledge within the university. Disciplines only infrequently converse with each other, and their crossdisciplinary contribution is limited by each discipline's self-protective strategy of specifying what counts as knowledge within its domain. Within the university's conception of knowledge, fact is separated from value and what is measurable is frequently separated from any notion of human purpose. In a world so divided, absolutists are told that their religious beliefs can have no justifiable bearing on a legitimate articulation of morality. Robert Bellah (1983) aptly captures the sentiment underlying university educational practice when he writes that:

> the ethos of the modern university [is] dominated by an Enlightenment tradition that viewed religion as a negative influence on human culture and one destined to be replaced by science. Even today university professors are among the least religious people in American society, although, ironically, natural scientists are somewhat more apt to be religious than their humanist and social scientist colleagues. (p. ix)

If this is an accurate depiction, we can begin to understand the posture of many absolutist students. These students find themselves being educated in an environment that breaks knowledge into discrete areas and denigrates beliefs that are central to their personal and social lives. In contrast to the experience of the common relativist, a challenge to the moral sentiments of the absolutist represents a challenge to her or his sense of self and place in the scheme of things. It should not, therefore, surprise us that these students are often defensive and adamant regarding their ethical convictions, and we can comprehend why one might refer to fundamentalism as "a religious ideology of protest" (Lawrence, 1989, p. 83).

RESPONDING TO THE ABSOLUTIST

The reader may ask why we should feel compelled to respond to the absolutist. We have already noted that serious negative consequences may accompany a substantive challenge to the absolutist's moral beliefs. The reader may even assert that in a society that advocates the freedom of the individual to follow the dictates of her or his conscience, the teacher should note the absolutist position but refrain from any response that might be construed as criticism. Such sentiments could seemingly be defended by a liberal conception of tolerance.

Even though we may understand the attitudes and circumstances behind the absolutist's behavior, a genuine discussion of ethics will require a response to absolutism that is comparable to that offered common relativism. The teacher's task is to do this without denigrating the absolutist. Why must the teacher respond, and what might she or he say?

One justification for engaging the absolutist comes from the activity of education itself. Although education is concerned with imparting information, it surely is not limited to this. A more adequate description of education would include its role in teaching students how to discriminate between the reasons for choosing one idea over another. Moreover, it seems realistic to expect that the nature and complexity of students' reasons for discriminating between ideas, and the instances of their use will become more sophisticated as the educational process proceeds.

The ability to identify "good reasons" for actions is a cornerstone of our conception of education, but as a justification, it still lacks an explanation for why we should *voice* our good reasons. Isn't it enough that we *have* such reasons? Why should the teacher and the absolutist student be required to expose their reasons to public scrutiny in the classroom?

A reasonable reply to these queries is suggested by the work of Hannah Arendt (1961, 1965, 1976). According to Arendt (1961), although in a democracy freedom to follow one's conscience proscribes coercion of belief, it also demands that one provide defensible reasons for actions within the public sphere. Further, the freedom implicit in democracy necessitates a public space within which these reasons can be articulated. For Arendt (1961, 1965), however, the ensuing exchange is not limited to mere discussion where the respective points of view are simply displayed and then returned to a mental cupboard for safekeeping. Rather, it entails a conversation whereby every participant's thought could conceivably be altered by the argument of another.

For one's thinking actually to be altered by a conversation presumes certain things about that exchange. The requisite truth-telling cannot be limited to merely saying what one believes, for to do only this is to endorse egocentrism. Participation in the public sphere requires that truth-telling extend beyond "what I believe" or "what the preeminent literature suggests" to include "why I think position X mistaken." In taking this additional step, the participant risks offending the holders of position X and being subjected to ridicule and rejection, but refusal to take this step precludes legitimate involvement in democracy and permanently relegates the speaker to the status of observer.

If Arendt is correct, as I believe she is, then democracy requires that the hard issues be discussed and that every participant's views be open to review. This means that teachers are compelled to address the controversial and seemingly irresoluble issues and to risk confrontation. It also means that instead of being exempt from discourse, the absolutist is obliged to confront those with differing views. He or she enters this exchange intending to persuade, but the nature of the public sphere dictates that the absolutist also entertain the notion that his or her position may be clarified by such an encounter. It is only in forming arguments capable of withstanding the barbs of those with whom we disagree that our own ideas become clear and begin to take a shape that permits others to "try them on." Prior to this, one's ideas remain securely one's own, but they contribute little to democracy or to moral progress.

How, then, does the teacher approach the discussion of ethics with the absolutist student? The teacher can begin by noting that the exploration of ethics is and *should be* troublesome. Moral considerations take place in all of our relations with the world, and the seriousness with which persons engage the moral debate speaks to the crucial role of ethics in human experience. Beyond establishing that the task is often not easy, the teacher must lay certain ground rules for ethical discussion—rules that apply to *all* participants. Three ground rules for ethical discussion are essential.

The first rule is that all participants be permitted access to the debate as equals. This requires that the conversation not be dominated by any person or persons, that it be free of coercion. It does not mean, however, that all moral stances are equal or that, as when viewed from a distorted understanding of tolerance, such stances are immune from criticism. Within the public sphere, equals may argue and conclude that a particular moral stance is quite wrong.

The second guideline is that participants be expected to enter into debate whether or not they are fully informed on the subject being discussed. Students typically assume that information precedes debate: one must have the "answer" before entering a conversation. While it is true that conclusions should be drawn from evidence rather than from mere opinion, students shortchange themselves and their peers if they remain silent until they have "the answer" and only then are willing to enter the discussion. What often occurs is that the perceived need for sufficient data translates into the conviction that one *never* had sufficient information to make an informed decision or to resolve a moral dispute.

Teachers must encourage all students to engage in the discourse before they have what they consider to be sufficient information, for what counts as a good reason or as sound reasoning often emerges from the conversation between persons immersed in a single, difficult question. In a circuitous manner, much of the necessary information comes from the debate itself.

The history of great ideas confirms that works of genius are seldom the product of individual thinkers working in isolation. More frequently they are the result of robust exchanges—conversational chain reactions—between individuals who, working alone, would not gather the critical mass of factual material necessary to reach the same conclusion. The debate itself contributes much of the material for discussion while it simultaneously inhibits the potential for discourse dominated by some at the expense of others.

The third ground rule is that the language used in the debate must be accessible to all. No participant can make a case by relying on arcane knowledge or a private language. Just as we would find it unfair if ethical discourse in the typical American classroom was only undertaken in Bengali, so it is when an individual's use of a private language excludes others from the debate. If anyone dismisses a challenge by claiming that the critic lacks the insight or the information to which only the speaker is privy, then that person has failed to make his or her case. And any argument won by trickery or by the critic's acquiescence reflects coercion rather than persuasion.

Participation in a democracy requires finding a language whereby parties with different interests or backgrounds can come to a common understanding. Every party to the debate, teacher and absolutist included, is required to give good reasons for belief and action—reasons capable of persuading the critic.

This will require a certain "bilingualism" on the part of the speaker. If the speaker is a religious fundamentalist, he or she will need to translate private reasons into a language that nonfundamentalists can understand.

This does not require the fundamentalist to disparage religious language nor to disavow its content. It does, however, stipulate that if the religious fundamentalist wants his or her moral considerations included in the debate within the public sphere, then his or her reasoning must be made accessible.

CONCLUSION

Throughout this chapter I have addressed the need for good reasons for belief and action. We asked if there were good reasons for accepting the claim of common moral relativism that there could be no *objective* morality, but only one born of cultural agreement and bound by time and geography. We found the reasons lacking, and with this discovery we were able to reject the popular notion that there is no point in discussing ethics since "everything is relative."

Good reasons for belief and action are required of the dogmatic absolutist as well. I did not ask whether moral absolutism was justified or whether it suffered from weaknesses comparable to those of relativism—that is a question for another time. The more pressing concern was whether there was good reason for the absolutist to assert, "there is no need to discuss ethics because we have the answer, and I will gladly tell you what it is." And although the absolutist could conceivably have "the answer," we found that it might be lost on his or her critics if it was not communicated in a language understood by all. The ability to persuade listeners that there are good reasons for the moral judgments of absolutism was dependent upon the willingness of the absolutist to enter into an honest, energetic, and undominated dialogue—simply asserting the truth is not enough.

Despite the tumult that has accompanied human civilization, we have good reasons for thinking that persistent dialogue will bring eventual resolution. History is replete with examples of communication between diverse peoples with quite distinct ideas, and such communication often reveals depth. We would, in fact, be hard pressed to find more than a few instances of culturally or philosophically sophisticated systems that had not been influenced by "many streams." This is not to claim that we are simply products of the cultures or ideas we encounter, but on the contrary, that we regularly break free of the confines of an isolated and idiosyncratic view of the world. And as a species we have often accomplished this under less than optimal conditions.

If we have good reason to be optimistic about dialogue on a grand scale, then surely there is reason to think that ethical discourse in the classroom will be fruitful.

NOTES

1. For examples of more sophisticated arguments for moral relativism consider: Gilbert Harman's *The Nature of Morality* (1977) or "Is There a Single True Morality" (1985); David B. Wong's *Moral Relativity* (1984); or the moral skepticism of Richard Rorty in *Philosophy and the Mirror of Nature* (1979) or *Consequences of Pragmatism* (1982).

2. I have intentionally failed to distinguish between skepticism and moral relativism in this argument, because although they represent distinct moral perspectives, teachers are apt to find that students have wedded the two concepts. Students often view skepticism as either a constituent of a larger relativism or as the principal justification for accepting a relativistic understanding of morality.

3. The anti-relativism portion of this argument parallels that offered by Irwin and is indebted to his insight and organization. See Irwin (1989) for a more thorough handling of the topic, or for a complementary argument see Louis Pojman's "A Critique of Ethical Relativism" (1989).

4. I have attempted to show that simplistic moral relativism is unreasonable, but it is equally clear that both relativism and sophomoric skepticism are impossible. Neither corresponds well with the day-to-day moral reasoning of most students or with the moral reasoning applied to real or hypothetical cases in the classroom. Teachers can successfully challenge the popular varieties of skepticism and relativism by applying them to real cases with actual implications.

5. While I have used the term *absolutism* to connote an extreme ethical stance, the argument's clear intent is to criticize dogmatism. As with the distinction between skepticism and relativism, the distinction between absolutism and dogmatism is often lost to the student, and the two are mistakenly seen as synonymous. Consequently the absolutist is perceived as arrogant, intolerant, and uninterested in the evidence. It is critical to note, however, that belief in objective, universal moral principles does not require that one embody these characteristics. The absolutist may be tolerant. And given the difficulty of securing an objective moral point of view, it is quite possible the absolutist will display humility in light of potential fallibility.

REFERENCES

Arendt, H. (1961). *Between past and future*. New York: Viking.

Arendt, H. (1965). *On revolution*. New York: Viking.

Arendt, H. (1976). *Eichmann in Jerusalem*. Middlesex, England: Penguin Books.

Bellah, R. (1983). Introduction. In M. Douglas & S. Tipton (Eds.), *Religion and America: Spirituality in a secular age*. Boston: Beacon Press.

Brandt, R. B. (1967). Ethical relativism. In P. Edwards (Ed.), *The encyclopedia of philosophy* (pp. 75–78). New York: Macmillan.

Harman, G. (1977). *The nature of morality*. New York: Oxford University Press.

Harman, G. (1985). Is there a single true morality? In D. Copp & D. Zimmerman

(Eds.), *Morality, reason, and truth* (pp. 27–48). Totowa, NJ: Rowman & Allanheld.

Irwin, T. I. (1989). *Introduction to ethics: Notes*. Ithaca, NY: Cornell University Press.

Lawrence, B. (1989). *Defenders of God: The fundamentalist revolt against the modern age*. San Francisco: Harper & Row.

Lyons, D. (1976). Ethical relativism and the problem of incoherence. *Ethics, 86*, 107–121.

Midgley, M. (1986). Trying out one's new sword. In C. H. Sommers (Ed.), *Right and wrong: Basic readings in ethics*. San Diego, CA: Harcourt Brace Jovanovich.

Pojman, L. (1989). A critique of ethical relativism. In L. Pojman (Ed.), *Ethical theory: Classical and contemporary readings*. Belmont, CA: Wadsworth.

Rawls, J. (1985). Justice as fairness: Political not metaphysical. *Philosophy & Public Affairs, 14*(3), 223–251.

Rorty, R. (1979). *Philosophy and the mirror of nature*. Minneapolis: University of Minnesota Press.

Rorty, R. (1982). *Consequences of pragmatism: Essays, 1972–1980*. Minneapolis: University of Minnesota Press.

Strike, K. A. (1990). Are secular languages religiously neutral? *Journal of Law & Politics, 6*(3), 469–502.

Wong, D. B. (1984). *Moral relativity*. Berkeley: University of California Press.

Part III

ETHICS AND INSTITUTIONS

9 Discovering How You Really Teach

GERALD GRANT
Syracuse University

You have been a principal for several years. You are accepted and respected by most teachers and staff. It is not a bad school, although there are some serious problems and morale is low. The previous principal was a self-styled innovator who brought in experts in attempts to start half a dozen new programs. A couple of these programs have caught on, but most are either languishing or have been rejected outright. Even the successful programs don't seem to have made a great deal of difference.

You have been open and listening carefully. You suspect the real problems have to do with deep-seated beliefs and attitudes that shape the moral climate of the school and the nature of interactions between teachers and students. Although you recognize there is sometimes a need for expert help from outside, you no longer believe in external change agents as the primary means of renewal. Experts and one-day workshops may be stimulating and useful when properly focused. But they are not the way to get at underlying beliefs. You are convinced that the capacity for real change lies in the hands of teachers who must assume and exercise moral responsibility for their profession. Your responsibility—your most fundamental responsibility—is to engage the faculty in genuine inquiry and reflection about how they really teach. The role of leadership is to stimulate and sustain a discovery process, taking a broad view of teaching as comprising all the formal and informal ways that teachers influence their students.

Any principal (or group of teachers exercising leadership responsibilities) ought to think hard about two critiques, described below, of the moral responsibilities of teachers. The rest of this chapter consists of two sections. In the first, we shall examine these critiques. In the second, we shall consider some effective ways of engaging teachers in reflection and action about these matters.

TWO CRITIQUES

Brain Checking

I borrow the title of this critique from Samuel Freedman's *Small Victories* (1990), a stunning examination of the life of one teacher, Jessica Siegel. She taught English at Seward Park High School on the Lower East Side of New York, still teeming with immigrant children today as it did more than a century ago. She taught her heart out, in contrast to many teachers at Seward Park who, Freedman tells us, didn't really teach or engage students as much as they allowed them to exempt themselves from tasks of thinking and learning:

> What have these students learned? What have they mastered? They have learned the use of image. They have mastered mirrors. Who has taught them? In part, their teachers. They understand from experience that if you show up (most of the time), hand in homework (every so often), and keep quiet (this is paramount), you will receive your 65 and be permitted to shuffle on towards a diploma and a mortarboard. Appearance is all. . . . "How about the content?" Jessica pled one time. She received only silence in response. It was a foolish question because any student knows that what is important is not comprehending the material; what is important is taking notes so the teacher can see you taking notes; what is important is less being a student than resembling one. The kids call the technique "brain checking." (p. 212)

Mike Rose, another gifted teacher who taught in the barrios of Los Angeles, issues a similar lament in *Lives on the Boundary* (1990). "What many students experience year after year is the exchange of one body of facts for another—an inert transmission, the delivery and redelivery of segmented and self-contained dates and formulas—and thus it is no surprise that they develop a restricted sense of how intellectual work is conducted" (p. 190).

Both Freedman and Rose give vivid content to what has been documented in more formal studies such as those by John Goodlad (1984) and Linda McNeil (1986). Goodlad's intensive study of what goes on in more than 1,000 classrooms provides a fascinating clock-hour portrait of life in American public schools. We know from his work, for instance, that teachers in the upper elementary grades spend an average of 7.41 hours a week on language arts, 2.93 hours on science, and 1.29 hours on art. He also provides a depressing picture of classrooms dominated by teacher talk, low engagement, and passive students. "A great deal of what goes on in the classroom is like painting by the numbers—filling in the colors called for by the numbers on the page" (p. 108). The pattern begun in the primary grades continues with only slight elaboration in the upper grades when students are asked to answer questions at the end of a few paragraphs of reading. Most of the time, teachers tell or explain rather than lead students to genuine inquiry. " . . . they ask specific questions calling essentially for students to fill in the blanks: 'What is the capital city of Canada?' 'What are the principal exports of Japan?' Students rarely turn things around by asking the questions" (pp. 108–109).

The pattern of testing often followed the dominant pattern of teaching: "At all levels these tests called almost exclusively for short answers and recall of information" (p. 207). Commercial workbooks and worksheets were often part of daily instruction and Goodlad's researchers saw "a kind of repetitive reinforcement of basic skills of language usage throughout the twelve grades" (p. 207) with quizzes emphasizing fill-in-the-blank thinking. Mathematics instruction was similarly routinized, taught "as a body of fixed facts and skills to be acquired, not as a tool for developing a particular kind of intellectual power in the student" (p. 209).

Linda McNeil's work (1986) goes beyond Goodlad's in that she not only confirms what Goodlad found but also offers a convincing explanation why many teachers teach in apparently thoughtless ways. Her analysis evolved from a project in which she attempted to find out what teachers actually taught in social studies classes, especially about economics. She suspected that many high school teachers presented a very conservative economic ideology, if they were not guilty of outright indoctrination. What she found was that most teachers, regardless of their ideology, presented a shamefully oversimplified version of their subject. Moreover, they elicited almost no sense of genuine inquiry. There was little dialogue or questioning or engagement of minds. In the place of an educational exchange, teachers provided lists to be copied and facts to be memorized.

Her book *Contradictions of Control* (1986), as Michael Apple pointed out in the introduction, is a case study of the trivialization of education. The forms are there but the substance is depleted. Economics was taught no differently from other social studies courses, which featured "lectures of facts, lists, abbreviated explanation, unelaborated abstract slogans, and other disjointed pieces of information" that students were expected to memorize and give back on tests (p. 71). Lists of things substituted for thought and discussion. Lists can be easily and efficiently taught, memorized by students, then cashed in for test points. Most students willingly cooperated in this limited exchange but in interviews revealed they did not trust teachers' simplified explanations and had little confidence in their ability to figure out things for themselves. Deep down, they were uneasy about the "client mentality" they had unwittingly developed.

When McNeil interviewed the teachers, she found their shortcomings were not that they were poorly educated or did not know how to teach. They said they taught that way because that was what the controllers of the system wanted. "Real teaching" would violate the expectations of the system. Administrators didn't want teachers who rocked the boat or contravened centralized controls. What the system wanted was to move pupils through as efficiently as possible. Keep the dropout rate down; turn out as many graduates with certificates as you can while keeping the peace. Thus teachers engaged in what McNeil calls defensive teaching: Control students by making the work easy. Teachers get students "to cooperate without resisting by promising that, in fact, the study of this topic will require no commitment of effort, and little time, on their part" (p. 175).

Not all teachers taught this way. In each of the four schools she studied (all of them regarded as "good schools" by their communities) there were some teachers who had high expectations, who did not conform to system "efficiencies." They sent students to libraries to look things up, and encouraged them to attend public meetings at which controversial issues were being debated and to interview citizens. Their tests asked students to take positions and defend them. Yet she also found major differences among the schools. Three of the four schools were dominated by different forms of the "contradictions of control." But the fourth, Nelson High, established an exemplary culture for learning, in part because the principal engaged the faculty in some of the ways we discuss in the following section.

Withdrawal

Are there other reasons why teachers fall into defensive teaching? McNeil suggests some of them in sketching the history of her four high schools. In *The World We Created at Hamilton High* (1988), Grant sees such teaching as but one aspect of a profound shift in the relations between students and teachers. In some places, like Hamilton High, it led to a virtual collapse of teacher authority. Police power was necessary to keep peace in the halls and classrooms. In many schools, especially in urban areas but not only there, teachers withdrew in varying degrees from the exercise of moral and intellectual authority. At its worst, they went into classrooms and locked their doors, holding sway by charismatic force, or cutting the kind of deal McNeil portrays. More usually, they kept a low profile and adopted the practice of not seeing anything that would cause them to challenge a potentially troublesome student.

What happened to cause teachers to abandon their responsibility for making a world, for creating a strong positive ethos? A school is a community that cannot disavow responsibility for either intellectual or moral virtue. The adults epitomize some version of character to pupils—by either ignoring or responding to incidents of racism, by the manner in which they answer a child's earnest inquiry, by the respect they show for qualities of intellect, by the agreements they make about what behavior will not be tolerated and what actions will be honored.

Teachers don't give up or turn lazy overnight. What happened at Hamilton High happened in varying degrees at schools across the nation as a result of a transformation in the network of authority relations within which all teachers work. In his biography of one school, Grant tells a complex story of change that begins in the 1950s and continues into the late 80s. Although the Hamilton High of the fifties was a smoothly functioning school that sent a high proportion of its graduates to college, this is not a nostalgic or reactionary tale. For Hamilton High of that era was also a school that was riven with class and racial inequalities and that conformed to the chauvinistic curriculum typical of the day. The unraveling of teacher authority was partly a result of teachers confronting their own unconscious racism, of realizing as a result of civil rights protests that they had been part of a system that denied equal educational opportunity. Others came to see in the Vietnam War protests and teach-ins that the version of American history they had been teaching was too pietistic. Teachers came to doubt their own authority, and divisions among teachers became more raw as some of those who participated in college protests joined the faculty and actively sided with the students. Faculty at Hamilton High were divided into at least three camps and gathered for lunch in three different caucuses. Some teachers deplored liberal attitudes about sex and saw the use of marijuana as a criminal offense, while others got high with students and a few had affairs with them.

Hamilton High tells the story of what it felt like from the inside as a series of social revolutions swept through the schools of America. Schools became in the 1960s and 70s the primary means of trying to create a more egalitarian society, often with disastrous unintended consequences in the short term. In the early years of large-scale desegregation, riots were followed by the rise of black separatism, in which black students elected to segregate themselves, and blacks who crossed color lines were treated as outcasts by their peers. Abolition of tracking intended to equalize educational outcomes initially led to students tracking themselves in a curriculum with many options; ironically, the gaps between white and black students widened as a result.

The power of central bureaucracies and the courts grew with the effort to put more egalitarian policies in place. Mandates and directives multiplied. Principals who had once acted with a fair degree of autonomy were now reluctant to act without consulting "downtown." Simultaneously, a children's-rights revolution grew apace as the courts redefined the prerogatives of young adults, granting them more formal equality in relation to parents and teachers. Several score of teenagers who attended Hamilton High lived apart from their parents in group homes or in their own apartments on welfare support. New due-process regulations stipulated that students be informed in writing of any charges against them and that the school be required to provide a lawyer to defend the student's interests, as well as a stenographer to keep a courtlike record in some instances. Teachers were hesitant to report serious offenses unless they had witnesses or evidence that would stand up in court. A parallel development encouraged students to bring suit for suspected abuses by parents or guardians, including teachers. Some pupils taunted teachers, "Don't touch me or I'll have you arrested." Grant reports that the shift in the psychological climate between teachers and students was reflected in a comment by a respected social studies teacher who said he began to feel, "Watch out, stay out of the way, don't get yourself in a situation in which these people can falsely accuse you" (p. 56).

Although we do not have the space to tell the story here, by the end of the 1980s there was evidence of much progress at Hamilton High. Although some racism remained, relations among whites, African-Americans, Asian-Americans, and Hispanics had been transformed. The gap between the SAT scores of white and black students had narrowed. It was a fairer, more democratic school, although also more bureaucratic and legalistic. However, the psychological residue of years of operating under mandates remained.

Members of the faculty hesitated to project any set of ideals beyond expectations of passive compliance with a minimalist, bureaucratic world. Some believed it was no longer possible to have the same set of ideals for students from such diverse racial, ethnic and class backgrounds. Teachers were confused about the grounds of their intellectual and moral authority. They felt like functionaires in a world created elsewhere. Although they no longer locked their doors, they felt little responsibility for what happened outside the classroom and often overlooked transgressions within it. The student handbook was legalistic, implicitly teaching that what was not illegal was permitted. Students learned how to manipulate the rule system in order to maximize their self-interest. They admitted there was widespread cheating in the school and said teachers often turned a blind eye to it (teachers said they wanted to avoid lawsuits). Some of the brightest students cheated the most in order to improve their chances for admission to the most competitive colleges. Some faculty were embittered. A few had given up, although they continued to show up. Most had withdrawn from any sense of responsibility for making a world, for creating a school with a strong positive ethos.

REFLECTION AND ACTION

Now we turn to the problem of how to engage the faculty in inquiry, reflection, and action. Do these critiques apply to your school? Let's look at three promising ways to find out: seminaring, shadowing, and researching.

Seminaring

A genuine seminar is a conversation in which the participants pursue questions occasioned by their reading of the text and compare what is said there with their own experience. It is a no-holds-barred opportunity to follow the question where it leads. It is not a lecture but an opportunity for members of the seminar to interrogate each other about the meaning the text has for them. The good seminar leader must have a thorough grasp of the text, pose provocative questions grounded in the text, and nurture the grains of truth that come forth from the members of the seminar, including questions the leader had not anticipated.

Assuming the approval of a representative body of teachers, seminar leaders should be selected from among teachers who have these skills and who represent a cross section of the school. Ideally, there should be one seminar leader for every ten teachers. The books mentioned above should be made available to them, and they should be assigned the task of planning a summer institute to consider these (and other) critiques. Leaders will need time to absorb the texts, discuss them among themselves, and make appropriate selections for distribution to the whole faculty. Such texts can serve to open a candid discussion of whether these critiques apply to your school. This process should not be hurried. Although eventually the seminar will want to raise the question of what is to be done, ample time should be given for analysis and exploration of how and whether this critique fits the school. It would be a rare school that absolved itself of any implication in these critiques. But even for those that did, a collegial seminar experience would strengthen consensus about the moral responsibilities of teachers and model a form of teaching that is sadly neglected in most schools.

Shadowing

After a decade of reform reports, there is relatively little evidence of significant reform in schools. One of the most promising exceptions has been the work of Theodore Sizer and the Coalition of Essential Schools he heads at Brown University. The Coalition is built around nine principles, which Sizer outlines at the end of *Horace's Compromise* (1985). No school may join the Coalition unless two thirds of its faculty endorse the principles, which argue that schools should strive to cover less material but engage students more deeply in what they do study; this is to be accomplished through teaching techniques that emphasize student initiative and place teachers more in the role of coaching than lecturing. As a prelude to discussing the principles, the Coalition urges that teachers test Sizer's critique of what's wrong with American schools by spending a day shadowing a pupil in their own school. They attend all that student's classes and tag along with students in between, as well as at lunch and in study halls. For many teachers who have long forgotten what it feels like to be a student, this is an eye-opening experience. It provides teachers with concrete data about the need for change and infuses the flavor of school life into any discussion of the principles teachers say they believe in.

Once schools have joined the Coalition, they learn that it is largely a teacher-driven enterprise. In summer institutes teachers from Coalition schools gather to work on such principles as new forms of assessment that require students to demonstrate what they've learned in exhibitions, debates, portfolios, reports and models. They also visit other schools during the course of the year to see what their colleagues have developed and to assess progress. It's a form of school shadowing, if you will. Schools differ markedly in the kinds of climates they create for pupils. Unfortunately, some teachers have never visited an outstanding school, and therefore they assume most schools are alike in character. They have little idea of how different things could be. These forms of shadowing can provide a great stimulus for reflection and action.

Recognizing that school visits can be expensive, teachers can make vicarious visits to schools and exemplary teachers by reading about them. Sarah Lawrence Lightfoot's *The Good High School* (1983) offers vivid portraits of six schools. Two of the best accounts of teaching yet written also convey a deep (and sometimes depressing) sense of the schools in which those teachers worked: Jay Mathews's *Escalante: The Best Teacher in America* (1988) and Samuel Freedman's *Small Victories* (1990). Philip Cusick's *Inside High School* (1973) remains one of the best examinations of student subcultures.

Researching

The book on Hamilton High was really a by-product of an unusual project designed to engage teachers in a discussion of what, if anything, might be wrong with their school and what they would want to do about it. I had been doing research on a federally funded project on the topic of what makes a good school when I gave a talk to a group of school superintendents. I had described Hamilton High in that talk in terms similar to those given here, and one of the principals surprised me by asking, "What would you do if you were principal of Hamilton High?" Such a role had never occurred to me, but I found myself improvising an answer that changed the course of my life for the next several years. I replied that I would try to hire the best anthropologist I could find who could pass for a teenager. I would turn him or her loose in the school for several months with the aim of writing a portrait of the moral life of the community. Then I would use that report to initiate a dialogue with all the members of the polity—students, parents, teachers, and staff. I would ask them, Is this portrait true? Is this the best we can do? If we repeated this experiment 5 or 10 years from now, what kind of school would you hope to see reflected in it?

As I wrote in the preface to *Hamilton High*, such matters are seldom discussed. There is no forum for such a dialogue in most schools, and nobody is asking these questions in a sustained way. In the ensuing months the colloquy with the superintendent kept coming to mind. But what principal could afford to hire an anthropologist, even if one could be found to meet my specifications? Then came the inspiration: Why not teach the students to be anthropologists? That is, teach them to observe, to take notes, to interview, to analyze data—and then guide them in analyzing life in their own tribe, so to speak. Their findings could be used to raise critical questions about how to improve the quality of life in the school. I did not expect the students to redesign the school or even to take responsibility for reshaping the climate, but I thought they could both learn some useful skills and open the dialogue in a compelling way.

Not only would it be good for students, such a process would also reverse the usual order of school reform. As Sarason (1971) has said so well, "The modal process of change in schools is one which insults the intelligence of teachers by expecting them to install programs about which they have not been consulted and which they have had no hand in developing or usually much say in modifying." Each of the three processes of initiating reflection described in this chapter has that aim, but using students to hold up a mirror to their teachers proved to be a particularly effective way of generating a serious dialogue about what ailed the school. When the process was first outlined to the faculty of ninety, all but three endorsed the idea. Twelve persons were elected to serve on a committee to assess the student research and to see what bearing it might have on the improvement of the school. They were some of the most able teachers, and they represented a good cross section by disciplines and departments.

Although the faculty reported a history of frustrating efforts at change that had operated in a top-down manner, their spirits were high at the first meeting of the new committee. They met fifteen times in the first year for sessions that lasted more than 2 hours each. They looked at videotapes students had made of their findings and at the results of other research gathered under my guidance. Some of the teachers began to do small questionnaires in their own classes and bring them to meetings. Teachers were highly engaged. They came early and stayed late. Absences were rare. The student research evoked deep feelings. Black and white teachers who had never talked to each other about their feelings at the time of the riots more than a decade earlier began to speak passionately about their different interpretations of those events. It was necessary to reconstitute their history, to understand where they had been, and to what place they had come before they could begin to chart a new course.

But to take responsibility for mapping that future was no simple matter. Teachers felt like "downtown" allowed the school and its teachers little autonomy. Central-office personnel issued directives and were condescending to teachers, who were "treated like children" and "expected to follow the schedules given to us," they reported. "You have made so many requests and have been turned down so much that you just give up or do your own thing" (Grant, 1988, p. 237). The teachers did not blame all the blockage in communication on the administrative hierarchy, however; they deplored the lack of collegial engagement on matters of substance. Heads nodded around the table as senior teachers considered how few conversations they had had with their peers about either ideas or teaching. A turning point in the teachers' consideration of their own responsibility for shaping the moral climate of the school came when one of the members of the group reflected that her own daughter would be entering Hamilton High in a few years. She raised the question of whether her child would encounter many faculty "who are positively indicating to her how much pleasure there is in simply knowing something. . . . I want her exposed in a positive way to learning that she enjoys, that is challenging to her, that isn't always going to be pleasant but that she thinks is something worthwhile to her" (p. 237). The librarian commented that Hamilton served the most disadvantaged students as well as the most able, but "I'm worried about the middle-of-the-road kid who is there every day, who does his or her homework, and who gets no extra attention" (pp. 237–238). A math teacher confronted the issue of teacher responsibility for school policy, noting that faculty meetings were occasions for dissemination, not real discussion. The meetings were "lists of points A, B, C, and D" when the issue ought to be "are we going to make decisions together as a faculty?" (p. 239). The principal, who had been invited to join the group after its first few meetings, expressed his doubts about the faculty's willingness to "sit together and say we're going to come up with some commonalities and say we're all going to get behind this" (p. 240). They might give lip service to the idea of school improvement, but too many "did not give a damn," and their diverse personal agendas came first.

The fifteen meetings were tape-recorded, and analysis of the transcript reveals that the dialogue developed five phases: (1) testing the need for change, (2) doubt and resistance, (3) emergence of belief that common action was possible, (4) development of shared meaning about desirable policies and practices, and (5) proposal of a strategy for schoolwide change. This process, treated at length in the epilogue of *Hamilton High*, can only be suggested here, but the fourth point, development of shared meanings, is critical. The complexity of the point can be best illustrated through a mundane example, a simple proposal by the principal to deal with the problem of tardiness.

The principal initially took the view that tardiness was a straightforward issue of faculty failure to enforce policy. Teachers should be out in the hall "getting [students'] butts in the classroom" (p. 251). Moreover, if teachers were in the hall between bells, "bad things wouldn't happen." Failure to enforce the policy was tantamount to insubordination and disloyalty. Some teachers vigorously agreed with the principal's account. Smiles spread across their faces, and their eyes settled on those teachers they regarded as slackers with respect to this policy. After a long moment of silence, one who disagreed spoke up and said she didn't think that was her job, teaching was her job, taking care of hall traffic was a job for corridor aides. Another said she saw the principal's point, but felt that standing out in the hall and screaming at kids to get them in the classroom was destructive to the kind of personal relationship she wanted to have with students inside the classroom. A teacher who recalled an earlier discussion about all the "legitimate" reasons students could be excused for class (she had listed seventeen reasons why students had been excused from her class in one week, ranging from band practice to senior pictures) asked whether anyone could believe that it was really important to get students to class on time if they could be back out in the halls 2 minutes later for all kinds of nonacademic functions. "Do we really want students in class? Do we really think every minute of class time is important?" she asked (p. 251). Over the course of several meetings, teachers discussed why the faculty might not feel loyalty to the principal on this issue, whether the authority of the corridor aides could be expected to substitute for faculty authority in essential matters, and how to resist the erosion of class time by what should be after-school activities. They did develop consensus about the need to reduce tardiness. It involved admitting and hearing their real differences, developing a policy that all could support (although not everyone had to do exactly the same thing), and recognizing that genuine commitment of the faculty required specific policies that made sense according to the overall philosophy of the school. These things do not occur unless a forum has been created for genuine reflection and time has been provided for building up the kind of trust to reveal one's honest feelings and to challenge one's colleagues in the way just illustrated.

Finally, the group proposed a strategy for schoolwide change. The crucial insight at this stage—which came midway in the academic year—was the realization that the members could not simply pass their conclusions to the faculty for ratification. If true commitment were to be developed, the faculty as a whole would have to have the opportunity to develop shared meanings and to undergo a process similar to that which the elected group had undergone.

Each of the three strategies for reflection and action suggested here can be a fruitful means for engaging the faculty in a genuine dialogue about the exercise of their responsibilities, and for reexamining and reconstituting their intellectual and moral authority. Obviously, aspects of these three approaches could be combined. A faculty committee with a year's lead time to plan a 2- or 3-week summer institute might ask a social studies teacher to organize an elective in which students conducted some research about their school. A half-dozen teachers might be asked to do the shadowing exercise during the spring term and another group asked to make visits to some exemplary schools. The institute could then be a lively seminar, perhaps with selections from some of the books we have suggested, punctuated by reports from student researchers and from teachers who have been shadowing and visiting.

REFERENCES

Cusick, P. (1973). *Inside high school: The student's world.* New York: Holt, Rinehart & Winston.

Freedman, S. G. (1990). *Small victories: The real world of a teacher, her students and their high school.* New York: Harper & Row.

Goodlad, J. I. (1984). *A place called school: Prospects for the future.* New York: McGraw-Hill.

Grant, G. (1988). *The world we created at Hamilton High.* Cambridge, MA: Harvard University Press.

Lightfoot, S. L. (1983). *The good high school.* New York: Basic Books.

Mathews, J. (1988). *Escalante: The best teacher in America.* New York: Henry Holt.

McNeil, L. M. (1986). *Contradictions of control: School structure and school knowledge.* New York: Routledge & Kegan Paul.

Rose, M. (1990). *Lives on the boundary: A moving account of the struggles and achievements of America's educational underclass*. New York: Penguin Books.
Sarason, S. B. (1971). *The culture of the school and the problem of change*. Boston: Allyn & Bacon.
Sizer, T. R. (1985). *Horace's compromise: The dilemma of the American high school*. Boston: Houghton-Mifflin.

10 Just Schools and Moral Atmosphere

F. CLARK POWER
University of Notre Dame

In this chapter I will argue that schools inevitably have moral characters or moral atmospheres that inform the moral education of students. In our individualistic American culture we have paid little attention to the moral quality of our institutions. This neglect has, I believe, adversely affected our ability to deal with many of the social ills that plague our society. To illustrate the necessity of taking the existence of moral atmospheres seriously, I will first consider *Meritor Savings Bank v. Vinson* (1986), a Supreme Court decision that sent a shudder through corporate America.

CASE

The case centered on a suit initiated by Michelle Vinson, who claimed that her supervisor, Sidney Taylor, had sexually harassed her while she was employed at the Meritor Savings Bank. On June 19, 1986, the Supreme Court declared that the bank was responsible for Taylor's acts of sexual harassment, even though he had acted contrary to the bank's stated policies and without the knowledge of bank officials. Robinson, Kirk, and Stephens (1987) concluded from the ruling that employers were to be held accountable for a sexual harassment policy that "works as well in practice as in theory" (p. 182). Consequently, Robinson, Kirk, and Stephens (1987) advised employers to monitor "the state of their own work environments" (p. 182). The fear of punitive lawsuits will surely force employers to assess the effectiveness of their harassment policies, particularly when the Equal Employment Opportunity Commission defines sexual harassment broadly as conduct that "has the purpose or effect of unreasonably interfering with an individual's work performance or creating an intimidating, hostile, or offensive working environment" (Murphy, 1987).

CORPORATE RESPONSIBILITY

The court's decision implies that Sidney Taylor was not acting as an independent agent, but as a member of a group. His employers were held responsible for allowing a situation in which he harassed Michelle Vinson in the blatant ways that she alleged (for example, by making repeated sexual advances, publicly fondling her, following her into the rest room, and raping her). There was no indication that the employers in any way sanctioned his behavior, but they did fail to establish procedures to check such outrageous conduct or to bring it to their attention. Thus responsibility for the bank's hostile work environment was imputed to the employers as well as to Sidney Taylor.

The Vinson decision calls attention to the elusive concepts of social environment and corporate responsibility. How can an environment be characterized legally by a subjective term like *hostile*? Furthermore, how can such an environment be immunized or rehabilitated? The difficulty with a notion like social environment is the relation between the group and the individual. Social environments are products of the individuals that compose them. Individuals can, and do, alter their environments by changing their social institutions and shared norms and understanding. Groups nevertheless exert undeniable influence over individuals, as common sense and a large body of social psychological research attest. Taylor was not just a perverted individual who abused Vinson because of an idiosyncratic psychological breakdown. His behavior was tolerated, even encouraged, by the bank's culture, a microcosm of a wider culture, which portrays women as sex objects. Given this relationship between the bank's culture and the wider culture, the failure of the bank's official antiharassment policies is not surprising. Establishing workplace norms that counter destructive influences from the wider culture is far more difficult than issuing policy directives.

THE SCHOOL ENVIRONMENT: A DISCUSSION OF STEALING

If the presence of a moral atmosphere is becoming a significant concern for corporate executives, it is all the more important for school administrators and teachers. School environments affect children, who are far more vulnerable than adult employees. Furthermore, as educational theorists from Plato to Kohlberg have argued, school environments can play a significant teaching role, especially in children's sociomoral development. Unfortunately, school environments bear an uncomfortable resemblance to the Meritor Bank environment in that they reflect the problems of the wider culture. Consider, for example, the following discussion with a class of high school sophomores concerning an incident in which a student had stolen a tape recorder from an unlocked locker and later bragged about it to his friends.

LEADER: Should his (the thief's) friends express their disapproval?

MARY: I'd say you'd better not brag about it. You'd better shut your mouth or you'll get caught.

SALLY: If somebody is going to be dumb enough to bring something like that into the school, they deserve to get it stolen. If you aren't together enough to lock your locker, then what can you expect? If somebody is going to steal, then more power to them.

LEADER: Is that what other people think? It's okay if you get away with it?

MARY: No, stealing is wrong.

LEADER: Well then, do you have a responsibility in a situation like this to try to talk the thief into returning the stolen goods?

MARY: You can't put pressure on students like that.

BILL: You can't ask that.

MARY: The school is responsible for enforcing rules. We're teenagers. We have our own responsibility, but we can't be responsible for everything. It's totally ridiculous to put it on the students.

BILL: Yeah, the kids come here to learn, not to patrol the hallways. They come here to go to school.

MARY: We're the ones who are teenagers. The teachers are grown up. They're the big people. They're supposed to control the people in the school. We're here to learn.

TODD: You shouldn't steal. But the way society is, everybody does it . . . [expressing disapproval] and doing something about it depends on a lot of things—[like] who is whose friend.

This discussion reveals a disturbing gap between the students' acknowledgement that stealing is wrong and their willingness to accept responsibility for stopping it. On a personal level, the students oppose stealing; on a cultural level, however, they are resigned to the inevitability of theft and tacitly support it. Mary, for example, warns the thief to be more discreet, whereas Sally blames victims who are "dumb enough" to bring valuables to school or to leave their lockers unlocked. Mary and Sally are not hardened street kids in a ghetto school, they are leaders in an affluent, high-profile, semi-urban high school. They and their peers have come to take stealing for granted; school is just like the rest of society, Todd tells us.

The students assume that responsibility for dealing with stealing clearly belongs to the faculty. Mary dismisses the suggestion that the students try to persuade the thief to return the stolen property as "ridiculous." She appeals to commonly accepted roles: the teenagers are in school to learn, the adults are there to teach and to keep order. Most teachers and administrators would, I believe, agree with her. They generally bear the burden of maintaining discipline, asking only that each student do his or her best to obey the school rules. Teachers and administrators, like students, generally accept the inevitability of stealing, and they counsel students to take precautions. What little can be done by way of providing harsh penalties, more secure locks, and surveillance, teachers and administrators typically try to do. What they do not typically try to do, however, is enlist students as partners in the disciplinary process. Instead of systematically attempting to secure student cooperation, they resort to largely ineffective external controls. Ironically, these external controls may contribute to the depersonalization of the school atmosphere and further aggravate the problem. To excuse this exercise of adult authority as a way of protecting adolescents from excessive pressures is to ignore the possibility that it may result in dissociating the students from the school community. Mary's comment that discipline is the responsibility of the *school*, not the students, signifies the significant problem of student alienation.

The cleavage between discipline and learning, presumed by students and adult authorities, presents a further problem. It is commonplace to think of discipline as keeping order or maintaining social control. Yet the word "discipline" is derived from the Latin *discipulus* meaning disciple or learner. We may be selling discipline short by failing to recognize it as part of the process of sociomoral education. Emile Durkheim (1925/1973) made this point in arguing for his collectivist approach to moral education:

> Too often, it is true, people conceive of school discipline so as to preclude endowing it with an important moral function. Some people see in it a simple way of guaranteeing superficial peace and order in the class. Under such conditions, one can come to view these imperative requirements as barbarous—as a tyranny of complicated rules. . . . In reality, however, the nature and function of discipline is something altogether different. . . . It is the morality of the classroom. . . . (p. 148)

If discipline becomes impoverished when divorced from its moral educational function, so too does the academic curriculum when it is detached from discipline and the wider social life of the school community. As John Dewey (1916/1966) explained, such disengagement comes with the development of formal schooling in which knowledge is abstracted from its context, making learning more arduous and less responsive to social purposes: "Formal instruction . . . easily becomes remote and dead—abstract and bookish, to use the ordinary words of deprecation" (p. 8). The challenge is to make the curriculum an agency of moral education by integrating it with social experience:

> When the acquiring of information and of technical intellectual skill do[es] not influence the formation of a social disposition, ordinary vital experience fails to gain in meaning, while schooling, in so far, creates only "sharps" in learning—that is, egoistic specialists. To avoid a split between what men consciously know because they are aware of having learned it by a specific job of learning, and what they unconsciously know because they have absorbed it in the formation of their characters by intercourse with others, becomes an increasingly delicate task with every development of special schooling. (Dewey, 1966, p. 9)

The issues raised by Durkheim and Dewey point to fundamental problems in contemporary schooling, problems that are not likely to be resolved using the usual administrative approaches to discipline and the curriculum. As we have seen in the Vinson case, a key to understanding such problems, and to remedying them, may be found by attending to the moral dynamics of the group or the moral atmosphere. The degree to which teachers and administrators have an ethical duty to examine the moral atmosphere of their schools is worthy of further reflection. Underlying the question of legal liability in the Vinson case—and of teacher and administrator culpability for problems like stealing—is the issue of collective responsibility. To what extent are those in positions of authority responsible for the actions of others when those actions are in some sense facilitated, or at least not resisted, by the social structure and culture of a particular group?

This is a very difficult issue because usually those in authority do not intend the harm done, in fact, they may even take actions to prevent such harm. Authorities cannot be faulted for not being omniscient or omnipotent, nor can they be expected to exercise surveillance and control that would undermine the autonomy of the members of the group. However, we may expect those in authority to do what they can to establish the conditions for a positive moral atmosphere.

In presenting the discussion on stealing, I have intimated that schools function in ways that absolve students of responsibility for school discipline and limit adult authorities to a counterproductive reliance on external measures of control. I could have used any number of issues—alcohol and drug use, truancy, violence, racial antagonism, vandalism, cheating—to make the same point. For example, cheating is a pervasive problem—

particularly in high schools with a high percentage of students going on to college. Teachers typically try to thwart it using threats, multiple versions of tests, careful proctoring, and the like. Some students regard this as a game of catch me if you can. One student put it this way: "At high school they [the teachers] assume you're going to cheat. The teacher says, 'Don't cheat,' and it's almost like inviting it. . . . It's always a challenge, let's see if we can beat this teacher." Most students, even the honest ones whose self-interest lies in thwarting cheating, will allow others to copy their answers, overlook their peer's infractions, and, of course, never even consider reporting a peer to the teacher.

Aggregate Counternorms

The pressure that even honest students feel to conform to peer expectations betrays the influence of what we (Power, Higgins, & Kohlberg, 1989), in our research on schools' moral atmospheres, have called *aggregate norms*. Aggregate norms arise within student peer groups without the reflection of discussion. Students follow them not because they believe that they are necessarily right, or even self-serving, but out of a desire to "fit in" or conform on a behavioral level with their peers. Sometimes these norms run counter to the rules of the school or to the expectations of administrators and teachers; for example, students report peer pressure to use drugs and alcohol, to exclude those not in their clique, to cheat, and above all not to report or even criticize a peer. Insofar as these *aggregate counternorms* make any moral appeal at all, it is to a protective sense of in-group loyalty. To report a peer is regarded as a betrayal of the in-group member to the alien out-group authority. Even to criticize a peer may be considered siding with the adults; the rule of thumb is to mind your own business.

BUILDING A POSITIVE MORAL ATMOSPHERE

Thus far I have tried to demonstrate that schools all too often engender atmospheres that fail, in rather obvious ways, to support moral reflection and behavior. As the case of sexual harassment at the Meritor Bank and the stealing discussion illustrate, institutions can even foster a culture that leads otherwise decent individuals to tacitly condone actions they know to be reprehensible.

We (Power, Higgins, & Kohlberg, 1989) have explored this negative cultural influence further by focusing on its effects on students' moral reasoning, evaluated by Kohlberg's measure of moral development. Previous research (Colby & Kohlberg, 1987) has shown that moral reasoning competence (determined by assessing responses to hypothetical dilemmas) develops through an invariant sequence of six cognitive stages grouped according to three levels: preconventional level (Stages 1 and 2), conventional level (Stages 3 and 4), and postconventional level (Stages 5 and 6). At the preconventional level, rules are obeyed for extrinsic considerations, such as reward or punishment. At the conventional level, rules are valued for their own sake. Finally, at the postconventional level, rules are justified by appeal to underlying principles. We tested the effects of the culture on students' moral reasoning by comparing their stage of competence with that of their performance (determined by assessing their responses to dilemmas based on everyday moral problems in their schools), and found their stage of performance lagging significantly behind their stage of competence.

We found that students generally resolved dilemmas about everyday moral problems in their schools at a half to a full stage below their moral reasoning competence. On the brighter side, we also found that not all school cultures exerted a negative influence. In our study of Just Community programs in which building a positive moral atmosphere was the primary goal, we found no gap between competence and performance. The Just Community programs succeeded to a large extent in providing an atmosphere that nurtures adolescent moral development. In this next section, I will offer suggestions for building a positive moral atmosphere, drawing in particular on what we learned from the Just Community programs.

School Size

The first step in building a positive moral atmosphere is to break down the division between adult and peer cultures in the school. This division is created not just by school structures but also by wider cultural forces that increasingly isolate children from adults. Large schools, in particular, contribute to the problem by minimizing the opportunities for meaningful teacher-student contact (Barker & Gump, 1964). Teachers are less likely to get to know students if they teach them only one course, and only a small percentage of students get involved in extracurricular activities. The students most likely to be neglected in large schools are the ones most in need of adult attention, those who are academically marginal and socially alienated.

Big schools have the advantage of providing students with superior physical resources and increased opportunities for specialization, but they are hardly conducive to the social and moral development of students. Nor is there any compelling evidence that big schools deliver a better all-around education, as John Goodlad (1984) concludes from his massive "Study of Schooling":

> I would not want to face the challenge of justifying a senior, let alone junior high school of more than 500 to 600 students (unless I were willing to place arguments for a strong football team ahead of arguments for a good school, which I am not). (p. 310)

If we cannot tear down large schools and start all over, what can we do? Many educational reformers advise restructuring schools into semi-autonomous subunits, each with its own curriculum. Such an arrangement would take advantage of the resources of the large school (for example, its language and science laboratories and wide range of specialized elective courses offerings), while providing students and teachers with a far more personalized environment. In such restructured schools, the now irrelevant institution of the homeroom would take on a new life.

Democratic Participation

Just restructuring schools will not solve the school culture problem, but it can provide the conditions for more fruitful student-teacher interactions. We must next consider how to improve the way in which students, teachers, and administrators communicate about school life and discipline. It is a commonplace that good discipline requires teachers and administrators to state their expectations clearly and enforce them consistently. However, this one-sided communication is likely to reinforce the cultural gap between students and teachers. More progressive approaches generally recommend student input into the rule-making process. For example, the Positive Discipline Approach of Keating, Pickering, Slack, and White (1990) states:

> Making appropriate decisions . . . is really what a happy, productive life is all about. . . . It is highly recommended that you and your students decide together what the expectations should be for your classroom. Students are willing to fulfill the expectations that they feel are necessary—ones they understand, and ones they have helped to select. (p. 77)

Students are far more willing to abide by, and enforce, the rules once they have shared the position of those in authority. The experience can potentially enlarge their perspective on discipline, as can be seen from the following reflections from a student member of a democratic discipline committee, who had himself appeared before the committee for skipping classes:

> It was certainly an eye-opener for me. I was having my own problems and some of those kids would come in with the same stuff. Then I would push myself much harder. I realized what it looked like from the other side. My view of the housemaster has changed radically. He is not much of a tyrant after all. . . . Being on the Disciplinary Committee, I started to feel a little more sorry for him. . . . Being on this [committee] really gives you a better view of the high school. It gives you a better idea of what happens in the school. (Kenney, 1983, p. 277)

Providing for student input into rule making seems eminently sensible and grounded in a long tradition of social psychology. Nevertheless, many teachers and administrators are reluctant to give students a meaningful role in decision making. Part of their disinclination stems from a belief that adults have the responsibility to protect the immature. They assume that adolescents left to their own devices lack the competence to make enlightened decisions. This seems to be true with regard to matters requiring specific expertise, such as the books to be included on a curriculum. On disciplinary matters, however, there is a long tradition of successful experimental democratic high school programs (Piaget, 1932/1965; Power, Higgins, & Kohlberg, 1989). These democratic experiments should be distinguished from the free schools of the late 1960s and 1970s. Many of those schools adopted a laissez-faire approach to discipline that led to serious disorder. Many teachers and administrators rightfully complained of the lack of authority in those schools. Democratic schools should not, however, be confused with free schools. Democratic schools infuse rules with a strong sense of authority because all of the members of the group are involved in process of making the rules and members are often expected to help enforce those rules.

The weakest objection to this, but the one I suspect accounts for much of the resistance to student participation, is the time and effort it requires. It seems, after all, much more efficient for teachers and administrators simply to lay down the law, especially when the laws are not all that controversial. Who, for example, could possibly be opposed to a law against stealing? The principal point of involving students in the process of resolving disciplinary problems is not, however, to enrich the problem-solving process, although this may very well occur. On a pragmatic level, involving students in the process encourages them to own the problems, thereby increasing their commitment to resolving them. And more importantly, on a moral level, involving students recognizes their dignity as moral persons.

Whether adolescent students can strictly claim that they have a right to such involvement is a matter of heated controversy (cf. Aiken & LaFollette, 1980). If adolescents are judged incompetent, then adult intervention may be warranted. Yet the case for adolescent incompetence is a shaky one, especially in a society that permits 18-year-olds to vote, serve on juries and in the military, marry, and enter into contracts. What makes an 18-year-old substantially more mature than a 15-year-old? Developmental research indicates that young persons at both ages are probably at Kohlberg's conventional Stages 3 and 4 of moral judgment. The attainment of autonomous moral judgment (the apex of moral maturity) does not generally occur until at least the mid-20s, if at all (the majority of adults do not develop beyond the conventional stages).

Therefore, a case cannot be made that adolescents are incapable of democratic participation, but can a case be made that adolescent development would be better served without it? Feinberg (1980), for example, argues that before adulthood certain paternalistic interventions may be necessary for the sake of fostering development and keeping the future open. Yet one can accept Feinberg's argument that adult interventions may be necessary for some choices that could have lasting negative effects while recognizing that such interventions may be unwarranted and counterproductive for others. Democratic participation is an application of the general axiom of learning by doing. Democratic participation provides a powerful means of helping young persons understand the reasons for the rules that they must follow and, more importantly, to develop themselves as autonomous moral agents and members of a democratic society.

MORAL DISCUSSION

The Positive Approach to Discipline recognizes many of these advantages of student participation. Missing, however, is an explicit connection between discipline and moral education. Positive discipline and other such approaches aim broadly at nurturing values, like self-control, without focusing on moral development. More than learning specific precepts or acquiring the willpower to resist temptation, moral development involves the capacity to make judgments based on considerations of fairness. If discussions of disciplinary issues are to have an effect on moral development, students and faculty need to consider not just behavioral expectations and consequences but the justifications for these expectations. I am afraid that it is all too easy for students and faculty to agree on behavioral expectations (for example, not to steal, cheat, or miss class) without ever pausing to ponder why, from a moral point of view, such expectations are important.

There is extensive research literature documenting the effectiveness of the moral discussion approach as a means of promoting moral judgment development (Higgins, 1980). Its method is to encourage students to reason at the next higher stage of development by creating cognitive conflict at the students' current stage of moral development (Blatt & Kohlberg, 1975). In theory, cognitive conflict is produced by the following: experiencing disagreement over the resolution of a moral problem, exposure to higher stage reasoning, and taking the perspective of others. Moral dilemmas such as the Heinz dilemma (Should a man steal a drug to save his dying wife?) are effective tools for launching a good moral discussion because they pose problems for which there are no ready-made answers and because they typically generate considerable disagreement.

The major limitation of hypothetical dilemmas is that they do not directly touch the real-life problems of students. Even when the dilemmas are taken from real life, the discussion seems artificial without a way of implementing group resolutions. Thus the moral discussion approach is most fruitfully employed when it is integrated with the process of democratic decision making. For example, the student comments on the stealing incident raise significant moral questions about the limits of student responsibility, the justifiability of blaming the victim for carelessness, and the duties to a friend who has violated the law. The best context for discussing these questions would be one in which the students felt their opinions really mattered. Democracy empowers students by giving them an opportunity to express their opinions and make decisions, and in so doing encourages students to reflect, to listen, and to deliberate. Democracy can be doubly empowering when students can be helped to see new possibilities for relating and working together. There is no reason why students should accept stealing, cheating, racial animosity, or a host of other problems as facts of life.

DEVELOPING COLLECTIVE NORMS

Democratic schools thus provide a rich opportunity for students to inquire into the kind of group life that they would like to have and the rules that must be followed to bring it about. Although research has shown that such discussions are valuable as a means of fostering moral development, the goal of these discussions is not philosophical exploration and debate but the building of shared expectations and values. Consider Phyllis's statement, made in a democratic meeting about a recent theft:

> It's everyone's fault that she don't have no money. It was stolen because people just don't care about the community. [They think] they are all individuals and don't have to be included in the community.

> Everybody should care that she got her money stolen [and therefore] we decided to give her money back to her.

When Phyllis says, "Everybody should care that she got her money stolen," it is clear that she is not simply voicing her personal opinion on the matter but intends to speak on behalf of a shared norm. In the context of this meeting, Phyllis and others who had previously discussed the matter in a small group had come to the conclusion that collective restitution was necessary. Phyllis offers two reasons for that conclusion, both related to the collective norm of caring. First, the theft resulted from a lack of caring and community feeling; and second, compassion for the victimized community member dictated that all share the burden of restitution. Phyllis's statement stands in marked contrast to those made in the previously cited discussion of stealing. Clearly Phyllis belongs to a group in which the students have developed a commitment to uphold common values. Phyllis does not have to convince students that they are as responsible as the faculty for responding to the theft; she merely has to remind them that they are a community.

BUILDING COMMUNITY

By community, Phyllis means more than the web of informal relationships among students and teachers or the feeling of school spirit that arises when a team is on the verge of winning a championship. For her, community is a normative concept that entails a valuing of the ideal of group solidarity and a commitment to norms of care and responsibility. Thus we can distinguish a community from a pragmatic association of individuals who cooperate for the sake of mutual advantage. This is not to say that pragmatic associations are unethical—their members recognize that they must be governed justly. But a community, as I am using the term, is a group committed to collective norms of caring, trust, and shared responsibility, norms that go beyond the strict requirements of justice.

Given its supererogatory nature, I do not want to suggest that teachers and administrators are obliged to build community. Furthermore, given the individualism of American culture (Bellah, Madsen, Sullivan, Swidler, & Tipton, 1986), I recognize that the goal of building community will undoubtably seem countercultural to most educators. I nevertheless recommend that schools become communities for at least four reasons.

1. The other-oriented values of community offer some counterweight to the excessive self-centeredness of our wider culture.

2. Community meets the need adolescents have for peer group identification in a way that nurtures moral development.
3. Community offers the kind of intensified moral experience so vital to serious moral education.
4. Living in a community reminds us of our interdependence, as one of the Just Community students put it:

> I know it sounds funny, but you can't look at it [that] just because you feel that no one else cares . . . you should suddenly stop caring. You are yourself. And in a community, I know it's true you can't do everything all by yourself, you need others to help. And right now I feel I don't want to lead a life where I have to do things by myself and I can't share things with anybody and no one can help me.

CONCLUSION

The moral atmosphere of the school is a tremendous resource for nurturing social and moral development. Unfortunately, it is all too often a squandered resource, insofar as well-meaning teachers and administrators are simply unaware of its potential for harm or good in the school. As increased attention is being given to the excesses of our individualistic American culture, we will be looking to our nation's public schools to embody the elusive values of justice and community.

REFERENCES

Aiken, W., & LaFollette, H. (1980). *Whose child? Children's rights, parental authority, and state power*. Totowa, NJ: Littlefield, Adams.

Barker, R. G., & Gump, P. (1964). *Big school, small school*. Stanford, CA: Stanford University Press.

Bellah, R. N., Madsen, R., Sullivan, W. M., Swidler, A., & Tipton, S. M. (1986). *Habits of the heart: Individualism and commitment in American life*. New York: Harper & Row.

Blatt, M., & Kohlberg, L. (1975). The effect of classroom discussion upon children's moral judgment. *Journal of Moral Education, 4*, 129–61.

Colby, A., & Kohlberg, L. (1987). *The measurement of moral judgment. Vol. I: Theoretical foundations and research validation*. New York: Cambridge University Press.

Dewey, J. (1966). *Democracy and education*. New York: The Free Press. (Original work published 1916)

Durkheim, E. (1973). *Moral education: A study in the theory and application of the sociology of education*. (E. K. Wilson & H. Schnurer, Trans.). New York: Free Press. (Original work published 1925)

Feinberg, J. (1980). The child's right to an open future. In W. Aiken & H. LaFollette (Eds.), *Whose child? Children's rights, parental authority, and state power*. Totowa, NJ: Littlefield, Adams.
Goodlad, J. (1984). *A place called school*. New York: McGraw-Hill.
Higgins, A. (1980). Research and measurement issues in moral education interventions. In R. Mosher (Ed.), *Moral education: A first generation of research and development*. New York: Praeger.
Keating, B., Pickering, M., Slack, B., & White, J. (1990). *A guide to positive discipline: Helping students to make positive choices*. Boston: Allyn & Bacon.
Kenney, R. (1983). *The creation of a democratic high school: A psychological approach*. Unpublished doctoral dissertation, Boston University, Boston, MA.
Meritor Savings Bank v. Vinson 91 U.S. L. Ed. 2d (1986).
Murphy, S. (1987). What makes a work environment "hostile"? [Case note]. *Arkansas Law Review, 40*, 857–876.
Piaget, J. (1965). *The moral judgment of the child* (M. Gabian, Trans.). Glencoe, IL: Free Press. (Original work published 1932)
Power, F. C., Higgins, A., & Kohlberg, L. (1989). *Lawrence Kohlberg's approach to moral education*. New York: Columbia University Press.
Robinson, R. K., Kirk, D. J., & Stephens, E. C. (1987). Hostile environment: A review of the implications of Meritor Savings Bank v. Vinson. *Labor Law Journal, 38*, 179–183.

11 Ethics Committees and Teacher Ethics

BETTY A. SICHEL
Long Island University

The quest for professionalism is one reason for the recent interest in the professional ethics of teachers, but other conditions also contribute to this attention: changes in student and teacher populations; legal intrusions into classrooms and schools; greater public awareness of, and concern about, professional misconduct; increasing parental involvement in schools; and new ethical frameworks that change our understanding of the dimensions and problems of professional ethics. In other professions, such as medicine, new institutional structures and techniques are now used to provide moral education and advice to professionals, to improve the moral climate of institutions, to heighten moral sensitivity and feelings, and to formulate ethical codes. In this chapter, I study how one new structure and method can improve professional teacher ethics and the moral life of schools.

Professional teacher ethics primarily concentrates on improving an individual teacher's ethical reasoning and judgments. Accordingly, a teacher should be an autonomous moral agent who individually makes and carries out ethical judgments. The existence of a just, humane, and caring school is dependent on each teacher becoming just, humane, and caring. With this additive approach, the sum of all just and humane teachers equals a just and humane school. The onus of moral responsibility is on each teacher. This focus ignores the school culture and does not consider the significant evidence that the culture, governance, and environment of the school affect teacher effectiveness and student achievement (Rutter et al., 1979; Grant, 1988). Similarly, it is argued here that the improvement of professional teacher ethics requires attention to the diverse institutional factors that comprise the moral climate of the school.

An earlier version of this paper was given May 1989 as the Presidential Address of the Middle Atlantic States Philosophy of Education Society. I thank Professor Bert Bandman for many invaluable suggestions. Another version was presented at the Fall 1990 South Atlantic Philosophy of Education Society meeting and a shortened paper was published in their proceedings.

One development in medical ethics provides a model for understanding how the school as an institution contributes both to the professional ethics of teachers and to the relationship between a professional and the institution, between the ethics of teachers and schools. During the last few decades, health care institutions have established institutional ethics committees (IECs) to provide education for members of the institution, to formulate ethical policy, and to be a consultative body for difficult, complex ethical dilemmas. This chapter argues that schools should create school ethics committees (SECs) analogous to the IECs of health care institutions.[1] To understand how the IEC model can inform teacher and school ethics, we examine first the development of IECs and then how a similar model would prove advantageous for teacher and school ethics.

THE INSTITUTIONAL ETHICS COMMITTEES IN HEALTH CARE FACILITIES

Approximately two decades ago, medical practitioners and health care workers realized that new technology and social conditions were producing difficult, complex moral dilemmas that could not be resolved with the old methods, categories, and assumptions. The combination of a cluster of court cases and proposed Federal regulations was a watershed that changed medical ethics and motivated the formation of IECs. One landmark court case,[2] that of Karen Ann Quinlan, pertained to a comatose patient in a persistent vegetative state who was attached to a respirator. Though irreversibly brain damaged, Quinlan was not brain dead. The Superior Court of New Jersey denied her father's petition to remove the respirator and justified its denial by citing expert medical testimony against the removal; by noting that the rapid advancement of medical knowledge made it impossible to foresee future prognosis; by recognizing the absence of medical tradition to warrant the act; and by arguing that the Constitution guarantees a right to life, not a right to die. On the basis of an individual's right to privacy, the Supreme Court of New Jersey reversed the first decision and authorized the removal of the respirator, but not the removal of all life-support systems (Rachels, 1986).

Only one aspect of the New Jersey Supreme Court decision is considered in the following discussion: the reason the decision drastically changed medical ethics, by focusing attention on the ways decisions are reached in medical institutions. The judge questioned why the health care institution in which Quinlan was a patient did not have a method, in the form of a committee of medical specialists that would adjudicate difficult ethical cases, or formulate policy about institutional ethical dilemmas such as whether a respirator should be removed from a comatose patient (Weir, 1977).

Although this legal decision referred to expert knowledge and a committee of medical specialists, the court recommendation had different consequences than originally imagined.

The judge had assumed that decisions in medical cases were matters of agreed-upon professional knowledge and practice, but health care workers understood that medical decisions often involve ethical, conceptual, and epistemological problems and include social, value, and legal considerations. For example, certain ethical dilemmas occur because of the state of medical knowledge, and the uncertainty about prognostication and treatment (Paget, 1988). Many moral dilemmas reach into uncharted medical and ethical territory and require multidisciplinary, multidimensional data and concepts. Finally, during this earlier period, patient participation in medical decisions increased significantly, much of the justification for this linked to "the idea of the moral autonomy of individuals" (Ladd, 1975, p. 99).

Because complex, diverse factors contribute to the difficulty of making medical ethical decisions and because of the legal ramifications of such decisions, health care facilities and personnel have supported the formation of IECs. These committees now make policy on a wide number of issues, examine complex ethical cases, provide consultative services for various medical professionals and staff members, give ethical comfort to health care workers, and offer various medical ethics educational programs.[3]

TEACHERS, SCHOOLS, AND THE IEC MODEL

We now turn to the main problem of this chapter, how the ethics of schools and teachers can be improved by using a model similar to that of an IEC. After an introduction that justifies school ethics committees (SECs), three sections focus on the main purposes of SECs: educational, policy-making and consultative. A final section briefly discusses the implications of SECs for professional teacher ethics.

Introduction

At the outset, there is the problem of why school personnel would agree that an SEC should generate ethical policy and moral codes, plan and offer professional ethics education, and consult on particularly difficult moral cases. School administrators may claim to have the authority, the right, and the responsibility to make decisions regarding the rules and policy governing school life. Some teachers may argue that the most successful means to change schools is through union negotiation of contractual agreements. Other teachers and staff may not want to take the responsibility inherent in an SEC. All school personnel may contend that moral conduct, even when connected with professional roles, is an individual matter and involves personal responsibility and autonomy. These common views are the remains of old attitudes and outdated ways of governing schools. The reasons to follow justify the efficacy of SECs and respond to older attitudes.

Pluralistic Moral Beliefs and Diverse Knowledge. Many moral problems in schools cannot be understood or resolved with the knowledge and skills of any one person, but require multidimensional input and the expertise of various specialists and school personnel. Different school personnel may view moral dilemmas in different ways, depending both on their personal views of the good and on their professional roles (Grant, 1988; Sarason, 1971). In a study of the role of personal views of the good for professional life, it has been argued that a looser coupling between person and profession[4] and between person and institution than existed in the very recent past is now developing. With looser coupling, issues such as personal views of the good, personal values, and different theoretical assumptions about the moral domain and moral standards affect professional moral decisions and actions.

Equally important, school personnel have different knowledge and skills, experiential backgrounds, and role expectations. These factors contribute to their interpretations of what a moral dilemma is; what moral policy is needed; what evidence, knowledge, or resources are required to resolve a moral dilemma; what moral judgment should be made; and what moral action is consistent with that moral judgment. An SEC overcomes the problem of diversity by avoiding the limitations of a single perspective and instead utilizing the strengths of diverse perspectives, resources, skills, and knowledge.

The Complexity of the School's Structure. The implementation of school moral policy and/or a moral code often involves aspects of the school organization that are beyond the control or authority of one person. For example, when contractual agreements ignore school organization, writing policy into a teacher contract with a district often does not improve teaching-learning conditions. Teachers often discover that the inclusion of policy in a contract has unanticipated consequences and little overall positive impact on the teaching-learning situation. One reason for unexpected results is that policy does not necessarily consider the structure of the school. Similarly, the establishment of moral policy or a professional moral code may have few expected consequences because the policy or code did not consider the institutional or structural character of the school. Since an SEC is comprised of people with different institutional roles and responsibilities, it can appraise the changes needed when making policy, consulting about moral dilemmas, and providing moral education.

In addition, an SEC can adapt the external constraints of government policy and judicial decisions to local conditions (Ladd, 1975). In connection with this function and the school's relationship with external authorities, John Ladd and, more recently, critical theorists would argue that this is not a positive feature, but a form of cooptation, a reason why administrators, central authorities, and government officials would support the formation of SECs. Criticism of SECs as a type of "social engineering" can be answered in two ways. First, as with IECs in health care institutions, SECs are not merely part of a procedure by which to carry out external policy, but are potentially a means to maintain the internal integrity and uniqueness of the school. Second, just as IECs have over time influenced government and legislative policy, SECs similarly can become a force to influence external authority and policy.

Participation and Democracy. A more salient justification for the formation of SECs is derived from the principles of democracy and how these principles should inform school life, and the school's decision-making procedures and governance.[5] One view of democracy, authoritative democracy, with its focus on the "wise" leader, assumes that an individual or a small elite possesses the knowledge, expertise, and wisdom to make important social and political decisions for everyone else (Barber, 1984). The primary problem with authoritative democracy is not how the elite is chosen or whether leaders are elected, but the conceptualization of human nature, human ability, and welfare that underlies it. In contradistinction to this view, advocates of "strong democracy," to use Benjamin Barber's expression, argue that each person has sufficient general intelligence and ability to contribute to decision making in areas that affect his or her life and community. All human beings can therefore cooperate and participate in the social and political life of the institutions of their communities. Autocratic or even authoritative administrative decision making would thus be anathema to the maintenance of a democratic school environment and structure.[6]

The consequences of denying roles in shaping a school's moral policy to teachers and other school personnel have been described by John Dewey (1971):

> It is still also true that incapacity to assume the responsibilities involved in having a voice in shaping policies is bred and increased by conditions in which that responsibility is denied. . . . Habitual exclusion has the effect of reducing a sense of responsibility for what is done and its consequences. (p. 113)

Elsewhere Dewey (1915) states:

> The two elements in our criterion both point to democracy. The first signifies not only more numerous and more varied points of shared common interest, but greater reliance upon the recognition of mutual interests as a factor in social control. The second means not only freer interaction between social groups . . . but change in social habit—continuous readjustment through meeting the new situations produced by varied intercourse. (p. 100)

These and other passages from Dewey's writings furnish reasons for instituting democratic methods for ethical policy making and improving the professional ethics of teachers.

First, to ensure the continuing vitality of a democracy, democratic procedures should exist in all areas of civic and institutional life. How does the school contribute to insuring the health of civic and political democracy, to transmitting and engendering a democratic spirit among students and teachers? One way is for the school itself to be a model of democracy and thus to illustrate how enlightened self-transformation can take place in a democratic society (Counts, 1932/1978). Democratic ideals can be nurtured if school personnel have roles in deciding the moral policy of the school.

Second, the inclusion of diverse interests and groups in the democratic procedures of an SEC strengthens school personnel's ability to make moral decisions, take responsibility for those decisions, and carry them out in action. The issue here is not merely that participation is advocated because it is a basic tenet of democracy, but rather that participation is essential because it achieves desirable collateral ends, such as enhancing a person's ability to make and carry out moral decisions.

Third, as Dewey recognized, not only does participation enrich the whole, but it equally enriches the person who participates (Dewey, 1954; *cf.* Care, 1987). Participation has the potential to encourage self-realization and the development of moral character, as well as to afford greater "political space" (Keim, 1975, p. 18). Exclusion, on the other hand, does not only lead to a personal incapacity to make decisions or an inability or unwillingness to take an active role in civic democracy. As important, exclusion from school governance has other consequences for school personnel, many of which are now discussed under various rubrics. For example, it can be questioned whether teacher burnout is primarily caused by classroom dynamics or features of the present school system that frustrate and affect teachers.

The Purposes of School-Institutional Ethics Committees

The Educational Purpose. If any purpose is fundamental to the workings of an SEC, it is the educational purpose. As will be noted, even the policy and consultative purposes can be understood as aspects of education. When considered as a separate purpose, the educational purpose of an SEC has two dimensions: first, the self-education of the committee, and second, furnishing moral education for the larger school community. The self-education of an SEC is propaedeutic to other purposes. Descriptions of the formation of IECs in health care institutions note that self-education takes from one to three or more years. Although it is prior to consulting on cases or formulating policy, self-education actually continues while the committee carries out these two other functions.

Self-education is exceptionally important for a number of reasons. Through such education, committee members become collaborative partners rather than adversaries. SEC members have different school roles that often require competition to obtain scarce resources. As SEC members, they must subtly shift roles. At the same time that they have special knowledge, expertise, and skill, SEC members need to collaborate with each other to be effective in SEC activities. Committee decisions should not be matters of victory or defeat, of a battle to sustain the interests of one group or person, but should recognize the diverse needs and interests of all parties. Although they have specialized educational knowledge, SEC members must also acquire an understanding of various ethical standards, ideals, and decision-making procedures. Finally, members of the committee should develop ethical attitudes, feelings, sensitivity, and imagination.

How can individuals with different interests be transformed into a collaborative network that uses each person's special knowledge and skill to improve the moral life of the school community? How do the members of an SEC acquire the theoretical and conceptual knowledge necessary for practical ethical decision making? A first step is to limit preliminary meetings to a program of self-education. These self-education meetings can be facilitated with the assistance of an ethicist and the presentation of ethical cases that steer the committee away from narrow, special interests and insure discussion among people with very different moral beliefs and interests (Lamore, 1987, especially Chapter 3).

Second, an SEC should provide moral education for the larger school community by organizing practical ethics seminars, workshops, and conferences. In hospitals, IECs often conduct ethical rounds for hospital staff to examine concrete cases and speculate about their resolution. Similarly, SECs can conduct simulations, use videotapes of class and school ethical problems, and examine various works on educational ethics (Strike, Haller, & Soltis, 1988; Strike & Soltis, 1985). Through its educational function, an SEC raises school personnel's moral consciousness and increases moral understanding. The moral education function of a school community is ongoing. As new types of moral dilemmas develop and as new ethical tools become available, an SEC continues to provide the moral education necessary to understand new problems and new ethical tools.

There is another essential aspect of the educational function of SECs. Benjamin Barber (1984) suggests that "without talk, there can be no democracy" (p. 267) and that such local talk can "instill civic competence" (p. 268). This emphasis on "talk," on communication and dialogue, is connected to the educational purpose of SECs in that education creates conditions for communication, dialogue, and networks of conversation.

The Policy Purpose. Even the suggestion that a committee, an SEC, should make policy or write an ethical code may cause uneasiness and criticism in that some may claim that SECs would usurp the rights and responsibilities of individual teachers. Who has ultimate decision-making authority in the use of moral policy and in making decisions about a moral code? Can an SEC override the moral decision of a teacher or criticize a teacher's moral actions? Such questions misunderstand the role of SECs. In one way, these questions assume that SECs are identical to Committees on Special Education (CSEs). Each CSE deliberation focuses on an individual case, the educational needs of an individual student. Although CSE deliberations probably require a wide variety of educational experiences, objectives, and resources, a single student is still the focus of each particular CSE hearing and decision.

While similar to CSEs in limited respects, SECs are different in numerous ways. SECs would have broader purposes, such as concern with ethical policy matters, facilitating communication, providing professional moral education, gathering information from various sources, developing moral policy or a moral code, giving ethical comfort, and providing consultative services. In some instances, a single concrete moral problem may trigger SEC deliberations, but these deliberations rarely focus on the culpability of individuals. Instead, the original problem may motivate deliberation about more general ethical issues and may be the starting point for consideration of ethical policy, a moral code, and a new program of moral education.

John Rawls's (1955) distinction between justifying rules and justifying actions under rules is helpful in understanding the policy role of SECs.

When justifying rules, the issue is: How does an institution (or an individual) justify general rules that would be standards for resolving a wide range of concrete moral dilemmas? In the case of justifying actions under rules, an agent who is faced with a concrete moral dilemma uses appropriate moral rules or principles to resolve the dilemma. This justification of actions under rules is not the mechanical application of a rule or set of rules to a moral dilemma, that is, having a formula to solve moral dilemmas within the appropriate class (Lamore, 1987). Nothing could be further from the practice! The resolution of a concrete moral dilemma requires cognitive thought, the delineation of the parameters of the problem, understanding what aspects of the larger experiential situation refer to the moral dilemma, deciding what moral principle or rule applies, and so forth. Two agents examining an identical moral dilemma may apply different moral principles or concepts to it. Even if they use the same moral principle, they may make very different judgments.

These two concepts, the justification of rules and the justification of actions under rules, can be applied to SECs. A committee would concentrate on the development of a local moral code or on formulating general policy. Individual agents, on the other hand, would justify decisions under the SEC code or policy. In ambiguous or controversial situations, individual moral agents would not necessarily agree about which concrete situations or problems should be included in the class of problems covered by the general moral policy, nor would they necessarily concur about which moral judgments should be made. In other words, moral agents could still disagree about whether a situation or dilemma is covered by policy, how to decide and what standards to use, and what action should be undertaken. There is even the possibility that a moral agent could use various moral standards and ideas not covered by an SEC policy or code. This controversial notion is based on the idea that a policy or code is highly general and there will be boundary areas and lacunae where other ethical views enter the picture; individuals will have to supply the details for particular situations, and make specific judgments for each concrete moral dilemma. Professional moral codes and policy statements provide a moral background, a structure, an environment within which a moral agent recognizes moral dilemmas and directs her or his moral attention, attitude, sensitivity, and imagination.

The Consultative Purpose. Teachers may request a meeting of an SEC to consider an ethical dilemma. This does not imply that the committee will solve the problem or tell teachers what decision should be made or what action they should take. Rather, as the term *consultative* suggests, school personnel consult with committee members to study the various possible responses to moral dilemmas. The consultative purpose of SECs includes at least two functions, each of which may involve different problems: Consultation may take place prior to a teacher's decision or subsequent to moral action.

1. *Consultation prior to decision and action.* Even if consultation with an SEC is optional, one may wonder whether the decision of a committee should be optional or mandatory. Should a teacher have the option either to accept or reject the committee's decision or should a teacher be required to accept an SEC decision? If acceptance of a committee's decision were mandatory, this would negate the meaning and spirit of the consultative purpose of an SEC. Even though the policy function of SECs may be analogous to quasi-legislative decision making, the consultative purpose is not analogous to legislative enactment or judicial decision. A very different type of relationship should exist between an SEC and teachers. A committee should not be a surrogate for a teacher's ethical decision making or a means for teachers to avoid the responsibility of decision making. Instead, when consulted, an SEC should assist the teacher with a professional ethical problem by clarifying issues, examining the problem in a variety of ways, bringing a committee's diverse knowledge to the issue, and so forth. A teacher, however, makes his or her own decision. The committee provides a forum within which a teacher can explore a variety of options and communicate with other professionals who have different perspectives on the situation.

2. *Consultation subsequent to decision and action.* After making a moral judgment and acting on that judgment, a teacher may consult with committee members. In retrospect, a teacher may be uncertain about the decision and its consequences or wonder whether a different decision should have been made. At times, the decision and action are not morally reprehensible or even questionable, but a teacher may be concerned about the ramifications of moral decision making and acting under situations of great uncertainty. A teacher may have regrets and feelings of moral inadequacy and doubt. She or he may realize that a variety of alternative decisions could have been made or that no matter what the choice, the results would have been unacceptable. In some cases, subsequent consultation with the committee may primarily be for ethical comfort, helping a teacher to accept the decision and recognizing its validity. In other cases, a teacher may develop new ways of looking at similar moral dilemmas and thus acquire greater understanding, skills, sensitivity, and imagination for resolving future practical ethical dilemmas.

Both prior and subsequent to making decisions, consultation can be seen as having a strong educational function. Through its consultative purpose, SECs assist teachers in acquiring greater understanding of what an ethical dilemma is, what its parameters are, what knowledge would contribute to an understanding and resolution of the dilemma, what types of ethical standards could be used to resolve the dilemma, and how the dilemma and its possible solutions might affect teachers, students, and others.

Certain types of consultation have not been common for teachers. Though physicians are viewed as autonomous agents, in actuality they are members of various professional, communicative networks. Although individual physicians are responsible for medical decisions, they often do not make decisions without considerable input from other professionals. This occurs in a number of ways, through formal and informal consultation with other physicians or health care experts. Members of IECs mention that when physicians accept the notion of an IEC, they informally consult with committee members about specific medical cases. Some IECs even have members on call so that a physician or other health care professional can speak with a committee member at any time of the day or night. Thus the consultative function of IECs is both formal and informal. Similarly, this range of consultative practices is advocated for SECs. Teachers would then become part of communicative networks that would allow for increased discussion about professional ethical matters and greater understanding of professional moral dilemmas.

AFTERTHOUGHTS

At this point, we need to return to some of the questions asked earlier, in particular, how SECs would help develop the professional ethics of the individual teacher or what the relationship should be between the institution, the school, and the individual, the teacher. No matter what the person's personal ethical commitments, each teacher is affected by the school's moral climate. The earlier claim that there is now developing a looser coupling between teacher and institution than had heretofore existed does not cancel the notion that the school as an institution affects the moral lives of teachers. Depending on the nature of the organization, its moral climate and values, its type of governance and social environment, a school can contribute to the moral growth of its members or constrain their behavior, can increase moral sensitivity or limit the development of moral feelings, can celebrate moral diversity or enforce narrowly conceived social rules.

To understand how the institution influences the individual, various issues still need to be investigated: whether the school is a unique social institution and whether the bureaucratic model should be the basis for studying school ethics and moral life; whether the school should be viewed as a community and what type of community schools can (or should) be; what type of good (or goods) the school as a community should seek to achieve (e.g., Moravesik, 1988); how to conceptualize the looser coupling between teacher and school, between person and profession, that is advocated here. We also need to investigate various aspects of how professional ethics develops within communities or institutions, and to what extent the social and moral climate and governance and structure of institutions affects the moral decisions and professional ethics of individuals within those institutions.

This chapter has presented one way to gain greater understanding of these various practical, theoretical, and conceptual issues. That way is to begin to improve the moral climate of the school and create conditions conducive for the nurturing of the professional ethics of teachers by creating SECs. SECs will not abrogate the moral decision making of teachers but will create a moral environment in which teachers can make more responsible and responsive moral decisions. SECs will create an environment in which teachers recognize that professional ethics is of fundamental importance for teaching and schools.

NOTES

1. Other professions are considering the IEC model; see Reamer, 1987. For studies of IECs, see Fost & Cranford, 1985; Rosner, 1985; Sichel, 1989. For a more complete bibliography, see Macklin & Kupfer, 1988.

2. Two other cases involved the care of infants: the Infant Doe of Bloomington (IN) case and the Baby Jane Doe case in New York State. Both cases concerned parents' decisions (following physician recommendations) to forgo surgery for their severely handicapped infants and to allow them to receive only "normal" care and to be kept comfortable. When these cases provided impetus for federal regulations regarding decisions about the care of severely ill neonates, there was further motivation for the formation of IECs.

3. For the function, operations, structure, dynamics, and methods of IECs, see Cranford & Doudera, 1984.

4. For a criticism and analysis of firm coupling between person and institution, see Ladd, 1970.

5. For a case study and analysis of democracy and participation in higher education, see Edel, 1990, which also includes his statement of the characteristics of democracy (pp. 121–122).

6. Similarly, Bayles (1986) argues that a considerable portion of the power and self-regulation of professions is unwarranted in that clients have the capacity to make judgments reserved for professionals.

REFERENCES

Barber, B. R. (1984). *Strong democracy: Participatory politics for a new age.* Berkeley: University of California Press.

Bayles, M. D. (1986). Professional power and self-regulation. *Business and Professional Ethics Journal,* 5(2), 26–46.

Care, N. S. (1987). *On sharing fate.* Philadelphia: Temple University Press.

Counts, G. S. (1978). *Dare the schools build a new social order?* Carbondale, IL: Southern Illinois University Press. (Original work published 1932)

Cranford, R. E., & Doudera, A. E. (Eds.). (1984). *Institutional ethics committees and health care decision making.* Ann Arbor, MI: Health Administration Press.

Dewey, J. (1915). *Democracy and education.* New York: Macmillan.

Dewey, J. (1971). Democracy and educational administration. In J. P. Strain (Ed.), *Modern philosophies of education* (pp. 108–114). New York: Random House. (Original work published 1937)

Dewey, J. (1954). *The public and its problems.* Denver: Alan Swallow. (Original work published 1927)

Edel, A. (1990). *The struggle for academic democracy.* Philadelphia: Temple University Press.

Fost, N., & Cranford, R. E. (1985). Hospital Ethics Committees. *Journal of the American Medical Association,* 253, 2687–2692.

Grant, G. (1988). *The world we created at Hamilton High.* Cambridge, MA: Harvard University Press.

Keim, D. W. (1975). Participation in contemporary democratic theories. In J. R. Pennock & J. W. Chapman (Eds.), *Participation in politics* (pp. 1–38), Nomos XVI. New York: Lieber-Atherton.

Ladd, J. (1970). Morality and the ideal of rationality in formal organizations. *The Monist, 54,* 488–516.

Ladd, J. (1975). The ethics of participation. In J. R. Pennock & J. W. Chapman (Eds.), *Participation in politics* (pp. 98–125). New York: Lieber-Atherton.

Lamore, C. E. (1987). *Patterns of moral complexity.* New York: Cambridge University Press.

Macklin, R., & Kupfer, R. B. (1988). *Hospital ethics committees* (pp. A5–A9). New York: Albert Einstein College of Medicine.

Moravesik, J. (1988). Communal ties. *Proceedings and Addresses of the American Philosophical Association, 62,* pp. 211–225.

Paget, M. A. (1988). *The unity of mistakes.* Philadelphia: Temple University Press.

Rachels, R. (1986). *The end of life.* New York: Oxford University Press.

Rawls, J. (1955). Two concepts of rules. *Philosophical Review, 64,* 3–32.

Reamer, F. G. (1987). Ethics committees in social work. *Social Work, 32,* 188–192.

Rosner, F. (1985). Hospital medical ethics committees: A review of their development. *Journal of the American Medical Association, 253,* 2693–2697.

Rutter, M., Maughan, B., Mortimore, P., & Ouston, J. (1979). *Fifteen thousand hours.* Cambridge, MA: Harvard University Press.

Sarason, S. B. (1971). *The culture of the school and the problem of change*. Boston: Allyn & Bacon.
Sichel, B. A. (1989). An ethics of care and institutional ethics committees. *Hypatia*, *4*(2), 45–56.
Strike, K. A., Haller, A. J., & Soltis, J. F. (1988). *The ethics of school administration*. New York: Teachers College Press.
Strike, K. A., & Soltis, J. F. (1985). *The ethics of teaching*. New York: Teachers College Press.
Weir, R. F. (Ed.). (1977). *Ethical issues in death and dying*. New York: Columbia University Press.

12 Ethical Discourse and Pluralism

KENNETH A. STRIKE
Cornell University

Becoming a morally competent person involves learning the intricacies of moral speech. If we wish to understand the responsibilities of teaching, we will need to understand the characteristics of moral speech in schools.

MORAL SPEECH AND PLURALISM

In our society people speak a variety of moral languages. In some cases this is because different languages are adapted to different purposes. In other cases it is because we deeply disagree, even concerning the right moral vocabulary to employ to characterize moral phenomena. Thus one way to begin to reflect on moral speech in public school settings is to consider the difficulties posed by the fact of significant disagreement.

Two conclusions emerge. The first is that it is hard to imagine a good school in which "values" are not dealt with. A recent RAND Research Review summarizes the results of one study.

> Successful schools . . . have missions that are simple and sharply defined—including a determination to mold students' attitudes and values—and organizations with on-site capacity to make decisions and solve problems. As a result, they are able to persuade their charges to follow rules and to achieve academically. ("Inner-city high schools," 1990, pp. 5, 6, 12)

Such sentiments are among the more common tenets of the effective schools literature. When schools lack a sense of purpose, when they project no clear idea about the kinds of people they expect their students to become, students are most likely to acquire their outlook from their peers or from popular culture. A world with weakened families and aimless schools is one where children find their identities in gangs and kill one another for gym shoes.

The second conclusion about teaching values in schools is that we cannot. As soon as any attempt is made to identify some set of values to teach, someone will drop by to inform us that whereas, of course, schools should teach values, unhappily this particular set of values is racist, sexist, Eurocentric, a manifestation of secular humanism, relativistic, absolutistic, Protestant, liberal, conservative, homophobic, feminist, Marxist, or a manifestation of some other This-ism or That-ism that the protestor knows to be perverse, unjust, and destructive of the moral fiber of American democracy.

Solutions to this dilemma fall into three groups. First are views that emphasize teaching ethical reasoning. They claim to teach students how to think but not what to think. Second are views that seek to differentiate and privatize the educational system so that students are freer to attend school with those who are like-minded. Third are attempts to discover a lowest-common-denominator morality. Each view has weaknesses.

The proposals for teaching students how to think but not what to think depend on the assumption that there is a language for making value judgments that is independent of particular viewpoints or communities and that can thus serve as an arbiter among them. This view of rationality has been thoroughly criticized in philosophy (Rorty, 1989). It is time for educators to give up on it.

The second and third views are more plausible. They respond to the dilemma of diversity in opposite ways. One seeks separation. It says that because we cannot agree and because we have a right to our own views, let us go our separate ways. Each community can transmit its own values to its children as it sees fit. It would be equally accepting of African American schools, religious schools, and schools for students interested primarily in the performing arts. The opposing voice responds that we must still live together and that we must therefore find something we have in common that we can transmit to our children. To minimize conflict, it seeks to identify a minimalist package.

These two views share some common ground in that both seek to balance moral diversity against the need to maintain a common morality. Each needs the other. A view that simply asserted the right of moral pluralism would be deficient in that it would fail to explain how people who inhabit different moral worlds, but who live in a common society, are to live together in peace. Also, unless there is some shared morality, it is hard to see how those who hold to some particular moral outlook are to secure tolerance for their own views, and it is hard to see how those who assert a right to moral pluralism are going to make sense of their claim to others. A common morality is necessary if we are to live in a society where reasoned discussion replaces coercion as a way of settling disputes and to be secure in the right to differ.

Those who argue for a minimalist common morality must recognize that the common morality they seek to promote is insufficient in that it will be designed to tell us how we are to treat one another insofar as we must interact, but it will not pretend to tell us much about many areas of life. Such a moral language is likely to have something to say about taxes, sewers, criminal statutes, military budgets, elections, and due process. Justice and democratic decision making are a part of it. But it will have little to say about God and goodness. It will be a poor resource when we want to conceive a vision of our own lives.

We need to avoid two extremes in our view of moral education. The first I shall call "liberal silence." Liberal silence occurs when schools try to avoid moral questions, making minimal efforts to teach only the common morality. In schools where liberal silence prevails, the voices of particular moral communities are silenced because they are not shared. We fear our differences and the controversy they invite, so we create schools that extol mutual respect and tolerance but resist any real exploration of competing moral visions.

The mirror image of liberal silence is "liberal balkanization." If we begin to notice that schools whose sole morality is a thin common morality require us to repress some of what makes us what we are for the sake of peace and tranquility, we may respond by transforming the demand for tolerance into a demand for radical separation in which each group has an equal claim on public resources.

Both of these visions are inadequate because both exclude the possibility of dialogue, and dialogue is essential for any reasonable moral education. Moral education requires at least two kinds of moral learning. First, students need to learn to speak a common moral language. If we fail here, we will have abandoned any hope of civil peace and mutual tolerance. Second, students need to learn to speak some particular moral language that allows them to think about the meaning of their lives and enables them to reflect on what vision of the good they will seek to realize in their lives.

As educators it is our task to represent both kinds of moral languages in our students' education, and it is our duty to do so while respecting the diversity of our students' orientations.

Why speak about moral languages? Talking about different viewpoints as languages allows us to focus on some of the things that make them different besides the fact that they assert different claims. Languages differ in that they have different vocabularies, different patterns of reasoning, and different standards of appraisal. Speaking of moral viewpoints as languages allows us to notice how much of what we believe is determined by how we talk. It also allows us to notice how much of an adequate moral education is a matter of learning how to talk in certain ways. To put the matter in a more esoteric vocabulary, a significant part of moral learning is the achievement of dialogical competence in moral languages.

Consider an illustration. Suppose one is interested in teaching students to appraise a sport. Let's take tennis. Students will need such concepts as "serve," "volley," "backhand," "service line," and "ace." They will need to be able to construct such sentences as "The depth of her approach shots is the reason why her net game is so successful." People who learn to say things like this are also learning how to *see* the game. Concepts are perceptual categories. Those who lack the concept of serve and volley can observe ball swatting and net rushing, but cannot observe a tactic in a game. They are also learning the standards of appraisal that pertain to the game. They are learning how to think about strategy and how to judge the aesthetics of the sport.

Thinking of moral learning as the achievement of dialogical competence means that educators need to develop an ear for moral dialects. Suppose Johnnie feels that he must fight anyone who insults him or his family. We need to be able to listen to Johnnie talk about this carefully enough to decide whether Johnnie has learned to speak a moral language in which honor has a significant place. And we need to understand why Johnnie sees fighting as a way of restoring his honor or that of his family. If we can enter Johnnie's moral outlook, we may help Johnnie to see that people who insult him dishonor themselves more than him, or that there is no sensible connection between hurting someone else and restoring one's honor, or that thinking of such matters in terms of honor is not a productive way of thinking. If we cannot enter into Johnnie's speech, we are likely to see his conduct as merely some form of social maladjustment and to see him as the object of therapy. We will then deal with Johnnie in a way that leaves his pattern of moral reasoning untouched and in place. But we can only engage Johnnie where he lives if we have developed an ear for moral speech.

We also need to think of what goes on in schools as occasions where moral dialogue can or does occur and where its characteristics can be noticed and reflected on.

Finally, if we think of moral education as involving an attempt to help students to achieve dialogical competence in moral language, we need to learn to stop talking the language of "values." Consider the following list of moral concepts: "honor," "redemption," "autonomy," "sacrifice," "character," "justice," "authenticity," "utility." These are concepts that have their linguistic homes in different moral outlooks. They are a rich resource for characterizing moral phenomena. When we reduce them all to so many "values," we impoverish moral speech. We are then only able to say that children should have values and to hope they will have good ones. But we cannot talk about them in any sophisticated way. When educators learn to talk the language of values, they make themselves morally deaf. A language for the description of moral phenomena in which the main noun is "value" is about as useful for ethics as a language in which the only noun was "stuff" would be for physics.

PUBLIC SPEECH AND MORAL BILINGUALISM

Children need to achieve competence in two types of moral language. The first—let us call it "primary moral language"—is language that will help form self-identity, help form attachments to members of a like-minded community of moral speech, help people to form and articulate some sense of the point of their lives, and help them to form and articulate some ways of thinking about what kinds of things are worthwhile. Primary languages live in our several heritages: our religions, our philosophies, our histories, and our ethnic backgrounds.

The second kind of moral language—let us call it "liberal-democratic speech," or "public speech"—is the common moral language. It is a kind of moral pidgin that we use to talk to each other about common concerns, despite the fact that we may deeply disagree about much that is central to our lives.

Public speech is a moral language that developed partly as a response to diversity in primary moral languages. Consider that after the Protestant Reformation, European societies faced a dilemma as to the moral basis of the state. It had been taken for granted that civil order and civic virtue were rooted in *the true faith*. If there is only one candidate for the true faith, such convictions are not overly disruptive of the civil peace. However, when there are two or more, civil peace is in doubt. People who dissent from the official religion will perceive the civil order as illegitimate. Moreover, they will experience conflict between their religious convictions and the demands made on them by the state. Conversely, from the perspective of those whose religion dominates, the loyalty of dissenters is always in question. When the civil order is rooted in religion, there is little difference between heresy and treason.

Under such circumstances there can be no civil peace. People find themselves divided by competing primary moral languages and lacking in ways to achieve reasoned agreements about civic matters with those who disagree. Thus they must either dominate or be dominated.

What is required to resolve this dilemma is a shared moral language. The task is to construct a way of talking that allows people to argue productively with each other and settle civic matters peacefully, and that all can speak conscientiously without disavowing their primary moral languages.

The enterprise of constructing a public language can be described as the development of a view of what can count as public reasons. There must be an overlapping consensus (Rawls, 1985). A language of overlapping consensus is characterized by a set of considerations that all agree to count as relevant considerations in public debates.

What features will characterize an overlapping consensus? I would propose the following as a partial list.

1. Tolerance of diversity and freedom of conscience
2. Equality of rights and interests
3. Participation and consent as legitimating factors in decision making
4. Respect for law
5. Fair procedures for resolving disputes

These can be given a common argument. Each is a moral precept whose justification consists in the fact that it is unlikely that any speaker of any primary language in a society with significant diversity in primary languages would be willing to join in a commitment to a common language unless it contained a provision of this sort. These provisions ensure that the diverse views and interests of each group will be treated with respect and given fair consideration. They prevent the domination of the speakers of one moral language by others.

For example, people would refuse to enter into an overlapping consensus unless it was assured that the power of the state would not be used to make some primary language mandatory for all citizens. People are not likely to agree to arrangements that may become an instrument for the oppression of those convictions that they hold most dear. Likewise, they are unlikely to join in an arrangement in which their interests, wants, and needs are treated as inherently less important than those of others. Nor will they agree to an arrangement whereby their political rights are less than those of others. Thus these kinds of moral conceptions state the minimal standards for a civil morality that people with diverse convictions are likely to agree to.

These conceptions provide a framework for civic debate and public criticism. Anyone who wishes to advance a public stance about some matter can be required to show that the position meets the standards required by this set of notions. Thus they will have to show that their position equally respects the various parties whose interests are affected by it, that each group has had a suitable opportunity to participate in deliberating about the matter, and the like. Proposals that turn out to advance the interests of some groups against others will be rejected. Thus the kinds of moral commitments that I have suggested are likely to be a part of an overlapping consensus that functions as a framework for public argument.

This view sees the civic arena as a kind of moral community, but as one with limited purposes and scope. It provides for a sphere of social cooperation where decisions about civic matters can be made for mutually acceptable moral reasons. But it also assumes that participants in this moral community can come to it without being required to abandon their primary moral languages. Thus the moral precepts that constitute the public moral language constitute a thin morality and a thin moral community. People will continue to understand both the ends they will pursue in their lives and the meanings of their lives according to their diverse primary moral languages.

PRIMARY MORAL SPEECH AND PUBLIC SPEECH: THEIR CONNECTION

Thus adequately morally educated individuals must be morally bilingual. They need to be competent in a primary moral language and in public speech. There is, however, more to be said. Human beings have a need for wholeness and coherence that might be thought to be frustrated by this moral bilingualism. If moral bilingualism is not to result in moral schizophrenia, then there must be connections between primary moral languages and liberal discourse such that people do not end up experiencing their moral bilingualism as a kind of schizophrenia.

Primary moral languages and liberal discourse are connected in a way that I shall describe as dialectical. This means that they interact in ways that diminish their mutual incoherence. People have to construct for themselves, within the structure of their primary moral language, an interpretation of the meaning of the public language such that they can give themselves reasons, in their primary moral language, for speaking the public moral language in public contexts. Thus a liberal democratic society is likely to develop various interpretations of the public language, each shaded so as to render it coherent with different primary languages. Moreover, the moral standards of the public moral language are likely to cause people to reinterpret their primary moral languages so that they are rendered consistent with the standards of the public language. In short, the interaction between the public languages and the various primary moral languages is likely to generate a process of mutual adaptation and adjustment.

If so, then the development and articulation of a common public language is not just a matter of discovering those moral concepts we happen to have in common. It is not a lowest-common-denominator ethic. Instead, the public moral language is a way of talking and thinking that is constructed by people who disagree about much to allow themselves to live their common lives in peace. It is created by real people and by real arguments. It is revised and maintained in the same way.

The public moral language requires educational attention. It requires forums wherein people can explore the public language and construct for themselves an understanding of it that allows them to live in the moral space delineated by their primary language while also enabling them to participate in public discourse. The young need to be initiated into this process of conversation. This, I think, is a central role of schools in moral development. It means that schools cannot settle for either liberal silence or liberal balkanization.

HERMENEUTICAL SPEECH

This vision of moral education seems incomplete in that it provides no perspective from which various primary languages can be criticized. Nor does it provide for the autonomy of children. It treats the notion that students will come into schools in possession of a primary language as an unchallengeable fact and emphasizes only a process of constructing a public language. Should we be satisfied with a view that allows children to be captives of the moral convictions of their parents and community?

One might reason that any public language that people would be willing to enter into would ensure that parents would function as the primary educators of their children. People would be unlikely to agree to a view of civic power that tolerated differences between adults but also allowed the civil authorities to dominate the moral education of children.

However, there is another side to the story. Any overlapping consensus is likely to include a demand for freedom of conscience and tolerance of diversity. The various primary moral languages in a society that has achieved such public language are likely to have undergone some transformation so that they will have constructed their own conception of the point of freedom of conscience and tolerance. If so, then they are likely to have constructed these ideas in a way that can govern the relationships between parents and children within a particular moral community. Such a society is unlikely to have very many who will interpret freedom of conscience and tolerance so as to give themselves an unencumbered right to dominate the outlook of their children. Instead, children will be seen as future citizens who, as they mature, have the right to a critical view about their own primary moral language and a right to their own views.

Then there must be something in a child's education that abets criticism of his or her own primary language. What are the sources of such criticism? One is the dialectical interaction between the primary language and the public language. However, people who disagree about important things need to do more than work out a common public language. They also need to learn from one another. The various primary moral languages in a culture are among the most important resources available to people to get a critical perspective on their own outlook. I shall call critical dialogue between various primary moral languages *hermeneutical dialogue.*

Hermeneutical dialogue has several purposes. The first is understanding. Part of the process of understanding another people is to be able to grasp how they think about their lives. The second is reciprocity. Reciprocity involves the capacity to put oneself in the other's place. The third purpose is criticism.

That hermeneutical dialogue involves criticism may not be seen as good news. People do not, as a rule, enjoy having their convictions criticized. Moreover, the suggestion that schools should provide forums where such criticism occurs might be seen not only as an invitation to much discord and contentiousness, but as intolerant. Why insist on criticism?

A primary moral language is a perspective from which people give reasons for their choices. When people give reasons for what they do, they understand themselves to be giving good reasons. Good reasons are reasons that can stand up to criticism. When we reject the idea that moral frameworks are objects of rational criticism, in effect we treat them as arbitrary expressions of will. They are merely chosen, merely happened upon, no better or no worse than any other arbitrary choice.

If primary moral languages involve criticism, to fail to treat them as objects of criticism misrepresents them. If we decline to treat primary moral languages as objects of rational appraisal, we may teach students to see them as objects of arbitrary choice, one as good as another. In short, we teach relativism.

The view that all moral perspectives are equal because they are all equally arbitrary and thus none can be shown to be better than another may seem the purest expression of tolerance, but, in fact, it is a view that is impossible to maintain. It requires us to believe that there is nothing critical to be said about moral perspectives no matter how brutal or absurd they might be. Genuine tolerance is not rooted in epistemological indifference. Tolerance is rather a set of reasons we can give ourselves as to why we should not use the power of the state to suppress our neighbor's errors. Tolerance thus precludes the state (and thereby public schools) from advancing some primary moral outlook. It does not require us to reject critical dialogue.

The second reason why criticism is important is that it is a condition of individual autonomy. The acquisition of competence in a primary moral language is essential to an adequate moral education. This is a reason why it is important for parents and communities to have a central role in the education of children, and it is a reason why schools should provide more room for expression of primary moral languages than they do now. It is not a reason to treat children as though they were lifelong cognitive captives of their parents or of their community. Children need the opportunity not only to acquire a primary language, but also to appraise it. An adequate opportunity to appraise one's primary language requires the opportunity to listen to criticism and to encounter alternative perspectives, and must involve the possibility of defection. I think it likely that many who are deeply attached to their primary languages will resist such a critical role for schools. That is understandable, but it is worth resisting. Moral pluralism is a central value of our society. It is rightly respected. But it does not require us to ghettoize our children or to regard them as irretrievably born to a particular moral outlook.

TEACHING AND AN ETHIC OF DIALOGUE

If dialogue is to occur in schools, it must be regulated by an ethic of dialogue. It will be the responsibility of the schools both to teach this dialogical ethic and to conduct moral dialogue according to its precepts. This ethic of dialogue should be seen as part of the public ethic and can be regarded as an extension of some of its concepts to include moral speech. Moral dialogue is a form of inquiry and reflection. Its central norms are those that govern the search for reasoned conclusions. Thus it is expected that participants will not lie or seek to manipulate or deceive one another. The process of dialogue must be open to all relevant evidence and lines of argument. Likewise, it must be open to all interested and competent speakers. Finally, outcomes should depend only on the open consideration of evidence and thus cannot be determined by power relationships or relations of dominance.

Educators must themselves learn and find ways to teach students and their communities the most difficult art of respectful discussion about important matters over which we disagree deeply. Moral dialogue requires a sensitive mix of passion and civility. The process of creating moral dialogues in schools needs to be open to criticism to ensure that it does not become a means whereby the views of some are imposed on others. The principal obstacle to effective moral education in schools is the chilling effect of public suspicion that any effort at moral education in schools will end up as a means whereby the views of some are forced on others. This distrust reduces schools to an unpalatable and miseducative choice between liberal silence and liberal balkanization. If trust is to be built, educators will need to learn the art of turning critics into participants. A dialogical view of moral education does not offer experts with a program. It offers an open and undominated moral conversation with room to participate for all.

This analysis has suggested that dialogical competence can be seen as having three components. There must be competence in some primary moral language. There must be competence in the public moral language. And there must be competence in hermeneutical discourse. Each component is incomplete without the others. A society that wishes to have rich sources for reflection on the ends and meaning of life but also wishes to have civil peace and a just scheme of cooperation between people who speak different primary languages must have robust primary moral languages and an adequate public language. Because these are dialectically connected, they cannot be understood independently of one another. Having achieved a public language, we will find that we have also achieved a level of moral understanding that leads us to see the importance of open, undominated, and critical dialogue between different primary moral languages.

We need a broad view of what counts as dialogue. A good moral education does not consist in placing students with differing moral outlooks in a room and letting them have at it. Whereas it is appropriate for schools to encourage students to discuss their views and their differences in a reasoned manner, children and adolescents are not likely to be the most sophisticated representatives of their own moral traditions. Thus students must study, discuss, and appraise texts (not textbooks!) that give authentic expression to various moral outlooks. Some of this can be done through an effective use of literature. Consider that the consequences of an ethic of honor is a theme of *Romeo and Juliet* and is discussed in *Huckleberry Finn*. Johnnie, our combative student mentioned earlier in the chapter, might get some insight into both literature and his own behavior if he could see himself as acting like the Montagues and Capulets.

We also need to do the kinds of things that those who urge a multicultural approach have recommended. That is, we need to read the works and the history of people who experience the world from diverse viewpoints. For similar reasons we will have to take religion more seriously as a topic of study, and this means both that we will have to be more accepting of students' expressions of their own spirituality in schools and that we will have to study texts that affirm religious sentiment. Finally, it would not hurt students to read some philosophy.

Because one purpose of dialogue is to help students enter into the public moral language, we must give significant place to texts that express this. Students need to discuss texts such as the Constitution and the Bill of Rights, the Declaration of Independence, and the Federalist papers. It also means that we need to exhibit these texts for what they are, as milestones in a search for unity in diversity. We need to exhibit them as the product of debate and compromise and imperfect realizations of an evolving ideal.

Much of the material for a moral education emphasizing dialogue is already in the curriculum. But it needs to be sifted and appropriated so as to exploit its potential for moral dialogue. And we will also need to do the work required to recover the moral potential inherent in a variety of cultural resources that we now largely ignore. Finally, we will need to master the difficult skills of productive discussion of things about which we deeply disagree. The "we" who must master these skills are the adults who occupy the schools and the adults who participate in the politics of schools as much as the children who attend them.

Unhappily, I do not think that current schools are healthy places for moral dialogue. They seem dominated more by a concern for economic productivity and careerism than by a concern to enable people to reflect on their lives and their society. Most attempts at moral education seem to me to be instances of what I earlier characterized as liberal silence. We occasionally try to teach a little of the public ethic. But we distort and trivialize even that because we disconnect it from dialogue and from its dialectical interaction with our primary moral languages. These we seek to keep outside the walls. If we are to recapture either a more robust sense of citizenship or a more robust capacity for reflection on our own lives, we need to invest more of our effort in promoting the varieties of moral dialogue.

IMPLICATIONS

This discussion has several implications for the moral role of teachers in schools and for the education of teachers.

First, let me reinforce a point that I argued in my discussion on teaching moral reasoning in Part I of this book. The central goal in teaching ethics to educational practitioners should be dialogical competence in the public moral language. It should be noted that the conception of a public moral language has been expanded to include the ethics of dialogue. Perhaps this is the most important thing we can teach in programs for aspirant teachers and administrators.

Second, it is vitally important that teachers acquire a good ear for the nuances of the varieties of moral speech in our society. If they do not, then they cannot hear what others are saying, and they cannot be the means of promoting moral dialogue in schools.

Listening is not only paying attention. It is fruitfully compared to interpreting a text. It is effectively promoted in situations where interpreting texts is the emphasis. I would insist that teachers spend some time studying literature and that this literature be decently multicultural in its composition.

Also, we need to rid ourselves of the habit of speaking a language in which all moral concepts are just so many values. "Values" speech has become a part of the professional culture of educators. It has the capacity to make its speakers simultaneously morally deaf and morally arrogant.

Finally, we need to enhance opportunities for moral dialogue in school settings. If school talk is inevitably strategic and if moral conversations in all their messy diversity are inhibited, there is little that a teacher education program can do to make things better. "Use it or lose it" is an aphorism that applies to any form of language, including moral speech.

REFERENCES

Inner-city high schools that work. (1990). *RAND Research Review, 14*(3), 5, 6, 12.

Rawls, J. (1985). Justice as fairness: Political, not metaphysical. *Philosophy & Public Affairs, 14*(4), 223–251.

Rorty, R. (1989). *Contingency, irony, and solidarity*. New York: Cambridge University Press.

13 Ethics and Teacher Professionalization

C. J. B. MACMILLAN
Florida State University

The central issue in teacher professionalization is autonomy in all its guises. Although it will not be the task of this chapter to resolve all the questions that arise in regard to teacher autonomy, it should be recognized that this is a pedal point in all that follows. To what extent can an ethical perspective infuse a profession like teaching when the profession is not in significant control of its ideals and practice? Can state- or district-imposed codes of professional conduct be anything other than bureaucratic regulations if individual teachers and the profession-at-large are not in control of their destinies? Can bureaucratic regulations become or stand in for professional ethics? These are the questions implicit in this chapter.

An essential part of any organized profession is how it encodes and enforces the ethical standards implicit in the profession's practices. The paradigm professions, medicine and law, have professional associations that control standards of preparation, service, and practice. Breach of standards by an individual practitioner can lead to loss of the right to practice. But it is not at all clear that teaching is a paradigmatic profession, and there are serious arguments about the viability of attempts to provide teachers with the kind of status and autonomy that medicine and law have achieved. (See especially Burbules & Densmore, 1991.)

It is almost definitional that a full-fledged profession is guided by a code of professional ethics (Sockett, 1990). In speaking of profession ethics, a distinction is necessary: what is the difference between professional ethics and the moral dimensions of any citizen's (or any human's) responsibilities? A member of a profession must of course be held to those characteristics of interpersonal affairs that are the responsibility of any person—honesty, for example, or fairness. In addition, however, the professional practitioner is bound by a sense of the ethical dimensions of the relations among professionals and clients, the public, the employing institution, and fellow professionals. It is beyond the scope of this chapter to examine all dimensions of these relations, but suffice it to say that professional ethics are those responsibilities whose abrogation subverts the possibility of professional practice. As such, professional ethics are derived not from the general moral code of any particular society, or even of any particular professional association, but rather from a conception of what constitutes the profession's purposes and characteristic activities or modes of action (Macmillan, 1990; see also Emmet, 1967).

It is necessary to encode and enforce professional ethics for the members of the profession. This serves two functions, as Sockett (1990) has pointed out:

> Ultimately, a code with sanctions provides the professional with two things: (1) pressure to adhere to the code as a guide to follow, not as a set of regulations to obey, and (2) confidence that competence, standards, and results can be measured because of the opportunity for the public to seek redress. (p. 239)

In the paradigmatic professions, professional associations take on this task. It should be noted that a member of one of these professions can use the association's code to insist that conditions for practice be such that the practitioner can adhere to the code. Physicians who take employment with private clinics or less typical establishments (the "Love Boat," perhaps) can insist that the conditions of practice be appropriate, and they can appeal to the profession's established code of ethics (as well as other standards) to justify these requirements.

SHOULD TEACHING BE PROFESSIONALIZED?

As mentioned above, there are serious arguments about whether trying to make teaching more like the paradigmatic professions is a worthwhile or viable program of action. Opinions range from Burbules and Densmore's (1991) outright condemnation of the program to Downie's (1990) urging that teaching become more like the paradigmatic professions.

By way of introduction, two points should be emphasized, as they have been by American defendants of professionalization (among them Shulman, 1987; Darling-Hammond, 1989; Sockett, 1990; and many of the other papers in Goodlad, Soder, and Sirotnik, 1990). The first is the dependence of professional practice (and status) upon an intellectually respectable knowledge base. The second is the presumed autonomy of the profession and its members, the freedom to make professional decisions without interference from nonprofessional persons or governmental bodies.

1. One of the central (and quasi-definitional) features of the paradigmatic professions is that practice is based on a scientific (in the case of medicine) or traditional (in the case of law) body of knowledge that is learned by professionals as the major part of their training. Few doubt that the extensive—usually university-based—training of physicians and lawyers has led to improved practice; but no one doubts, either, that the same extensive training limits access to the professions for the most part to those who have great financial and intellectual resources. The question is whether teaching has an identifiable knowledge base that justifies professional status and privileges, including autonomy. More on this issue later.

2. A central characteristic of the paradigmatic professions is their autonomy. Professional autonomy has two aspects: On the one hand, there are some decisions that are left to members of the profession-at-large to make without veto power or interference by nonprofessional (lay) sources; on the other hand, individual practitioners are given considerable freedom to determine appropriate treatment for their clients. These are related, of course, but the autonomy of the profession-at-large sets up a range of discussion, defense, and discipline that is insulated from professional/lay conflict; the profession-at-large reserves for itself matters that it views as peculiarly requiring professional expertise for determination. Individual practitioners are given the right to make decisions within the realm of professional competence, subject to professional discipline. There are no "lone professionals" whose practice is independent of possible review, but that review is reserved for the profession-at-large.

Most arguments about the professionalization of teaching take place in a context where the purpose of the discussion is to find ways of improving public schools. Downie (1990) is possibly an exception: He directs his "philosophical concern" to the "evaluative question of what enables professions to perform a unique and socially valuable function, distinct from business or commerce" (p. 147).

Downie establishes six "ideal characteristics" in his evaluative analysis of the ideal of a profession. The professional (1) "has skills or expertise which proceed from a broad knowledge base"; (2) "provides a service to clients by means of a special relationship . . . authorised by an institutional body and legitimised by public esteem"; (3) "has the social function of speaking out on broad matters of public policy and justice"; (4) "must be independent of the influence of the state or of commerce"; and (5) "must be educated as distinct from merely trained in a narrow sense." (6) Finally, "Insofar as criteria 1–5 are satisfied a profession is morally and legally legitimate" (pp. 154–155).

Downie (1990) does not argue that these exactly fit teaching, but rather presents them as ideals to which teaching should aspire; of particular importance is the threat to the autonomy of the teaching profession.

> The Government [of Great Britain] has attempted to introduce market forces, and in particular, competition into the professions. Now in a market there are two sorts of competition; merchants compete with other merchants, and merchants compete with customers. No doubt the Government intends to introduce only the first sort of competition into the professions with the aim of improving the service to the customers. But it is arguable that the first sort of competition will lead to the second, for it will lead both professionals and clients to "shop around" for the best deal, and the search for the "best deal" by professionals and clients will destroy both the professional relationship and the independence of the professions. (p. 158)

Downie seems not to doubt that achieving or approaching these ideals would improve both the status of professional teachers and the delivery of education in schools.

Burbules and Densmore (1991), on the other hand, have severe doubts that "professionalizing" teaching—by whatever criteria—is a positive move when the task is to improve the education of all children. "In the present instance," they state, the ideal of a teaching profession

> leads to a self-defeating political strategy by alienating the very groups whose support is essential for school reform, by making it more likely that teachers can be "bought off" with short-term concessions, by raising expectations among the public that will give impetus to other reforms which teachers will not like, and by importing assumptions and objectives that conflict with the values of democratic public schooling. (p. 59)

Professionalization, they argue, is a "package deal,"

> and if teachers were to become fully professional in the traditional sense of the term, it would have detrimental effects on their students, the parents of their students, other local community interests, and particularly the many current teachers who could not remain in this newly constituted field. (p. 59)

For the topic of professional ethics, the importance of this argument lies in another question: is an autonomous profession, governed by an independent professional association, a necessity for the development and enforcement of a code of ethics? More basic, perhaps, is the question of whether teaching can be autonomous, given the nature of the profession as it is currently defined and understood in the United States. I shall turn to the latter question first.

THE INSTITUTION-DEFINED PROFESSION

In the United States—and most Western nations—teaching is an institution-defined profession. So also are the other "educational" professions subsumed under the general label of "school administration." This simple fact has enormous implications for the development and enforcement of a code of professional ethics.

Ordinary intuitions give a clue as to what it means to say that teaching is an institutionally defined profession. Imagine an airplane conversation between seatmates who have not met before; etiquette in such occasions does not permit asking names, at least until the flight is almost over: the exchange of personal information is limited to locations (Where do you live?) and occupations (What do you do for a living?). "I'm a doctor," reports your seatmate. "Where do you practice?" is the next question. The doctor's answer might range across a wide number of possibilities: a hospital, a private practice in a small town, an industry or factory, the "Love Boat," or even—and this is important—"I'm not in practice at the moment."

No answer the doctor gives will change the fact that he is a doctor by profession.

Now imagine: "I'm a teacher." "Where do you teach?" If the answer to that question does not indicate or name a school or an educational institution of some sort, doubt is cast upon the teacher's claim to the status of teacher; a teacher who is not employed by one of a relevant range of institutions (which includes private schools, public schools, universities, and so forth) doesn't fit our expectations. If a person claims to be a teacher, the implication is that that person is working as a teacher in a school. The teller in a bank who has a teacher's training and certificate is not (now) a teacher; nor is the businessman with a teacher's credentials. Too much should not be made of this, perhaps, but it indicates the point about teachers' professional status: It depends more on actual employment than on training and certification.

The doctor's status, on the other hand, is a reflection of just those things—training and certification by established authorities.

The converse of this point is that we live under a "warm-body" theory of teachers' status: Employment as a teacher in a recognized institution determines one's status as a teacher; if a school were to hire someone with no formal credentials to fill a position as teacher, that person is still—and thereby—entitled to professional status. "I dub you teacher," says the administrator faced with a shortage of certified personnel, and it is done. (Imagine a hospital, law office, or engineering firm run on similar principles: "I dub you brain surgeon.")

This feature of the teaching profession raises an important question: Does teaching really depend on a recognizable knowledge base, on special training that is necessary for engaging in the profession's characteristic activities, on the type of esoteric learning that justifies the autonomy and monopoly of the paradigm professions? I can do no more than raise this issue here and point to the ongoing debate. (See, e.g., Bull, 1990; Sockett, 1987, 1990; Macmillan, 1988; and Pratte, 1988.)

But other evidence supports the intuition that teaching is an institution-defined profession; consider the title of that otherwise excellent collection of papers, *The Moral Dimensions of Teaching* (Goodlad, Soder, & Sirotnik, 1990). Only one chapter—Fenstermacher's "Some Moral Considerations of Teaching as a Profession"—sees moral dimensions in teaching as an activity or practice that might take place outside the context of the institution of schooling, and even Fenstermacher is most concerned about the moral problems facing school teachers:

> What makes teaching a moral endeavor is that it is, quite centrally, human action undertaken in regard to other human beings. Thus, matters of what is fair, right, just, and virtuous are always present. Whenever a teacher asks a student to share something with another student, decides between combatants in a schoolyard dispute, sets procedures for who will go first, second, third, and so on, or discusses the welfare of a student with another teacher, moral considerations are present. The teacher's conduct, at all times and in all ways, is a moral matter. (Fenstermacher, 1990, p. 133)

Although many moral and ethical problems arise from the peculiar relationship between those who teach (including, for example, parents and friends) and those who learn from teachers, the central concerns in the professional literature arise from the fact that teachers are functionaries in schools, people whose status derives not from their training or their typical activities as professionals but rather from their place in the employing institution. The problems of professionalization of teaching—including the development and enforcement of codes of professional ethics—arise from the institution and not directly from noninstitutional crises of the sort that arise in paradigmatic professional practice.

Bruce Kimball (1988) has shown the import of being an institution-defined profession, given the nature of school control in the United States. "There is scarcely a 'professional' decision," he states, "that a teacher makes that the local politician or used-car salesman on the school board is not legally empowered to reverse" (p. 8). He continues:

> The "professional" judgment of teachers and school administrators in the United States is directly subject to that of publicly elected officials. Their professional expertise is therefore subject to majoritarian will, and the struc-

> tural analysis that is applied to other professions suggests that any endeavor to "professionalize teachers" by raising standards or inducements or the level of training is therefore doomed to failure. The endeavor is doomed by the fact that teachers cannot control decisions relating to the expertise upon which their guild is founded. (Kimball, 1988, p. 9)

Faced with this situation, most commentators on the control of schools argue for some form of "democratic interaction" between professionals and public, either through an elected school board or through participatory arrangements in individual schools. (See, e.g., Gutmann, 1987; Strike, 1989; Bull, 1990; Sockett, 1990; Burbules & Densmore, 1991; Fenstermacher, 1990.) Practically no one explicitly argues that teachers or professional educators should be granted full autonomy in the running of schools, although the Carnegie Report's (1986) emphasis on collegial control moves in this direction.

But Kimball (1988) shows the problem with all public control of schools:

> It should be clear that a price is paid for majoritarian and political control of teachers' every decision. If local Boards of Health could overrule the diagnoses of doctors or if Boards of Aldermen could reverse the rulings of judges or pass bills of attainder, then medical and legal professionals would be in the same position as teachers and school administrators, and medical diagnoses and criminal trials would be hopelessly politicized, as are the schools. (p. 9)

Kimball's conclusion is clear: Attempts to raise the professional status of teaching will not or cannot succeed as long as teachers do not have the authority to make and carry out decisions within their realm of expertise.

But the type of control evident in the United States is not the only problem that stands in the way of professionalization. The mere fact of institutional definition of the profession puts a kibosh on the possibility of autonomy. Imagine a school that was controlled not by a school board but by a group of teachers; even here, the teachers would not have the support and comfort of the profession in defining and evaluating the conditions for practice; their status, privileges, and autonomy would still come from the employing institution rather than from their own training and expertise. And the legitimacy of that school itself would depend upon state approval of some sort.

CERTIFICATION, THE STATE, AND SANCTIONS

In the United States, teacher licensure (or certification) is a state function; that is, it is the state government rather than the profession itself that determines who is allowed to teach in public (and often in private) schools. The professional associations of the paradigmatic professions, on the other hand, are the bodies that determine what qualifications are required for individuals to practice medicine or law.

The converse of this is that the determination of who will not be allowed to teach because of breaches of professional codes of ethics is not a function of the professional organizations. A teachers' union or professional organization might establish a code of ethics—as has the National Education Association (NEA)—and even enforce it by denying membership to those who have broken its rules, but that enforcement would be without teeth, insofar as membership in the organization is not a requirement for employment in most states. A teacher who is fired because of unethical conduct might move to another district—or state—and find another teaching position. Hence, codes of professional ethics as established by educational professional associations in the United States are codes without severe sanctions. Only insofar as the states themselves keep and exchange records on disqualified teachers are there teeth in professional codes of ethics. And the states themselves differ considerably in their willingness to do this.

The point of having teeth in codes of professional ethics is rather more subtle than might be thought; it is, as Sockett (1990) points out, a matter of establishing trust in the profession. "Sanctions," he states, "protect the weak. The willingness to put oneself under a sanctions system is, in part, to offer trust" (p. 238). By establishing and living by a sanctioned code of ethics, members of a profession protect themselves and their professional realm of autonomy by assuring the public that all members must live up to the profession's ideals.

One thing should be clear: A code of ethics does not make individual professionals ethical. The development of a sense of ethical propriety is something that should be part of professional education, but learning the profession's code will not guarantee ethical conduct. That is most likely a matter of personal commitment to, and understanding of, the profession's ideals as exemplified in standards of practice. The code itself stands as a warrant to the public and to other professionals that the ideals and standards are taken seriously in a formal way.

But how can a profession establish and enforce codes of ethics in the face of the constraints of institutional definition and state control? Recognizing that the context of the discussion of professional ethics is "a tension between public and professional control," Sockett (1990) proposes that a partnership of the public and the professional be the means by which the tension is resolved and professional accountability of a new sort is developed. Local codes could be "built by schools in discussion with their constituencies" in order to establish the trust between public and profession that such codes help to ensure (pp. 241–242).

> There will be no professional accountability until the pattern is much more localized and professionals display the standards to which they are committed; until professionals, aware of their own problems but thoroughly confident of their competence, can invite the individual and the public to judge a teacher and call that teacher to account in terms of these standards; until there is a developed partnership between public and professional control. (p. 243)

But Sockett quotes Corwin (1965): " . . . professional status is most effectively guaranteed when professional codes are safeguarded by law but enforced by their own members" (1990, p. 243). It is hard to see how a general code of ethics can be developed from local codes; indeed, as I have argued elsewhere, there is something wrong with seeing the content of a professional code of ethics for teachers as a function of any existing professional or political community rather than as a statement derived from the ideals and purposes of the activities of teachers (Macmillan, 1990).

The enforcement of a code, however, must be both local and more general, in that if teachers found unethical at local schools can simply move to others, the code might be otiose.

THE FLORIDA EXPERIMENT

The state of Florida has established a procedure for enforcing a code of ethics for the "educational profession" that seems to solve this problem. By state law, two bodies have been established; the first, the Education Standards Commission, is charged with recommending a code of ethics and "principles of professional conduct" that have the force of law to the State Board of Education (which consists of the governor and the elected cabinet); the second, the Education Practices Commission, enforces the principles of professional conduct as a low-level court. The latter has the power to discipline teachers who infringe the principles by fine, reprimand, and suspension or revocation of teaching certificates.

The code of ethics and the principles of professional conduct developed by the Education Standards Commission has a striking resemblance to the NEA code of ethics; both codes concern themselves with relations of teachers with students, with the public, and with other members of the profession. They differ primarily in details of wording rather than of content. This code has been the basis of the actions of the Education Practices Commission since 1982.

Prior to the establishment of the Education Practices Commission (EPC) in 1980, the State Board of Education served as the highest in-house disciplinary board; only this body was entitled to pass judgment on teachers and other educational personnel. With its establishment, matters changed:

> The EPC was created as an autonomous quasi-judicial agency attached administratively to the Department of Education (DOE). The Commission is the final agency in matters pertaining to disciplinary action against holders of Florida teaching certificates and is composed of five teachers, five administrators, and three lay people, two of whom are district school board members. (Florida Education Practices Commission, 1987–88)

Members of the EPC are appointed by the State Board of Education upon nomination by the Commissioner of Education (who is elected in statewide elections) and approval by the Florida State Senate. They employ an executive director who handles the bureaucratic side of code enforcement.

> The Commission operates like a circuit court and is not responsible for investigations and prosecutions. These functions are the responsibility of the Commissioner of Education through the staff of Professional Practices Services which functions somewhat like the State Attorney's Office. The EPC is the final agency to hear certificate disciplinary cases and to render decisions in regard to penalty. . . . The decisions of the Commission are appealable to the First District Court of Appeals. (Florida Education Practices Commission, 1988)

The effects of this organization on the policing of the profession are considerable. In 1987–88, for example, 165 cases were filed before the EPC. These resulted in 68 revocations of certificates (50 permanent, the remainder for periods of 1 to 10 years); 23 suspensions of certificates for periods up to 3 years; 6 denials of certificates (usually for fraudulent applications); 6 grantings of certificates after bureaucratic denials; and 62 other penalties, including reprimands, fines, probations and limitations on a teacher's scope of practice. Some infractions received more than one penalty, so the figures do not quite tally (Florida Education Practices Commission, 1987–88, p. 8).

Because the EPC is not limited in its concerns to matters encoded in the Principles of Professional Conduct adopted by the State Board of Education, many of these cases involve other ways in which professional teachers and administrators can go astray: incompetency, breach of contract, and criminal conduct not involving school-related matters.

How is this mechanism to be assessed as a way of establishing and enforcing a professional code of ethics? It has the advantage of being statewide; the penalties assessed by the EPC cannot be ignored by any districts in the state as they hire teachers. Reciprocal relations with other states make it unlikely that a penalized teacher will easily find employment elsewhere in public school systems. It should be noted, however, that private schools in Florida are not required to hire certified teachers, so the EPC's actions are felt not by the profession as a whole but only by those who are employed by the public school system.

In all but one of Florida's sixty-seven districts, teachers are represented by either the American Federation of Teachers or the NEA. But the professional organizations are not officially involved in the EPC, although active members of both associations have been appointed to the Commission. The code and principles of conduct are not official doctrines of either organization.

Yet the EPC prides itself on its professional makeup and on being the voice of the profession. The flyer describing the EPC to the public cites these "advantages":

1. Unlike most states, the education profession in Florida truly sits in judgment of its peers through the EPC.
2. The EPC removes politics from the arena of decision making.
3. The EPC has the flexibility to render judgments and assess penalties compatible with the severity of the infraction.
4. The profession is able to govern the behavior of its practitioners through the setting of standards (Education Standards Commission) and enforcing adherence to them (Education Practices Commission).
5. The profession's public image is raised by demonstrating its ability to set rigid standards and to enforce them. (Florida Education Practices Commission, 1988)

To the extent that the commissions have majorities of professional teachers and administrators, these claims ring true; but if they are viewed as creatures of the state legislature (as they must be) rather than of a profession attempting to assert its own accountability, it could be that they reflect not trust in teachers but mistrust of the profession as a whole.

For the reassurance of the public, even a professionally staffed state enforcement agency like Florida's does not have the power of a strongly enforced code established by the profession itself, for the appearance of professional concern is central to that function of the code. In such cases it is the state's concern and lack of trust of the profession that is the message, not the profession's self-concern.

Insofar as the code of ethics and principles of professional conduct are known by, and consciously adopted by, individual teachers and professional organizations, the Florida system can serve as a model; but there is considerable doubt that this sort of commitment (or even knowledge) is present. To the extent that this is so, the EPC remains a mere bureaucratic creature of the state — a comfort, perhaps, to the public, but not a reassurance to the profession.

CONCLUSION

In this chapter I have tried to summarize the major issues involved in the professionalization of teaching, particularly with regard to professional ethics. Underlying my discussion is a belief that without considerable autonomy, teachers will continue to be hindered, individually and collectively, from developing the skills and ethical commitments that are essential to high-quality professional practice. The manner in which American schools are currently organized does not bode well for the provision of the sort of autonomy that could lead to this end; but there is some hope in recent developments that require teachers to take more responsibility for the operation of schools, for only as autonomy is required of teachers will they be able to grasp it.

REFERENCES

Bull, B. (1990). The limits of teacher professionalization. In J. I. Goodlad, R. Soder, & K. A. Sirotnik (Eds.), *The moral dimensions of teaching* (pp. 87–129). San Francisco: Jossey-Bass.

Burbules, N. C., & Densmore, K. (1991). The limits of making teaching a profession. *Educational Policy*, *5*, 44–63.

Carnegie Task Force on Teaching as a Profession. (1986). *A nation prepared*. New York: Carnegie Forum on Education and the Economy.

Corwin, R. G. (1965). Teachers as professional employees: Role conflicts in the public schools. In R. G. Corwin (Ed.), *A sociology of education* (pp. 217–264). New York: Appleton-Century-Crofts.

Darling-Hammond, L. (1989). Accountability for professional practice. *Teachers College Record*, *91*, 59–80.

Downie, R. S. (1990). Professions and professionalism. *Journal of Philosophy of Education*, *24*, 147–159.

Emmet, D. (1967). *Rules, roles and relationships.* New York: St. Martin's Press.
Fenstermacher, G. (1990). Some moral considerations of teaching as a profession. In J. I. Goodlad, R. Soder, & K. A. Sirotnik (Eds.), *The moral dimensions of teaching* (pp. 130–151). San Francisco: Jossey-Bass.
Florida Education Practices Commission. (1987–88). *Annual Report, July 1, 1987 through June 30, 1988.* Tallahassee: The Education Practices Commission.
Florida Education Practices Commission. (1988). *Education Practices Commission: Professionalism through integrity.* (Pamphlet/Flyer). Tallahassee: Author.
Goodlad, J. I., Soder, R., & Sirotnik, K. A. (Eds.). (1990). *The moral dimensions of teaching.* San Francisco: Jossey-Bass.
Gutmann, A. (1987). *Democratic education.* Princeton, NJ: Princeton University Press.
Kimball, B. A. (1988). The problem of teachers' authority in light of the structural analysis of professions. *Educational Theory, 38,* 1–9.
Macmillan, C. J. B. (1988, November). *The very idea of a knowledge base for teaching.* Paper presented at the annual meeting of the American Educational Studies Association, Toronto.
Macmillan, C. J. B. (1990, April). *Professional ethics for teachers: A "transcendental" view.* Paper presented at the annual meeting of the American Educational Research Association, Boston.
Pratte, R. (1988, November). *The knowledge base for teaching: A response to Macmillan.* Paper presented at the annual meeting of the American Educational Studies Association, Toronto.
Shulman, L. (1987). Knowledge and teaching: Foundations of the new reform. *Harvard Educational Review, 57,* 1–22.
Sockett, H. (1987). Has Shulman got the strategy right? *Harvard Educational Review, 57,* 208–219.
Sockett, H. (1990). Accountability, trust, and ethical codes of practice. In J. I. Goodlad, R. Soder, & K. A. Sirotnik (Eds.), *The moral dimensions of teaching* (pp. 224–250). San Francisco: Jossey-Bass.
Strike, K. (1989). The ethics of educational evaluation. In J. Millman & L. Darling-Hammond (Eds.), *The new handbook of teacher evaluation: Assessing elementary and secondary school teachers.* Newbury Park, CA: Sage.

14 The Legal Context of Professional Ethics

Values, Standards, and Justice in Judging Teacher Conduct

JAMES GROSS
Cornell University

The greatest evil in the world is the waste of a human life. Each human being is an unprecedented wonder, with a unique personal potential and gift for the world, possibly never before seen on the earth. Yet, in the words of James Joyce's hero, "When the soul of man is born into this country there are nets flung at it to hold it back from flight" (Campbell, 1970). How sinful and unfair if educators, the ones supposed to help and inspire humans to "take flight" by opening minds, developing confidence, and freeing the wings of creativity, are instead among the many wielders of those nets. These are at root questions of applied ethics—matters of right and wrong actions, just and unjust purposes, moral obligations as well as human rights and duties.

The central objective of ethics is to determine what is good, or what is right, or what one ought to do. Unfortunately, discussions of moral and ethical principles are often dismissed as "idealistic," that is, unrealistic and impractical guides to making one's way in the "real world." A recent report on teaching ethics at a nationally known business school concluded, for example, that such courses would make little difference in the way people behaved:

> As long as you have a business culture that puts people in impossible situations—"your division has to grow 7 percent in the next year or else we're going to be No. 2 in the field and if we are, you're going to be job-hunting"—you're going to have people shipping inferior goods, juggling the books, bribing when they have to, trampling workers beneath them and generally conducting themselves in the time-honored tradition: Results and only results count. (Wilkes, 1989)

The pressure for quick results through rapid educational reform is also intense, particularly because the current national concern about the effectiveness of our schools has become a highly publicized political issue. Much of the blame for the problems with education has been put on teachers. The popular press, for example, repeats the themes of why teachers fail and describes in detail deteriorating discipline and declining scores on standardized tests, as well as the tenure laws that make it increasingly difficult and costly to dismiss incompetent or otherwise unsatisfactory teachers. It is precisely at such times that the greatest vigilance is needed to protect people's lives and careers against any rush to action based on unstated values and presumptions rather than fact. Fairness as well as effectiveness require that values be made explicit and that fact rather than assumption be the basis for assessing blame for deficiencies in education and for formulating solutions.

My recent study of "conduct unbecoming a teacher" and "incompetence" cases decided pursuant to the New York State Education Law (Gross, 1988) raised interesting and important questions of nationwide applicability concerning the nature of teaching, the conception of teachers as role models, the standards of conduct and performance to which teachers are held, the objectives and purpose of education, what constitutes "good teaching," the measurement of good teaching, and the obligation to provide remedial assistance to teachers who need to correct teaching deficiencies and improve. The study demonstrated, however, that decision makers' conceptions of the way things ought to be and beliefs about the way things presumably are—unchecked and unverified by empirical evidence about the way things actually are—often lead to unjust decisions about teachers' conduct and performance and to outcomes that are detrimental to teaching and learning. Injustice and inefficiency will persist as long as policy makers and decision makers operate without sufficient evidence.

JUSTICE AS ADJUDICATION OF RIGHTS AND OBLIGATIONS

The term *justice* is used here only in the juridical sense, that is, adjudicating rights and obligations in conformity with, and as determined by, laws or administrative or contractual rules and imposing punishments for wrongful violations of such regulations. Some rules are necessary to maintain a reasonably stable and harmonious social order, to resolve conflicts, to restrain certain actions and encourage others, and to let people know what is expected of them and the consequences of noncompliance. People obey rules for various reasons, some because of a positive sense of duty, others because they have been well-trained in obedience and find it more expedient or profitable to go along, fear the consequences of disobedience, or want to avoid the shame of public embarrassment or disgrace.

In part because the consequences of injustice are often so severe, no one ought to be punished for any wrongdoing unless responsible for it. For punishment to be just (and, by implication, for decisions to be just) what was done must be unlawful (or in some other way a violation or misdeed) and, before a person may be held responsible for that wrongdoing, a link comprised of substantial persuasive evidence (proof) must be made between the wrong done and the person being punished:

> Adverse decisions against an individual should not be based on anything except what are indeed facts, and facts in the public domain, not predictions which may yet prove false, or truths locked in somebody's breast, which cannot be surely known. (Lucas, 1989, p. 64)

These requirements, among others, are interposed between the allegation of wrongdoing and the imposition of punishment to reduce the chance that undeserved punishment will be inflicted on the innocent.

Punishments justly imposed are more than deterrents; they communicate condemnation and disapproval to offenders, vindication to victims—as well as the message that society is determined to uphold their rights—and to bystanders, a clear statement of what the society's values are and of a determination to uphold them. A false conviction, however, is a lie. The injustice of a penalty imposed on someone for something they did not do, or could not reasonably have known to be wrong, or over which they had no control, is doubly unjust and particularly obnoxious—not only because the outcome was undeserved but also because insult is added to injury. Granted, because there will be some too hardened to care, punishment, particularly of teachers, means public disgrace—for many, the worst part of the punishment and sanction enough (Lucas, 1989).

In the end, the final cause of law and its administration is the welfare of society. But laws are created by human beings to regulate human conduct. They embody the values of the people who made them—that is, their conceptions of the way things ought to be—and in their implementation they are filtered through the values of judges or other decision makers. As former Supreme Court Justice Benjamin Cardozo said, "Ethical considerations can no more be excluded from the administration of justice which is the end and purpose of all civil laws than one can exclude the vital air from his room and live" (Cardozo, 1921, p. 66). The search for excellence and justice in teaching is a search for ethics.

CONDUCT UNBECOMING A TEACHER

Certainly the phrase *conduct unbecoming a teacher* does not define itself, but some forms of alleged misconduct can be classified in the category of "conduct unbecoming." My study of panel decisions involved, in the main, the following alleged misconduct: physical abuse of students (30%); sexual activities (18%); dishonesty (16%); abusive classroom comments and related actions (6%); disrespectful relations with the administration (9%); criminal convictions for off-duty conduct (8%); fighting with other teachers (3%); bizarre behavior (3%); and other miscellaneous behavior, such as causing upset in a community. Classifications of conduct, however, are not standards of conduct, and any person subject to disciplinary penalties for misconduct has a right to know the standards by which his or her conduct will be judged (Gross, 1988).

Some of the actions engaged in by teachers in these cases, such as sexual abuse of a student or unrestrained and unwarranted attacks on another person, certainly are by their nature wrongful and punishable—whether committed by teachers or anyone else. Other conduct would be deemed wrong not because it is inherently evil but because some authority in society or at a workplace prohibited it. Because this conduct is not inherently evil, elemental fairness and procedural due process require that those subject to these prohibitions be given fair warning of prohibited conduct and be provided with a standard against which conduct can be uniformly judged by panels, commissioners of education, court justices, and administrative agencies. My study demonstrated, however, that no precise and useful standard of conduct has been developed for teachers or for the various bodies that pass judgment on their conduct.

Since a "judge's power of interpretation is in inverse proportion to the clarity and precision of the law" (Perelman, 1967, p. 29), the imprecision of the statutory phrase "conduct unbecoming a teacher" maximizes the influence of personal beliefs and values on the judgments of judicial and quasi-judicial decision makers. It means that personal views of ethics, humanity, law, private property, economics, and the nature of the employment relationship—what Cardozo called "inherited instincts, traditional beliefs, acquired convictions [and] the resultant outlook on life" (Cardozo, 1921, p. 12)—not only condition the thinking of decision makers but also provide them with ultimate standards for judgment. These value judgments also pre-position a decision maker's approach to particular case situations, thereby exercising a powerful influence on the outcomes (Gross & Greenfield, 1985).

In many of the "conduct unbecoming a teacher" cases decided pursuant to New York State education law, the standards of conduct were fashioned so generally and were thus so useless that they were not standards at all. Teachers were told to comport themselves in a "professional manner," to use "appropriate classroom language" rather than "student language," to exercise better sense and taste, to adhere to the "requisite standard of professional conduct," and that certain actions were "inconsistent with conduct which can reasonably be expected of one charged with the responsibility of guiding young people." Some of the vaguest standards were applied to alleged sexual behavior where panels found teachers guilty, for example, because they did not conduct themselves "in a manner which would uphold the dignity" of the position of teacher and conform "to a generally accepted level of proper behavior" for teachers, and for failing to fulfill their obligation "not only to avoid impropriety but with equal vigor, to avoid the appearances of impropriety" (Gross, 1988).

In other sexual misconduct cases involving teachers, vagueness is compounded by the application not of an absolute standard of conduct applicable to all teachers but of a subjective-relative standard whereby the appropriateness or inappropriateness of a teacher's conduct depends on how that conduct is perceived by students and/or the "community." One panel not only made the appropriateness of a teacher's conduct dependent on the perceptions of students but also made the teacher responsible for knowing when some unmarked boundary line had been passed. In considering charges against a demonstrative teacher who put his arms around students' shoulders and often hugged them, a panel admitted that there was a "fine line between demonstrative behavior and behavior that is or can be construed as being improper or sexual." Because this distinction is so fine and so subjective it is an inadequate standard for judgment.

It is also not a standard fashioned out of the available evidence concerning effective teaching styles. Many educators contend, for example, that gently touching students in appropriate ways increases their sense of self-worth, gives them needed encouragement and support, helps them to see their teachers as real people who personally care about and like them, soothes them, eases feelings of depression, and helps them to overcome loneliness—all of which make teachers more effective and learners more receptive and involved (Sawrey & Telford, 1973). Those panels that focus on how touching could be perceived, or misperceived, are in effect endorsing a hands-off, keep-your-distance teaching style without any consideration of the effect of that style on children and their education. It certainly is Orwellian, and contrary to traditional notions of excellent teaching, for one panel to tell a teacher to avoid danger "by non-involvement with students" and another to say, "teachers must not touch the merchandise" (Gross, 1988, p. 16).

The use of vague and subjective-relative standards has seriously unjust and harmful consequences. A panelist's personal views and the perceptions of students and "community" cannot be appropriate standards for determining proper behavior for a teacher or for making judgments directly affecting teachers' careers. The use of personal views and the perceptions of others as standards is also unfair because it denies a teacher any useful guide to acceptable conduct before acting, deprives an accused teacher of any reasonable opportunity for self-defense—how can one defend against the personal views of judges and the perceptions of accusers?—and resolves doubts about guilt against the accused contrary to the traditional principle that a person is innocent until proven guilty. Moreover, the potential career-ending consequences of misinterpretations and misunderstandings, potential or real, have inhibited teachers from freely expressing affection for children, thereby diminishing both teaching and learning (Gross, 1988).

THE CONCEPT OF ROLE MODEL AS A STANDARD OF DISCIPLINE

Another imprecise and even more powerful presumption about teachers' conduct that influences the outcome of the whole range of unbecoming conduct cases is that teachers must be held to a *higher standard* of personal behavior than persons engaged in most other pursuits. The higher standard presumption is based in great part on the conception of teachers as role models.

The process that psychologists call modeling certainly exists. All of us in one way or another "are dependent on one another for what we are, what we know, and what we prize" (Cohen, 1980, p. 186) and values, attitudes, and even personality traits are influenced by contacts with others. However, the problem with using role modeling as a basis for determining the nature of conduct unbecoming a teacher, and assessing appropriate penalties, is that no one is certain exactly how models are selected, particularly outside a child's home. The determinants of whether a role model's behavior will be adopted are many and complex, including the observer's personal characteristics and past experiences, the nature of the model's activities, the situations in which the interactions between the role model and the observer take place, the anticipated satisfactions or observed benefits of the modeled action, and the perceived risks or observed social barriers and economic constraints of engaging in the model's behavior. People, including young people, "resist accepting innovations that violate their social and moral convictions" (Bandura, 1977, pp. 24–25, 47, 53–54). Parents are the first and most important models of behavior: "their influence endures and is frequently ineradicable" (Cohen, 1980, p. 186).

A teacher cannot help but exercise power in influencing student participation in the learning process but teachers exercise this power in different ways and for different reasons. Generalizations about teachers as role models presume a "Mr. Chips" teaching style, personality, and environment for teaching that simply does not apply to all, or even most, teachers and teaching situations. Different teaching styles, personalities, and situations can weaken or strengthen the possibility that a student might choose a teacher as a role model.

Some teachers, for example, function on the basis of a power to punish. Properly applied, this is not an illegitimate or illegal approach (most parents probably use it), but rather than inspiring role modeling, it weakens the teacher-student relationship. Other teachers, like parents and employers, rely on their position in the accepted hierarchy of power to influence students' behavior. Students who submit to such authority show respect for the teacher's position, not necessarily for the teacher as a person. Some teachers rely on special knowledge or expertise, in part personal and in part related to their position in the hierarchy. Students' reactions to this approach depend greatly on the extent to which they come from homes with a respect for knowledge and position. Teachers also influence students' behavior by distributing or withholding rewards, which often involves the manipulation of people and may entail consequences not likely to inspire role modeling (Tauber, 1985).

Certain teachers, however, do exercise personal power over students based "on a student's identification with the teacher" and the student's desire to be like him or her. The person, and not necessarily the position, is respected; it is in these relationships that role modeling is likely to result. But not all teaching results in a "teacher, once looked up to" but now "shown to have cheated, lied, or done something similarly damaging" being pulled "down off a pedestal" (Tauber, 1985, pp. 2–3). Once again, however, it is mainly the students' perceptions that determine not only whether role modeling takes place but also what being pulled down from a pedestal will actually mean—simply rejecting the teacher as a role model, rejecting the teacher as a teacher, or possibly, as inferred in most role model-based decisions, being dragged down themselves by compulsively emulating their role model's lying, stealing, drug dealing, alcoholism, sexual abuse, or other offenses.

The assumptions are only subjective and speculative because there is no conclusive empirical evidence to establish just how wide a sphere of influence the teacher as role model has over students. The presumption that any misconduct by a teacher is harmful to students' educational growth makes the central factual or evidentiary question simply whether the alleged misconduct occurred. If it did, a detrimental effect on students is automatically assumed, and the magnitude of the assumed effect becomes a function of how abhorrent the misconduct is to judicial and quasi-judicial decision makers. However, fairness demands that there be an evidentiary base for the use of the role model concept as a standard for discipline.

The absence of empirical evidence that students either do or do not emulate their teachers' conduct and of the process of emulation (if it does occur), combined with the fluidity of the phrase "conduct unbecoming a teacher," inevitably lead to decisions based on the idiosyncratic mores of communities, school administrators, and other decision makers, rather than on professional job-related standards of conduct (Willett, 1973; Winks, 1982). Even the most elaborate procedural safeguards in a statutory or contractual disciplinary system are useless if teachers' conduct is measured against subjective standards. It is unjust to prevent teachers from practicing their chosen profession, or to deny them the right to live their personal lives free of employer interference, merely on some deciding body's recitation of the immorality of certain actions or the invocation of the role model concept (La Borde Scholz, 1979).

THE NEXUS REQUIREMENT: ON- AND OFF-DUTY CONDUCT

The highest court in New York State has ruled that disciplinary charges against teachers are not criminal proceedings and that their primary function is not punitive but to determine the fitness of accused teachers to continue to fulfill their professional responsibilities. Only an objective analysis of the evidence, if any, of the job relatedness of a teacher's alleged misconduct does justice to that purpose; merely declaring conduct morally abhorrent and proclaiming disastrous results does not. The job-relatedness test should replace the role model notion in both on-the-job and off-duty conduct cases.

As a generalization, when a teacher's misconduct is directed at children, particularly the students he or she teaches, and particularly when it endangers their mental health and physical safety, it is most directly job related and most likely to result in serious punishment including discharge. Teachers have been discharged justifiably for such acts as reaching inside the trousers of an 11-year-old student and fondling the student's penis while class was in session and for having frequent sexual intercourse with a female student with a record of truancy and drug use. These teachers used their power to exploit the vulnerability of the young people under their control. They used young children as the means to their own self-gratification rather than respecting them as persons with rights and dignity.

The job relatedness of teachers' conduct is not always so direct, particularly in situations involving off-duty conduct. Again, the highest court in New York State has ruled that private conduct can become the lawful concern of school officials only if the alleged conduct is explicitly linked to the performance of a teacher's job responsibilities, that is, "if the conduct directly affects the performance of the professional responsibilities of the teacher or if, without contribution on the part of school officials, the conduct has become the subject of such public notoriety as significantly and reasonably to impair the capability of the particular teacher to discharge the responsibilities of his position" (Gross, 1988, pp. 33–34).

Unfortunately, the New York State Commissioner of Education subsequently ruled that a criminal conviction "created a rebuttable presumption" of conduct unbecoming a teacher that the teacher would have to rebut (Gross, 1988, p. 35). Whether a teacher's conduct is legal or illegal has no necessary relationship to the individual's fitness to teach, which is a question of fact and must be based on evidence not on some talismanic significance of a criminal conviction. In any attempt to discharge or in some other way punish a teacher for disciplinary reasons, the charging party should have to prove that the accused teacher is no longer fit to teach. In other words, there ought to be a presumption of fitness. Equating criminal conviction with unfitness to teach shifts the burden to the accused teacher to prove fitness and relieves the accuser of the responsibility to produce *evidence* of unfitness. Thus a teacher can be dismissed, or otherwise severely disciplined, on the basis of a record that contains no persuasive evidence of such fitness or unfitness.

Even under the role model theory, one could just as easily speculate that seeing models punished tends to inhibit similar behavior in others (Bandura, 1977); that seeing a convicted teacher return to the classroom "as an example of society's willingness to permit a worthy individual to redeem himself after suffering appropriate punishment for wrongdoing" would show youngsters that after they are punished for their misconduct, "they can go on then, life is not over" (Gross, 1988, pp. 38–39); and that students benefit by working with reformed teachers and counselors who had histories of drug addiction and drug-related convictions and showed students not only the consequences of such terrible mistakes but also that these mistakes could be overcome (Gross, 1988). Clearly, speculation concerning the role model effect of a teacher's misconduct can produce equally plausible but absolutely contradictory conclusions. Speculation, however, is the basis of injustice not justice.

THE NATURE OF THE EDUCATIONAL PROCESS

In determining whether the educational process has been affected by a teacher's misconduct, a deciding body must do more than analyze the misconduct; it must also determine the nature and meaning of the educational process itself. "Good" teaching is often described in education literature as educating students for emotional and intellectual independence rather than dependence and for creative rather than imitative thinking, in an honest and open "free flow of feelings and thoughts in a pleasant relaxed atmosphere" (Goodman, 1964; Muschel, 1979, pp. 6, 11).

The style and quality of teaching that actually occurs, however, is directly influenced by many considerations, including the existence of multiple and often conflicting educational objectives. For example, should schools teach students to be society makers or to adjust to and conserve the existing one; stress individualism and competition or social cooperation; stress facts or concepts; prepare the young for employment emphasizing obedience to authority or for self-determination of the meaning of their lives and life goals (Taylor, 1981)?

In general, there are two fundamentally different conceptions of teaching. Put in somewhat oversimplified terms, one, prescriptive education, involves value inculcation whereby "information and accepted truths are furnished to a theoretically passive absorbent student." Traditionally, this approach has characterized elementary and even secondary education in this country. The second conception, analytical education, is more likely to be found in higher education, where teachers and students are supposed to be active participants in a search for truth through research and inquiry that challenges all dogma "by bombarding students with all conceivable ideas, from which they may discern truth, if it exists, by and for themselves" (Goldstein, 1976, pp. 1297, 1342, 1350). Neither approach is constitutionally compelled, in that the Supreme Court has endorsed both (Gross, 1988).

Whereas prescriptive education appears to predominate over analytical education in elementary and secondary schools, the need for creativity and inventiveness requires a substantial degree of analytical education at all grade levels (Smalls, 1983). No evidence concerning the implementation of either or both of these approaches to education has been considered or even introduced in any of the conduct unbecoming cases examined in my study. Evidence concerning the nature of the education process is important because in the prescriptive model, for example, a teacher may be simply a mechanical instrument of a school board's rigidly predetermined design. Conduct at variance with that design—particularly when the design includes the inculcation of "right" values — becomes conduct contrary to the educational purposes of that district. Inherent in the analytical, or marketplace-of-ideas, approach is a much wider tolerance for diversity of teacher conduct in and out of the classroom.

A few years ago, in New York City, a panel imposed a one-semester-without-pay suspension on an inner-city high school teacher who distributed leaflets urging students to walk out (and eventually some of them did) to protest allegedly racist conditions at the school. The teacher had taught for 13 years and was commended by the panel as an "excellent and dedicated" mathematics teacher, a "role model," and a professional who spent "long hours" beyond the regular workday "giving special help to students." The teacher was a member of the high school's Committee Against Racism, which for at least a year had been meeting, handing out leaflets, and petitioning the school administration to eliminate "racist conditions" in the school building including poor physical conditions, lack of heat in the classrooms, overcrowding in classes, and too few English teachers for a school population that was 60% Hispanic and 40% African American. The panel commented only on the physical conditions of the school, which it found "abominable and revolting" (Gross, 1988, pp. 48–49).

Yet the panel ruled that this teacher had interfered with the work of the school, which the panel defined as "teaching and attending classes as scheduled and assigned," and with the rights of other students, including the right "to instruction by their own teacher," and had violated the rules and regulations that required students to attend classes. The panel asserted further that "as a teacher, he should have been setting a good example, not prompting students to break these rules" (Gross, 1988, p. 49).

What did the educational process require under those circumstances? Apparently no one in authority really cared that the school was a dump. The educational process was teaching these young Hispanics and African Americans that no one really cared about them as people. This was spirit breaking. In his own defense, the teacher argued that the purpose of education required him to teach his students to demand respect as human beings. As he put it, "The important lesson for all students and all workers is not just for students to go to school, but to teach them in school to realize that you have to stand up to injustice" (Gross, 1988, pp. 49–50).

Values have always been taught in our schools. The panel and the teacher in this case had different conceptions of what constituted ethical conduct, responsible teaching, and good citizenship. Such differences should not be resolved without evidence of the effects on students of the two approaches to teaching.

PROFESSIONAL CODES OF ETHICS: TIGHTENED DISCIPLINARY CONTROL OR PROFESSIONAL FREEDOM AND PARTICIPATION?

Many current proposals for the reform of education seek teacher "accountability" (a dangerously vague term) in part through the development and enforcement of a professional code of ethics for teachers. A code of ethics for teachers might be valuable to the extent that it could inform teachers, at least in a general way, about what conduct their profession expects of them. It could also be valuable to the extent that it demonstrated a concern for doing the "right thing" (thereby encouraging public trust and support) and marked elementary and secondary school teaching as a profession serious about regulating itself.

However, there are reasons to be cautious, or possibly even suspicious, of the calls for a code of ethics for teachers. There is a Hobbesian undertone to some code advocacy—an assumption that since nobody would act ethically except under immediate threat of punishment, there is a need for greater power to coerce them into acting responsibly. In that sense, a professional code of ethics could become merely an employer handbook of rules for teachers and thus make it easier, as one advocate put it, to obtain redress of grievances against teachers (Sockett, 1985).

On the contrary, rather than further restricting teachers, a code of professional ethics presumes a profession and professionals who, in varying degrees, exercise independent judgment in the decisions that affect them. Yet, at the same time that a code of ethics for teachers is being urged to promote professional conduct, school administrations retain control over decision making by enforcing a hierarchical authority structure and resisting "encroachment" by teachers on "management rights"—particularly when teachers seek control over the decisions that affect their work and careers. Teachers are thus saddled with professional responsibility without commensurate professional authority (Kleingartner, 1973).

Ironically, the attempt to control teacher conduct by more disciplinary rules and punishment may actually cause more disciplinary problems. This is a low-trust approach to teachers that reduces their discretion to a minimum and leaves them only trivial opportunities for choice, decision, and the acceptance of professional responsibility. Low-trust attitudes are usually reciprocated by "subordinates," often with antagonism, attempts at counterexploitation, and other consequences of alienation (Fox, 1974). The use of people as means to some organizational end violates a fundamental ethical principle.

If the move toward a professional code of ethics for teachers is part of a move toward recognizing and treating them as professionals, that is, with trust, and granting them real authority to make the decisions that affect their own professional status and the performance of their jobs, then it is likely that such high trust will be reciprocated with improved morale, increased creativity, pride in their work, innovative ideas and approaches to teaching, and fewer disciplinary problems (Berger, 1990; Daley, 1990). People usually become more responsible when they share in responsibility.

Finally, advocates of a code of ethics for teachers maintain that such a code would assure "clients" that professional services would be provided in accordance "with reasonably high standards and acceptable moral conduct" and would establish "uniform rules and behavioral standards by means of which professional conduct can properly be regulated" (Rich, 1985, pp. 21–22). There will always be a need for rules because there will always be conflicts and disputes and evildoers and deadbeats. But, when proposed as a basis for conduct regulation and punishment, phrases such as "reasonably high standards" and "acceptable moral conduct" are just as empty as "conduct unbecoming a teacher."

Just and productive educational reform can occur only after a national commitment to research produces substantial and reliable evidence concerning the nexus between teaching styles, teacher behavior, and student learning, and provides the basis for valid, reliable, and empirically derived measures for assessing teaching performance. Then the work and results of education can be more objectively assessed, corrective approaches more likely to succeed can be designed and corrective actions taken, and improvements can be more definitely determined.

My study revealed the serious injustices that result when decision makers operate without objective standards or reliable evidence concerning the educational consequences of various teacher behaviors both in and out of the classroom. Of course, educational reform involves matters of productivity and performance as well as equity, and the objective should be to maximize learning and teacher effectiveness in ways consistent with justice and equity for teachers, students, and administrators.

These comments could be read as recommending changes that will further retard educational achievement by making it more difficult to dismiss incompetent and immoral teachers. On the contrary, by demonstrating that the unfairness of the present disciplinary system is caused by the same lack of evidence about teaching and learning that prevents equitable and productive educational reform from taking place, these comments should spark an all-out effort to acquire the evidence needed to determine what constitutes good teaching and how to achieve and measure it. Recognizing that teachers are professionals and supervising them on the basis of empirical evidence rather than unsubstantiated personal values, preferences, and assumptions—in other words, treating them justly, with respect and compassion—is more likely to evoke their loyalty and best efforts in return.

REFERENCES

Bandura, A. (1977). *Social learning theory*. Englewood Cliffs, NJ: Prentice Hall.

Berger, J. (1990, November 13). Teachers and principal begin sharing power, but gingerly. *The New York Times*, p. 1.

Campbell, J. (1970). Mythological themes in creative literature and art. In J. Campbell (Ed.), *Myths, dreams, and religion* (pp. 138–175). New York: E. P. Dutton.

Cardozo, B. (1921). *The nature of the judicial process*. New Haven, CT: Yale University Press.

Cohen, S. R. (1980). Models inside and outside the classroom: A force for desirable learning. *Contemporary Education, 51*, 186.

Daley, S. (1990, November 21). A school in Minnesota doesn't have a principal. *The New York Times*, p. B11.

Fox, A. (1974). *Beyond contract*. London: Faber & Faber.

Goldstein, S. R. (1976). The asserted constitutional right of public school teachers to determine what they teach. *University of Pennsylvania Law Review, 124*, 1293–1357.

Goodman, P. (1964). *Compulsory mis-education*. New York: Random House.

Gross, J. (1988). *Teachers on trial: Values, standards, and equity in judging conduct and competence*. Ithaca, NY: ILR Press.

Gross, J., & Greenfield, P. (1985). Arbitrable value judgments in health and safety disputes: Management rights over workers' rights. *Buffalo Law Review, 34*, 645–691.

Kleingartner, A. (1973). Collective bargaining between salaried professionals and public sector management. *Public Administration Review, 33*, 165–172.

La Borde Scholz, J. L. (1979). Comment: Out of the closet, out of a job: Due process in teacher disqualification. *Hastings Constitutional Law Quarterly, 6*, 663–717.

Lucas, J. R. (1989). *On justice*. New York: Oxford University Press.

Muschel, I. (1979). Dependent teachers, ineffective principals, failing children. *Education, 100*, 6–17.

Perelman. C. H. (1967). *Justice*. New York: Random House.

Rich, J. M. (1985). *The role of professional ethics in teacher education*. Paper presented at the Northern Arizona University Center for Excellence in Education.

Sawrey, J. M., & Telford, C. W. (1973). *Educational psychology*. Boston: Allyn & Bacon.

Smalls, O. (1983). A legal framework for academic freedom in public secondary schools. *Journal of Law and Education, 12*, 529–559.

Sockett, H. (1985, March–April). *Towards a professional code in teaching.* Paper presented at the annual meeting of the American Educational Research Association.

Tauber, R. (1985, April). *French and Raven's power bases: An appropriate focus for educational researchers and practitioners.* (ERIC Document Reproduction Service No. ED 258 962)

Taylor, R. (1981). Finding the school board's philosophy: A role following model. *Education, 101,* 206–209.

Willett, R. E. (1973). Unfitness to teach: Credential revocation and dismissal for sexual conduct. *California Law Review, 61,* 1442–1462.

Wilkes, P. (1989, January 22). The tough job of teaching ethics. *The New York Times,* Sec. 3, p. 1.

Winks, P. L. (1982). Legal implications of sexual contact between teacher and student. *Journal of Law and Education, 11,* 437–477.

CONCLUSION: Summary and Recommendations

KENNETH A. STRIKE AND P. LANCE TERNASKY
Cornell University

We indicated in the introduction that ethics might be applied to education in three principal ways. Ethics could assist in educational policy-making, assess the school's role as a moral educator, and inform standards to govern the conduct of educators. We divided the book into three sections to facilitate examination of these roles. Broadly, the sections explored the philosophical thought on which ethical policy and curricula were founded, the pragmatic considerations of how ethics is taught in schools and which factors interfere with such instruction, and the ways in which institutional issues, often outside the purview of the teacher, influence the role of ethics in the classroom. Each contributor addressed one or more of these issues. Rather than summarizing, we think it more instructive to consider five of the common themes that emerged across the chapters.

AN EXPANDED UNDERSTANDING OF ETHICS

The reader unfamiliar with the literature on ethics may have been struck by what we considered to be ethical. Many preservice teachers have a lay definition of ethics, which reduces the subject to a review of the rules of right conduct. Given this narrow view, all that prospective teachers would need to know is that they should not slap or sleep with their students, that they should keep their personal lives private, and that they should keep their hands out of the till. In contrast, our contributors proposed a much broader understanding.

They stressed that ethics is not solely a personal endeavor of limited scope because ethics is not advanced if individual teachers and their students merely refrain from breaking a circumscribed set of rules. According to Noddings, teachers and schools are in the business of "shap[ing] acceptable people." Her description of a "distinctive moral orientation" suggests that teachers are molding character so that students can, in Bricker's words, "see" the world ethically.

This world is characterized by personal ethical encounters, but it is also influenced by contact with extrapersonal entities such as educational bureaucracies and social and economic realities. If teachers are to behave ethically, then as Howe notes, they must understand that access to education, employment, and the requisites for self-respect are also ethical issues. Further, as Strike's chapter on ethical reasoning suggests, the mere articulation of ethical principles is not enough. For ethics to work for teachers and students, schools must become places that practice the principles taught in classrooms. Our understanding of ethics must extend beyond the concern for producing virtuous teachers and obedient students to include serious consideration of just what constitutes an ethical environment.

REASONS EDUCATORS SHOULD CARE ABOUT ETHICS

An expanded conception of the ethical permits a more profitable examination of the reasons educators should care about ethics. Several such reasons were mentioned in the introduction to this book. One was that with each account documenting some misdeed comes the charge that schools are not performing their assigned task of producing moral citizens and the call for schools to provide the moral education that students apparently are not receiving elsewhere. By this civic leaders and employers often mean that schools should graduate persons who display loyalty, responsibility, and respect for private property. Although these may be legitimate goals for the school, they are inadequate given the role we see for ethics.

That these are insufficient goals can be seen in the second reason: we stand in need of wisdom about how to treat one another. This refers to how students are to relate ethically to others and to the social and political systems within which they interact, but it also includes the ways the school and its representatives should behave toward students. Typically, when the issue of ethics in education is raised it focuses on *what* students should be taught rather than on *how* they should be treated and on what lessons are ultimately learned in the exchange.

Schools wield considerable power. They confer privilege and mete out punishment throughout much of a person's youth. And in a meritocratic society such as ours, relative success or failure as an adult disproportionately results from one's relationship with this institution. Consequently, if schools and society limit their interest to desired moral outcomes (e.g., fewer crimes committed by youth) without considering the kinds of persons we want to become and the way we want to see the world, then our moral education programs will likely be disappointing, for we will have confused ethical development with temporary, social problem solving.

The final reason given for educators to be concerned about ethics was the proposed connection between a code of ethics and the establishment of a teaching profession, and contributors ran the gamut. Sichel envisioned such a code as an evolutionary structure that educates educators while it suggests policy and provides solace for teachers struggling with difficult decisions. Macmillan agreed that a code need not be a taskmaster, and further, that it may increase teacher confidence by clearly stating not only what is expected of the teacher but also what the teacher can expect of the institution. Nevertheless, he lamented the current "toothless" state of the code. Here his emphasis shifted to the educational consumer, and the apparent motivation for a code of ethics became increased consumer confidence in educators. Gross acknowledged both positions when he stated that such a code may imply either that teachers care deeply about ethics or that they must be chided or threatened into behaving acceptably.

What makes the difference between seeing a code of ethics as boon or bane? The reply depends on its source and inspiration. In the case of a code born of Sichel's school ethics committees, the intent is less one of standardization than of an attempt to meet ethical needs in a specific setting. As this model's contemplative education, consultation, and support emerge from the actual conditions of a particular school, teachers will likely welcome the input on ethics. If, however, the code is imposed on teachers by those outside its ranks, then it may denigrate teachers and produce the undesirable antagonism that Gross says accompanies "low-trust" models of management.

The Florida experiment described by Macmillan may represent the middle ground. Here the governing bodies are staffed principally by teachers and administrators whose joint decisions are binding for state educators. Macmillan notes, however, that as "creatures of the state legislature" the existence of the commissions may denote societal mistrust of educators rather than the elevated public image educators desire.

Regardless, the question remains as to whether a code of ethics will serve to resolve the debate about whether teaching is a paradigmatic profession. Proponents of professionalization must demonstrate how the teaching that occurs in schools is different from that found in homes, offices, and places of worship. If teaching is to be a profession in the way that law and medicine are, then it must be shown that teachers possess knowledge that is unavailable to the uninitiated. Using Macmillan's example, we cannot imagine the person on the street being dubbed "brain surgeon," but it is unclear whether a comparable reaction would follow were the person on the street dubbed "teacher." Unless we can coherently argue that teachers possess essential knowledge other than that of their subject matter, we cannot claim that teaching is a profession in the traditional understanding of the term.

If there is no arcane knowledge base for teaching, we might ground a teaching profession in the characteristic activities and commitments of its practitioners. Thus, rather than an esoteric body of knowledge we would find the practices and attitudes without which a person could not be said to be a member of the profession. One obvious difficulty with such a proposal is that those outside teaching may without training or intent possess comparable characteristics, and because one of the prerogatives of a profession is to establish standards for admission, the possibility of the untrained satisfying entrance requirements would mark teaching as a most peculiar profession.

If teaching is notably unlike the paradigmatic professions and yet desires the respect and rewards that accompany them, then it may choose to imitate the acknowledged professions and, in the process, to be held accountable to standards and expectations it may not be able to meet. Or it may seek the respect it deserves not by comparing itself to other vocations, but by focusing on the role and importance of teachers' moral and intellectual commitments in the lives of students and in society. What alternative models might resemble remains an open question.

IMPEDIMENTS TO ETHICS EDUCATION

The above discussion suggests that our expectations of ethics education have not been fulfilled. What, then, are the educational factors that interfere with ethical development in educational settings?

Bull raises a host of issues. He suggests that we are unclear about the place and purpose of ethics education in the preservice curriculum, and that the realities of teacher training programs contravene the establishment of ethics as their central organizing principle. His doubts especially warrant consideration for those who hold that ethics education offers the means for transforming teacher education programs.

Grant suggests that the common and miseducative patterns of "brain checking" and "withdrawal" are impediments. Students and teachers engage in a dance that has less to do with mastering and applying knowledge than with maintaining a fragile peace. Students *behave* as though they are learning and refrain from seriously challenging the teacher. In exchange, teachers place few demands on students in the classroom and even fewer outside it.

Teachers accept minimal responsibility for what transpires in the classroom. They feel an obligation to transmit the material required by the standardized tests and to require that students adhere to certain basic standards of behavior (i.e., that they demonstrate a modicum of respect for the teacher and fellow students by refraining from overtly violent acts and by remaining seated and relatively quiet). Students abide by these rules and come to think they are responsible only for themselves.

Consider, for instance, Power's discussion of stealing. His first group refused to confront the thief and sent everyone else to their respective responsibility corners. The person from whom the tape recorder was stolen was responsible for having brought it to school where theft is possible. Whereas Power's respondents believed that the thief was wrong to steal the recorder, his primary error was in failing to be discreet about his actions. And rather than examining their own responsibility, the students chastised school officials for failing to prevent theft.

Grant speculates that such attitudes find their origins in the "social revolutions" that swept the nation's schools during the past three decades. During this period society faced clashes over civil rights and the Vietnam War, and shifting mores in nearly every area of life. The authority of persons, positions, and institutions was questioned. Students began demanding their "rights" to various freedoms, and the resulting clash produced a contentious atmosphere that prompted legalistic and bureaucratic compensation.

This adversarial atmosphere inhibited communication at a time when it was most needed. Each party viewed the others with distrust. No longer did students and their parents presume that teachers knew what was best and operated free of ulterior motives. Teachers were required to justify every action, and, to their dismay, teachers often discovered that they lacked such justification.

Into this void rushed those willing to "set things right." The need to contend efficiently with legal and ethical challenges produced new agencies and authorities whose unspoken responsibility was to devise what were disparagingly called "teacher-proof" systems. Much of this activity took place sans substantive thought and evidence, and as Gross notes, the failure to build expectations for teachers on a defensible foundation propagates highly interpretive and potentially pernicious regulations. Teachers may subsequently be held to standards they do not, or cannot, know about. And even in those instances when teachers are confident regarding an ethical or curricular decision, a local school board with little understanding of the issues and perhaps with a skewed political agenda can, as Macmillan indicates, override teachers' best judgment. It is not surprising that teachers often chose a minimalist and defensive approach to education.

Just as students and teachers developed a moral myopia, so those establishing moral education programs often overlooked variables outside the individual classroom. As Power noted, they failed to consider the moral climate of the school. Schools are communities situated within a larger culture. As such, schools have characters, and the failure to research whether ethical aspirations for a school are commensurable with its character (i.e., how decisions are made, how persons are treated, and how it envisions its purpose) invites disillusionment.

If moral climate is ignored, any success that accompanies moral curricula will be short-lived and restricted. If we believe that rules or policy-making or a curriculum alone can transform an environment, we will be disappointed. The resultant failure to achieve tangible, widespread moral growth will open every suggestion for change to the charge that "nothing has ever worked before, so why should it now." If we refuse to assess the school's decision-making hierarchy, strategies, and unspoken rules, then we can expect little more than unintended consequences from attempts at ethical reform.

THE MORAL INFLUENCE OF TEACHERS

We mentioned several factors that impede ethical development in schools. Several contributors leveled serious charges against schools and teachers. Consequently, a central question is what real impact can educators have on the moral development of their students?

We are not asking whether a particular moral curriculum could be effectively introduced—in fact, the writers here have avoided discussion of packaged programs. The question is whether teachers, as a result of the roles they fill, can influence their students' moral development. Can we expect teachers to embody attitudes that students will emulate? What can teachers reasonably be expected to model for their students?

Gross is emphatic regarding the paucity of convincing evidence of a relationship between the behavior of teachers and the morality of their students. He argues that we do not understand how or why a person stands as a role model for another and that until we do we cannot use such criteria in our assessment of teachers. From the standpoint of procedural justice, Gross's comments are irrefutable. The idiosyncratic perceptions of students or their parents cannot be grounds for teacher censure or dismissal. However, Gross is not saying that teachers are not, or should not be, role models—only that we do not know how the process operates and we must not judge teachers by amorphous standards. More importantly, it would be an unflattering picture of anyone (teachers included) to claim that his or her only reason for behaving morally is the impact it might have on others.

We have argued that there are good reasons for being moral, and aping morality for the sake of appearances is not one of them.

If we currently lack evidence of how the role-modeling process functions, what can we legitimately expect of teachers? We can begin by acknowledging that teachers *do* influence students. Every student can recall the name of an influential teacher: someone who contributed to the student's eventual success or failure. It does not matter that some students are drawn to model their teachers' attitudes and actions, whereas others find them uninfluential. What matters is that teachers realize that their willingness to buy peace in the classroom with assurances of limited demands on students or to ignore instances of violence or racism in the hallway while off duty conveys messages that stand in contrast to the goals espoused by most schools. When Grant states that teachers disclose their characters and commitments by their actions, and when Power rejects an interpretation of discipline that equates it with the mere behavioral control of students, both are asserting that the behavior of teachers reveals their moral vision. And it seems unlikely that most students could acquire society's paramount moral tenets from teachers whose words stand in marked contrast to their actions.

PRACTICAL SUGGESTIONS

Before reviewing the proposals, let's consider what no one suggested. There was no call for an immediate and substantive increase in either teachers' salaries or the overall number of staff positions, or the number of hours in the school day or days in the school year. The fact that they were not mentioned does not mean that they are unimportant or that they may not be ethical concerns, but it does suggest that we see no ineluctable correlation between increases in any of these and an improved moral atmosphere in schools.

Further, no one proposed that the moral cures for the school reside in the unattainable. Were moral reform held hostage to the claim that the nation must first undergo, say, dramatic socialistic or spiritual revival, the efforts of our contributors would clearly be wasted. Although the suggestions require both time and perseverance, each is achievable in today's schools.

Structural Changes

Two structural changes are suggested by Power. The reduction of school size, either by maintaining community schools rather than centralizing or by implementing a house plan (school-within-a-school) in large schools, is already being considered by many districts in order to improve the moral and social climate of public schools. To guarantee ethical considerations a more central role in education we must challenge physical structures (such as size) that exacerbate the impersonal and egocentric inclinations present in most schools.

Reduction in size is most effective when coupled with another of Power's suggestions: democratic reform. This may at first seem to be a contradiction, for are not American schools the bastions of democracy? In actuality, democracy stands as little more than an icon in too many schools. If one were to ask whether understanding the democratic system was important, the answer would be yes. However, if one asked where, specifically, such principles operated in educational settings many would be at a loss to find a single instance beyond the election of student body officers and local school board members.

Many educators cannot even imagine what a more democratic school would resemble. This lack of vision is not indicative of a cognitive deficit but reflects the scarcity of tangible examples of democratic action in the teachers' own preservice training. It is common to find professors extolling the virtues of democracy to prospective teachers without once venturing beyond autocratic methods that would be as comfortable in the educational system of any fascist regime. Often teachers cannot envision a more democratic system because they have never seen one, and into this lacuna run the fears that the introduction of *real* democracy will mean relinquishing control of the schools to children, thus further reducing the respect and status of teachers. Fortunately, such an image is viable only if one conflates democracy with the most miseducative forms of child-centered education. This is not the image Power offers nor is it representative of the best and most successful of the democratically run alternative schools.

Teachers (and possibly even preservice teachers in their colleges and universities) could establish the school ethics committees (SECs) that Sichel describes. This option would permit educators to wrestle with a "worked example" of democratic decision making. It would assist them in making difficult ethical decisions. And it would serve to further educate teachers by providing them with material, a structure for reflection, and the prospect of substantive conversation with colleagues rather than the plaintive prattle characteristic of so many exchanges.

Sichel's proposal parallels the seminaring, shadowing, and researching that Grant offers. Although Grant's intentions differ from Sichel's, both make proposals that are constructed on an inquiry-reflection-action model. This three-part system offers a reasonable strategy for principled problem solving. The absence of any of the three components represents a serious omission, but reflection is the part most frequently overlooked and often with grave consequences. Without a structure for reflection, the unexpected and unintended consequences of action encourage slippage into the pessimism born of the failure of well-conceived plans to accomplish their goals swiftly. Moreover, the introduction of philosophical reflection restrains the purely strategic thinking—thinking limited to cause-and-effect relationships and unconcerned with the placement of the problem in a larger social and philosophical context—that Strike resists in his chapter on ethical reasoning.

Finally, teacher training curricula must be altered. Preservice teachers will need course work in ethics of the sort described by Strike. This will permit discussion of ethics with students, and it will also sharpen teachers' sense of teaching as moral craft. As moral craft, teaching will require not just that teachers treat their students fairly and with respect. It will also require that teachers comprehend the complexity of the ethical landscape.

Curricular change also requires enhanced disciplinary knowledge. If, as Strike suggests, students' moral growth benefits from a dialogue between private moral language, the public language, and a language of criticism, then prospective teachers will require greater familiarity with the foremost voices of the moral traditions of their students. Further, if the desire for greater recognition for teachers cannot be secured by reference to a distinct knowledge base for teaching, then teachers may choose to ground their status in a visible mastery of their subject matter. Recognition would then follow not from the attribution of "teacher," but from that of historian or artist or scientist who teaches.

Attitudinal Changes

These are inseparable from structural changes. The principal difference is that the implementation of attitudinal changes requires a more radical rethinking of the purpose and operation of the schools. Here we can apply Power's three remaining suggestions for building a "positive moral atmosphere." He suggests that the existence of clear behavioral expectations for students and explicit consequences for those failing to meet them is insufficient if our goal is not mere discipline but moral development. The goal of moral development demands that we seek justification both for the moral tenets about which there is already general agreement and for those still in their incipiency. If we want persons to think ethically, they must know more than which acts are wrong. They must comprehend *why* they are unacceptable.

Delving into the nature of moral issues serves a reflective role for the school comparable to that mentioned above for SECs. Just as reflection provides insight into the relationship between inquiry and action and mollifies the pessimism about unintended consequences, identifying core principles sharpens students' understanding of problems and assists them in the development of a viable and coherent moral outlook. If moral education is restricted to mere strategic thinking (e.g., "How do we get them to stop smoking in the rest rooms?"), then we will miss the subtleties and will find that we lack the critical insight for effecting real, lasting change.

This search for underlying principles is a necessary precursor to the development of collective norms and community building that Power advances. The school Power seeks is one in which a constructed common ground stands in opposition to particularistic conceptions of what counts as ethical. His vision contradicts the popular impression that common ground is no longer possible; but more than this, he challenges the idea that an ethical school is comprised of individual, ethical persons. In a truly ethical environment a public language can be spoken, and concerns other than self-interest can prevail.

One of the most dramatic attitudinal shifts is that of seeing noneducators as "partners" in moral education. It would be naive to suggest that this is novel. But in light of the efforts of the past two decades to elevate the status of teachers by certifying them as "experts" in education, it was an idea intentionally understated.

Macmillan proposes a partnership between the public and the profession to ensure teacher accountability. In his essay on pluralism, Strike attacks public suspicion by turning fearful critics of heightened moral discourse into participants in the conversation. Students may, however, be the group most in need of inclusion.

In the objectionable school portrayed in Grant's historical account, students are teachers' adversaries. And according to Gross and Howe, teachers who do not consider students the enemy often view them in an equally unflattering light as passive, immature beings to whom education is applied or performed. Students will be disinclined to help create a positive moral atmosphere if educators retain the perception that youth are creatures to be controlled or fixed.

Interactional Changes

Throughout the text, the importance we place on dialogue has repeatedly surfaced. Certain additional characteristics must be suggested, however, because perceived examples of dialogue often leave us less than enthusiastic about its prospects. At the time of this writing, the final Senate confirmation hearings for Justice Clarence Thomas have just concluded, and the Middle East Peace Conference has just begun. In both instances, the participants mistook *talking* for genuine discourse. Such examples represent the antithesis of the dialogue we intend.

What keeps real dialogue from occurring? The list may well be endless, and we would refer the reader to Chapters 7, 8, and 12 for more systematic discussion, but let us mention just two factors here. The first is what John Rensenbrink of Bowdoin College calls the "protest mentality." Although indignation can prompt dialogue, and there are instances where protest is the only viable option, used exclusively protest proscribes dialogue. Why is this? The apparent reason is that protest forces the recipient into a defensive posture. The protesters may eventually secure what they desire, but this may result more from acquiescence or extortion than dialogue. Unfortunately, results obtained by protest often produce policy that is formal and minimalistic rather than heartfelt and substantive.

The less apparent reason that protest prohibits dialogue may actually be more important. Rensenbrink (1992) argues that a protest mentality inhibits the development of an ethical, political consciousness. It does so because it presumes that *someone else* is in charge and alone capable of resolving the difficulty. Rather than negotiating from a position of strength, protesters operate from powerlessness and displaced responsibility. Consider again Power's case of the stolen tape recorder. For the most part, students held that the difficulty arose because all the other parties were not doing their jobs: school officials failed to prevent theft, students foolishly brought valuable items to school, and thieves were indiscreet. If ethical dialogue is to take place, conversants must ask what role they personally play in the issue and what responsibility they bear, even in their silence.

The second, related factor is an antidialogical competitiveness. This is not a blanket condemnation of competition, but it suggests that competition is counterproductive in dialogue. Too many people view ethical dialogue as a team sport in which each team's most erudite players score points against the opposition. As in the characteristic debate team, we find the keenest voices locked in heated exchange—often defending positions to which they cannot honestly accede. The elite compete while the masses watch, thus offering a picture not unlike Sichel's reference to Barber's distinction between authoritative and strong democracy. We are not proposing the abolition of debate competitions, but imagine how differently a victory would be received if such teams could win competitions only by swaying their opponents or moving their listeners to reflective action.

One of the key discoveries of grassroots activists during the past three decades is that victory must not be understood as winning the battle (something often accomplished by legislative or judicial edict) but by the number, and conviction, of the persons who come to be actively engaged in an issue. When real dialogue operates, we get Grant's "shared meaning." Without it, suggestions and concerns may be experienced as impositions. Debate pits the most articulate spokespersons against each other toward victory or defeat. Dialogue invites widespread participation toward resolution.

Multiple factors interfere with dialogue. What suggestions might our contributors offer for promoting it? Recall the following six:

1. Establish the ground rules for dialogue before the conversation begins.
2. Maintain an open exchange that is not dominated by any person or group. As Ternasky suggested, although dialogue permits conflict and may lead to the conclusion that someone is actually wrong, this can justifiably occur only if these criteria are satisfied.
3. Hold adamant convictions in suspense. This does not imply that persons should avoid nonnegotiable topics or seek Strike's "liberal silence." It does assert, however, that if one enters a conversation convinced that everyone else is dreadfully wrong, and one is further prepared to inform the infidels of their error, then we may call the ensuing exchange many things but not dialogue. As Ternasky mentioned, if we are to converse in the public sphere we must risk having our ideas altered by the thinking and experiences of others, and this cannot happen unless we entertain the idea that those with whom we disagree may have something to teach us.
4. Attend to the real-life experiences of participants. Hypothetical situations are valuable tools for manipulating ideas, but the resulting insights often transfer poorly to day-to-day life.
5. Reflect on the ethical principles underlying one's convictions before rejecting another's position or advancing one's own. In so doing, we can seek to discover both whether our convictions are justified and whether our proposed response sensibly follows from acceptable principles.
6. Anticipate insight from unexpected sources by carefully listening to the contribution of the typically silent member of the group or that of the person not intimately involved in the issue. Also, tap frequently ignored sources: original ideas embedded in, say, religious thought, history, or the literature on culture or gender bias.

Given the diverse thought and orientations of our contributors, we would be hard pressed to identify the pivotal points in this volume. We would be satisfied, however, if preservice teachers and administrators came away with four concepts.

First, moral beliefs are objects of rational assessment. Few argue convincingly that the ideals they hold most dear are arbitrary constructions.

Persons generally insist that good reasons exist for their beliefs. If there are good reasons, then the beliefs are subject to examination, and the holders are responsible for explicating to those with different viewpoints why particular ideals are worth holding.

Second, as both Bricker and Strike have suggested, when one begins to think about something in a new way, one begins to see it differently. No one suggested that requiring a course on ethics in the preservice curriculum would produce more ethical students. To the contrary, they argued that such measures are unlikely to be successful, and that the amoral person would not be swayed by such efforts. It is also evident that many students possess an intuitive grasp of what is moral. Given this, the purpose of ethics in the preservice curriculum is not to make students moral but to make their knowledge of ethics explicit.

Third, preservice educators must sense the breadth of ethical consideration. Teachers and students should understand what it means to be an ethical individual. They must also perceive that extrapersonal variables (i.e., the moral climate of the school and the community) carry moral weight.

Finally, the tolerance that marks legitimate ethical exchange must be understood to flow not from indifference or uncertainty but from a commitment to basic ethical and political principles. Consequently, we enter ethical dialogue not as a second-best strategy for problem solving, but as the most fruitful means of securing a sensitive mix of passion and civility. If this volume assists toward that end, we count it successful.

REFERENCE

Rensenbrink, J. (1992). *The Greens and the politics of transformation.* San Pedro, CA: Miles.

ABOUT THE CONTRIBUTORS

INDEX

About the Contributors

David C. Bricker, Professor of Philosophy at Oakland University, Rochester, Michigan, concentrates on ethics and political theory. His initial appointment at Oakland was in the School of Education, where he had ample opportunity to listen to experienced teachers comment upon their difficulties at translating professional ideals such as fairness into practice.

Barry L. Bull is Associate Professor of Education at Indiana University, Bloomington, Indiana. He received his PhD from Cornell University in 1979. He has taught at a number of universities and worked at the state departments of education in Washington and Idaho. His research focuses on the ethical justification of educational policies. Teachers College Press is publishing a book he has co-authored, entitled *The Ethics of Multicultural and Bilingual Education.*

Gerald Grant is Professor of Cultural Foundations of Education and Sociology at Syracuse University. He is the author of *The World We Created at Hamilton High* and is currently at work on a study of new roles for teachers, examining changes in nine schools in four school districts.

James Gross has published a two-volume (about to be three-volume) history of the NLRB (*The Making of the National Labor Relations Board: A Study in Economics; Politics and the Law, 1933–1937*; and *The Reshaping of the National Labor Relations Board: National Labor Policy in Transition, 1933–1947*); and a recent book, *Teachers on Trial: Values, Standards and Equity in Judging Conduct and Competence.* His other research on various topics in labor law and labor arbitration have appeared in the *University of Buffalo Law Review*, the *Cornell Law Review*, the *Syracuse Law Review*, the *Industrial and Labor Relations Review*, and *Arbitration Journal*, *Labor History*, and the *Labor Law Journal.* Dr. Gross teaches labor law, labor arbitration, and a course entitled Values in Economics, Law, and Industrial Relations at Cornell University, Ithaca, New York. He received his BS from LaSalle College, MA from Temple University, and PhD from University of Wisconsin. He is a member of National Academy of Arbitrators and serves on the labor arbitration panels of the American Arbitration Association, Federal Mediation and Conciliation Service, and Public Employment Relations Board, as well as being a panelist named in several contracts.

Kenneth R. Howe is Associate Professor in the School of Education, University of Colorado at Boulder, specializing in educational ethics and philosophy and educational research. His articles have appeared in the *American Journal of Education, Educational Researcher, Educational Theory, The Journal of Moral Education,* and *The Journal of Special Education*; a book, the *Ethics of Special Education* (with Ofelia Miramontes), is forthcoming in 1992. He is currently a Spencer Foundation Fellow, pursuing a project entitled "The Many Faces of Equal Educational Opportunity."

C. J. B Macmillan is Professor of Philosophy of Education at Florida State University. His PhD was awarded by Cornell University in 1965, and he taught at UCLA and Temple University before moving to Tallahassee in 1970. He was President of the Philosophy of Education Society in 1984 and is co-author of *A Logical Theory of Teaching,* published by Kluwer in 1987. He is currently working on a book on censorship and the schools.

Nel Noddings is Professor of Education and Associate Dean at Stanford. She is president of the national Philosophy of Education Society. She was a Phi Beta Kappa Visiting Scholar for the year 1989–1990. In addition to four books, *Caring: A Feminine Approach to Ethics and Moral Education, Women and Evil, The Challenge to Care in Schools,* and (with Paul Shore) *Awakening the Inner Eye: Intuition in Education,* and two coedited volumes, she is the author of more than seventy articles and chapters on various topics ranging from the ethics of caring to mathematical problem solving.

F. Clark Power is Associate Professor in the Program of Liberal Studies at the University of Notre Dame. His research focuses on moral development and education. He is the principal author of *Lawrence Kohlberg's Approach to Moral Education,* co-author of *The Measurement of Moral Judgment, Vol. II,* and co-editor of *Self, Ego, and Identity: Integrative Approaches* and *The Challenge of Pluralism: Education, Politics, and Values.*

Dawn E. Schrader is Assistant Professor of Educational Psychology at Cornell University, Ithaca, New York. She received her Ed.D. from Harvard University Graduate School of Education in 1988. Her doctoral dissertation explored the concept of metacognition and its relationship to moral development. Her current research interests include the interactive relationship between metacognition, moral judgment, and moral action, particularly as applied to professional and self development.

Betty A. Sichel is Professor of Education at Long Island University, C. W. Post Campus, Brookville, New York. She received her PhD in philosophy of education from New York University in 1969. She has published articles and books on a variety of topics, including philosophy of education, moral education, professional ethics, the educational ideas of classical Greek philosophy, and most recently, feminist ethics. At present, she is completing work on a book on academic ethics and researching a study of feminist ethics and moral education.

Kenneth A. Strike is Professor of Philosophy of Education at Cornell University. He received his BA from Wheaton College, and his MA and PhD from Northwestern University. His principal interests are ethics and political philosophy as they apply to the professional ethics of educational practitioners and to educational policy. His recent works include *The Ethics of Teaching* (with Jonas Soltis) and *The Ethics of School Administration* (with Jonas Soltis and Emil Haller). Both books are published by Teachers College Press. He is also the author of *Liberal Justice and the Marxist Critique of Schooling*, published by Routledge, Chapman & Hall.

P. Lance Ternasky was previously a member of the faculty of the Alfred North Whitehead Center of the University of Redlands, Redlands, California. He is currently completing doctoral studies in philosophy of education, philosophy of science, and ethics at Cornell University.

Index